UNDERGROUND CURES

THE MOST URGENT HEALTH SECRETS

E D I T I O N III

Published by Agora Health Books
Anne Kelly, Publisher
Alice Jacob, Copy Editor
Martin Milner, N.D., Medical Editor

ISBN 1-891434-10-1

Additional orders and inquiries can be directed to Agora Health Books, Customer Service Department, 819 N. Charles Street, Baltimore, MD 21201; tel. (508) 368-7493, fax (410) 230-1273, e-mail ahb@agora-inc.com.

Table of Contents

Introduction

The inaugural edition of *Underground Cures*, published in 1998, brought together for the first time the most urgent health discoveries from the world's most progressive health clinics and research laboratories. This year, Agora Health Books has once again partnered with Health Sciences Institute to bring you the latest updated edition of *Underground Cures*, which contains a hidden universe of remedies and healing possibilities you never imagined existed. The mainstream medical establishment and even many alternative medical communities have yet to discover these advanced, underground cures and urgent health breakthroughs.

This edition of *Underground Cures* is packed with 30 new chapters containing secrets for enhancing your health, extending your life, and liberating yourself from the devastating effects of many serious conditions. We've also reorganized the contents so you can quickly find the section you're looking for, whether it's breakthrough solutions for immuno-support, degenerative or autoimmune disorders, viruses, cancer, brainpower, mental health, energy, sexual health, heart health, pain relief or anti-aging secrets.

Every day, around the world, researchers and scientists are making exciting medical breakthroughs and health discoveries. Yet, you are often deprived of these healing possibilities. Your doctor may be too busy to sift through all the latest research. Or maybe he is overly influenced by the big pharmaceutical companies. Or perhaps a potentially lifesaving treatment is trapped in the tangles of government bureaucracy. The bottom line is this...for one reason or another, you are not getting the health information you need when you need it.

In 1996, a small, private group of conventionally and holistically trained doctors formed a network through which they could rapidly exchange news of the latest, most innovative cures and overcome bureaucratic blocks and delays.

This network is the Health Sciences Institute, dedicated to uncovering and researching the most urgent advances in modern underground medicine, like those in this book. The hard work and commitment of these "underground" health pioneers brings these cures to light...so that you can use them today.

The Health Sciences Institute now has over 80,000 members worldwide. As it grows in international reputation, more and more laboratories and scientists send news of their research directly to the institute. The editors at HSI research the truly revolutionary breakthroughs for safety, efficacy, and availability.

Every day, stacks of letters arrive from people whose lives were changed by a breakthrough they learned of through the HSI network. The institute maintains a file of members who have overcome such diseases as arthritis, prostate disorders, fatigue, and depression...of members who, although they had nearly given up hope, experienced dramatic recoveries when they tried a remedy they read about in an HSI publication. Please turn to page 225 to find out how you can receive regular news of the latest medical breakthroughs by becoming a member of the Health Sciences Institute.

Super Immunity
for the Millennium

In today's world, we are constantly assaulted by a growing number of environmental and biological threats to our health. There's simply no way to avoid the drug-resistant bacteria, industrial chemicals, and nutrient-depleted foods that depress our natural immune responses and leave us vulnerable. The best defense? To develop disease resistance at the cellular level—in short, to achieve superimmunity.

In this chapter, you'll learn about a new generation of natural immune-system boosters that may provide the most effective health insurance you can buy. Read on to learn how you can resist and overcome the most serious health threats of our age.

Calcium Elenolate:
Nature's Most Powerful Antibiotic
Tomorrow's #1 threat to your health is here today

You may not believe it now, but infectious "smart bugs" are going to be the No. 1 threat to your health. In the past 15 years, death by infectious disease has already gone from being the fifth-leading killer in the United States to being the third-leading one!

And now, nine disease-causing bugs—bugs we thought we'd beaten long ago—have returned, stronger than the original strains...bringing a plague of dangerous and even deadly illnesses, including blood poisoning, tuberculosis, meningitis, pneumonia, sinusitis, gonorrhea, and bacteremia.

Once, doctors could destroy these bacteria with powerful drugs. That was back in the golden age of antibiotics. Today, it doesn't matter how quickly we invent drugs to kill them. Faster than we can create new antibiotics in our laboratories, deadly bacteria are developing resistance to the potent but limited drugs. There is one way, however, to stop these superbugs. We can outsmart them, using the tremendous protective power of nature.

Nature's most promising antibiotic, antiviral, and antifungal agent is a compound derived from the olive leaf, called calcium elenolate. As the number of drug-resistant superbugs continues to increase, so will the urgent need for olive-leaf extract.

This plant extract not only helps your body battle the dangerous bugs that cause infectious disease but also detoxifies your entire system, enhances your energy, improves your circulation, activates key components of your immune system, and has beneficial effects on cholesterol and blood-sugar levels.

The history of calcium elenolate

Treatments made from the olive-leaf extract have been around for at least 150 years, with records dating back to 1827, when it was used as a treatment for malaria—with no side effects other than those produced by the ethanol wine used in these special ethanolic preparations. In 1906, the olive-leaf extract was reportedly far superior to quinine for the treatment of malaria, but quinine, because it was easier to administer, became the treatment of choice.

In 1957, the active ingredient of olive-leaf extract, oleuropein, was isolated and studied as a treatment for high blood pressure and other types of heart disease, again with no mention of toxic or other side effects.

From 1970 to the present, a hydrolyzed form of oleuropein has been tested and found effective against dozens of different viruses and many strains of bacteria. None of these experiments noted any toxicity.

Now in tablet form, olive-leaf extract is making a comeback. From Mexico we have reports describing dramatic malaria remissions, but the therapeutic potential of the olive leaf is much more far-reaching. It's been proven to work in a number of specific ways:

- It stunts the growth of viruses or bacteria by interfering with certain amino-acid production processes necessary for those pathogens to grow.

- It inhibits the spread of the pathogen by preventing shedding, budding, or assembly at the cell membrane (i.e., it inactivates the virus or bacterium).

- It can enter your infected cells and shut down viral replication processes.

- In the case of retroviruses, such as HIV, it neutralizes the production of enzymes that are essential for a retrovirus to alter the RNA of a healthy cell.

- It directly stimulates phagocytosis—your immune system's ability to "eat" foreign microorganisms that don't belong in your body. Clearly, this substance is highly complex— much more so than synthetic antibiotics—and this complexity is one of the keys to its success.

The importance of natural antibiotics in a dangerous age of infectious diseases

Independent research has shown that olive-leaf extract can be used as an adjunct treatment for influenza, meningitis, the Epstein-Barr virus (EBV), encephalitis, the common cold, herpes I and II, HHV-6, HHV-7, shingles, HTLV-I, HTLV-II, HIV/ARC/ AIDS, CFIDS, CMV, hepatitis B, pneumonia, sinusitis, tuberculosis, gonorrhea, malaria, bacteremia, urinary-tract infections, severe diarrhea, blood poisoning, and surgical infections.

Because it's a natural substance, olive-leaf extract has a much wider range of actions than man-made antibiotics. It contains a maze of chemicals—harmless to us—that lie in wait for invading bacteria. In this way, olive-leaf extract is very much like garlic, the traditional herbal cure-all. Garlic contains 17 amino acids, and 33 sulfur compounds, plus copper, germanium, selenium, zinc, calcium, iron, potassium, magnesium, and vitamins A, B-1, and C-2. As you can imagine, it is much more difficult for an invading bacterium to develop resistance in the face of such a complex mixture of active chemicals.

Plant medicines like olive-leaf extract offer a great deal of promise for the future treatment of infectious diseases. According to experts at the Centers for Disease Control in Atlanta, medicine must continue to probe natural resources if it is to provide effective health care for all. Nature has evolved germ killers far more potent than any that laboratory scientists can invent. The olive-leaf extract is one of these germ killers.

The safety factor

In 1970, the Upjohn Pharmaceutical Company conducted and published a safety study on the use of olive-leaf extract in lab animals. An extrapolation of Upjohn's figures reveals that even at doses several hundred times the recommended amount, no toxic or other adverse side effects are likely to appear.

Bonus heart-health benefits of this special olive-leaf compound

The Mediterranean diet, rich in vegetables, fruits, grains, and olive oil, has recently been linked to a low incidence of heart disease. According to many studies, the olive-leaf compound has been found to serve as a vasodilator (it opens up your blood vessels), to prevent LDL oxidation (which causes hardened arteries), and even to help with diabetes and high blood pressure.

It thoroughly cleanses and detoxifies your system. In fact, the manufacturers of olive-leaf-extract supplements warn that you may experience significant detoxification symptoms. These symptoms—which can vary from stomach rumblings and other digestive disorders to mild headaches—are positive signs that the supplement is "at work." You can lessen these side effects, however, with a program of vitamin C supplementation, taken to bowel tolerance, and/or a probiotic formula to ensure strong, beneficial microflora in your bowel.

Generally, the recommended amount of olive-leaf extract is one or two 500-milligram tablets daily. After about two weeks, you can increase the amount to six or eight capsules daily. When you begin to feel better, reduce the amount to one or two capsules daily.

Please turn to the "Guide to Sources and Availability" on page 215 for information on obtaining olive-leaf extract (calcium elenolate).

CHAPTER **2**

Lactoferrin:
The Healing Mystery of Mothers' Milk

History may reveal the discovery of lactoferrin to be among the most important medical advancements of the 20th century. This potent, natural immune booster has been reported to hinder tumor growth and metastasis, relieve the suffering of AIDS-related complexes, and protect the immunologically vulnerable from deadly viruses and bacterial infections. In healthy individuals, it can mean near-total immunity from colds, influenza, microbial parasites, and infectious bacteria. Its healing powers appear to be unrivaled. And yet, lactoferrin remains largely unknown and poorly understood, even in the alternative medical community.

What is lactoferrin and where does it come from?

Lactoferrin is an immune chemical produced by the body as part of its shield against infection. In a healthy individual, it's found in secretions like tears, perspiration, the lining of the intestinal tract, and the mucous membranes that line the nose, ears, throat, and urinary tract—in short, any place that is especially vulnerable to infection.

But by far the highest concentrations of lactoferrin are found in a substance called colostrum (or "first milk"), produced by a new mother in the first few hours after she gives birth. For the newborn, lactoferrin provides crucial immune-system stimulation, helping the new baby to survive in its new germ-laden environment outside the womb.

Recently, scientists have discovered that using lactoferrin in the form of a nutritional supplement can significantly boost the immune system and greatly enhance the body's ability to withstand and recover from infection and other illness. Lactoferrin supplements are produced using bovine colostrum. The process used to create the commercial preparation leaves the lactoferrin protein intact and chemically unaltered. (For those who are allergic to milk or lactose-intolerant, please note that the milk sugars responsible for lactose intolerance and the proteins responsible for cow's-milk allergies are largely absent in bovine colostrum. Except in the case of extreme sensitivity, lactoferrin usually presents no problems for those with milk sensitivities.

Have you noticed? The "common" cold is becoming a thing of the past

It used to be that you could expect to get one or two colds a season—a few days of sinus congestion, maybe a scratchy throat. Nowadays, it's not uncommon to suffer half a dozen major viral infections a year. Family physicians report the increasing prevalence of "super cold" viruses—colds that wipe you out for two weeks or more with bone-wearying fatigue, debilitating throat and sinus pain, and a nagging cough that drags on for weeks or even develops into bronchitis.

For anyone who is immune-impaired for any reason—recovering from surgery or cancer therapy, for example, the stakes are much higher: Even one bad cold can lead to hospitalization, or even become life-threatening.

And then there's the flu. Even flu shots can't adequately protect you. New and increasingly dangerous strains of the flu appear each year, circling the globe with astonishing speed.

Your only defense is a strong immune system

You can't avoid exposure to these infections, but you can help ensure that your immune system is strong enough to knock the bugs out before they take hold in your body. Research indicates that lactoferrin supplementation may be your key to developing this kind of superimmunity. Lactoferrin increases both the number and the activity of at least half-dozen different types of specific immune cells that help your body fight infection.

By taking supplemental lactoferrin daily (100 to 300 mg) as a preventive regimen, you're more likely to stay well while co-workers and acquaintances pass around the same cold or flu. When you sense that you might be "coming down with something," you can increase the amount (to 500 mg) in order to increase the level of protection.

Lactoferrin's actions extend far beyond the "cold and flu" season. Research has documented a long list of remarkable benefits, especially against retroviruses and malignancies. Lactoferrin can inhibit the growth of both tumors and metastasis, and scientists studying it report that it may be one of the best protective regimens against tumor formation and excessive cell proliferation available.

How does lactoferrin work?

Lactoferrin is a type of cytokine—an immune chemical that helps coordinate the body's cellular immune response, defending against invaders like bacteria and viruses. In particular, it functions as a type of border guard: It patrols the tissues at the openings of the body-nose, eyes, and mouth, as well as cuts or abrasions in the skin-for pathogens that can harm you. In the event of an invasion of microbes, your body increases production of lactoferrin, which is directly toxic to bacteria, yeast, and molds.

The most distinguishing characteristic of lactoferrin is its ability to bind to iron in the blood, denying tumor cells, bacteria, and viruses the iron they need to survive and multiply. But as researchers continue to test lactoferrin against various disease processes, several more important functions have been revealed. Lactoferrin also has been documented to:

- enhance natural "killer-cell" activity (which targets specific types of tumors and virus-infected cells)
- activate neutrophil cells (which surround and digest foreign bodies)
- prevent bacterial overgrowth in the gut, preventing dysbiosys
- prevent viruses (including those that cause AIDS, herpes, heart disease, and some types of cancer) from penetrating into your healthy cells
- inhibit tumor growth and metastasis
- reduce inflammation—which can reduce pain and increase mobility

- inhibit Candida albicans and other Candida strains
- inhibit free-radical production—fighting the aging effects of cellular oxidation
- function as an inhibitor of mammary cell growth—which means it may hold promise for prevention or treatment of breast cancer
- play a role in lessening ocular disturbances—which means it may help with vision problems
- act as a potent antimicrobial agent against Candida albicans

Studies suggest that with lactoferrin, "more is better." The more lactoferrin that is present in the body, the more effectively it performs its many immune-stimulating functions. There appears to be no toxic dosage—which is not surprising when you consider that high concentrations of lactoferrin are well tolerated by newborn infants.

Widely used to support recovery from cancer

Numerous studies have documented the benefits of lactoferrin against many types of cancer, including leukemia, Hodgkin's disease, and cancers involving the colon, breast, and lung.

Many holistic practitioners use it to achieve great effects by combining it with other immune-enhancing natural cancer therapies. In one widely reported case, a patient who had not been responding particularly well to a program of natural cancer therapies suddenly showed almost miraculous improvement when lactoferrin was added to her regime. This seemingly "hopeless" case was transformed into a remarkable recovery.

Other case histories indicate that the negative effects of conventional cancer treatments like chemotherapy and radiation are drastically reduced or eliminated with supplemental lactoferrin. (The amounts of lactoferrin used in these reported cases ranges from 500 to 1,500 mg per day.) Again, it should be noted that lactoferrin appears to be perfectly safe, even in high amounts.

Lactoferrin in stroke recovery

A member of the HSI network had suffered three strokes by the age of 68.

After two days of lactoferrin supplementation, she reports, "I was in the house cooking, doing everything I'd always done. I'm still taking my medication for my heart attack, but I feel great! I have a lot of energy.

"Before, I couldn't speak plainly because of the stroke, but I can talk now! My speech has come back. Also, I hadn't been able to drive because my eyesight was so bad, but after a short time on the lactoferrin, I can drive again!"

Lactoferrin appears to have a profound effect on degenerative (as opposed to infectious) disease. Although we can't say yet exactly how, it's very possible that lactoferrin's antioxidant action plays a key role. As you know, free radicals oxidize the LDL (bad) cholesterol, which causes arteries to harden and circulation to suffer.

Hope for autistic and brain-damaged children

Lactoferrin may even hold significant hope for children with autism or brain injuries. Nutritional biochemist Patricia Kane of Millville, New Jersey, has begun working with autistic and brain-injured children and has witnessed surprising results with the administration of lactoferrin.

Although autism is a brain dysfunction, Dr. Kane points out that, because of the involvement of the entire body, improvement can only come about by embracing all the systemic interactions—a holistic approach. The use of lactoferrin represents significant progress toward this goal. Protection against the cryptosporidium parasites Cryptosporidium parasites cause acute diarrhea in people with strong, healthy immune systems but can be life-threatening in those who are immune compromised. Studies published in *Infection & Immunity* (no. 61, 1993, pp. 4079) have shown that colostrum is able to ameliorate or completely eliminate the clinical symptoms of those suffering from cryptosporidiosis.

Stops lethal and debilitating viruses—
including HIV and herpes—from replicating

Lactoferrin appears to be able to interfere with the replication of certain viruses, including some herpes viruses. These viruses have been linked to heart disease, inflammatory bowel disease, shingles, and chronic fatigue. Lactoferrin's antiviral properties have been proven effective against HIV. (In fact, one of the first big breakthroughs in lactoferrin research occurred six years ago when a medical journal reported its success in helping AIDS patients reverse the potentially life-threatening condition of chronic diarrhea.)

Lactoferrin—a healing revolution

When you look at the number of very different immune-enhancing functions that lactoferrin performs, it's easy to wonder: Is there any health condition that lactoferrin won't help? And the truth is that doctors and healers are discovering new uses for lactoferrin almost as quickly as they can test them. Even more importantly, you now have direct access to this revolutionary new tool for immune system activation. For information on purchasing lactoferrin, see the "Guide to Sources and Availability" on page 195.

Actions:

- Activates DNA that launches the immune response
- Activates neutrophil cells that surround and digest foreign bodies
- Binds with iron in the blood
- Acts as an antioxidant
- Acts as an anti-inflammatory

Benefits:

- Enhances natural killer (NK cell) activity that targets specific types of tumors and virus-infected cells
- Nutritionally deprives cancer cells and bacteria of the iron they need for metabolism and proliferation
- Prevents bacterial overgrowth in the gut, preventing dysbiosis
- Inhibits free-radical production
- Reduces inflammation, which can reduce pain and increase mobility

References

"Bovine Lactoferrin and Lactoferricin inhibit tumor metastasis in mice," Jpn. J. Cancer Res. vol. 88, pp. 184-190, 1997.

"Human lactoferrin inhibits growth of solid tumors and metastases in mice," Cancer Research, vol. 54, no. 9, pp. 2310-2, 1994.

"Modulation of natural killer and lymphokine-activated killer cell cytotoxicity by lactoferrin," J. Leukocyte Biology, vol. 51, pp. 343-349, 1992.

"Influence of lactoferrin on the function of human polymorphonuclear leukocytes and monocytes," J. Leukocyte Biology, vol. 49, pp. 427-433, 1991.

"Lactoferrin inhibits bacterial translocation in mice fed bovine milk," Applied and Environmental Microbiology, vol. 61, no. 11, pp. 4131-4134, 1995.

"Inhibition with Lactoferrin of in vitro infection with HHV," Jpn. J. of Medical Science and Biology, vol. 472, pp. 735, 1994.

"The Role of Lactoferrin as an anti-inflammatory molecule," Advances in Experimental Medicine and Biology, vol. 357, pp. 143-156, 1994.

"Killing of Candida Albicans by Lactoferricin B," Medical Microbiology and Immunology, vol. 182, no. 2, pp. 97-105, 1993.

Infopeptides:
The Next Generation Immune Booster

The Health Sciences Institute has been tracking the progress of a truly amazing natural product that has successfully treated everything from acute viral attacks to serious, chronic, and even life-threatening disorders. But until recently, this substance was available only to the small number of physicians involved in or aware of the research. We can finally share news of the healing potential of infopeptides, because an infopeptide product is now available to you.

On the basis of research done thus far, infopeptides have the potential to revolutionize at least three major areas of treatment:

(1) immune dysfunctions (from minor to major, including AIDS)

(2) childhood diarrhea

(3) myalgias and muscle pains, including arthritis and fibromyalgia

Recently, physicians at one of the most important and successful cancer centers in the world, Klinik St. George in Bad Aibling, Germany, became aware of this research. They are so impressed that they are using this product, along with lactoferrin (see Chapter 2) to treat 100 cancer patients.

Biochemical research finds a previously unknown compound in colostrum

Infopeptides are a type of peptide found in milk and colostrum (the mother's "first milk") and were not previously known to exist. They are fundamentally different from whole colostrum and from lactoferrin because they appear to have no direct antiviral or antibacterial properties of their own. They do, however, contain chemically coded instructions that appear to be vitally important to a properly regulated immune system.

Infopeptides, however, are not found naturally in breast milk. The longer peptide chains have to be broken down into shorter segments in order to work. This appears to happen naturally in the process of sucking milk from the breast—probably a result of a combination of physical manipulation and enzymes in the mouth of the newborn. Once they are activated in this way, infopeptides have an impressive ability to trigger powerful antiviral, antibacterial, and antiprotozoal immune functions. In that sense, their action is more hormone like than nutrientlike. But they seem to be self-regulating in a way that artificial hormones are not. As noted by Staroscik, et al. in *Molecular Immunology* (vol. 210, no. 120, pp. 1277-82):

A small-chain polyprotein-rich peptide in colostrum...has the same ability to regulate the activity of the immune system as the hormones of the thymus gland do. It activates an underactive immune system, helping it move into action against disease-causing organisms. It also suppresses an overactive immune system, such as is often seen in the autoimmune diseases.

It also appears to act on T cell precursors to produce helper T cells and suppressor T cells. The effect is similar to that of thymus hormones.

(Note: This country's most widely prescribed drug—synthetic estrogen—reduces the function of the thymus.)

Infopeptides are unique because of their ability to control both underactive and overactive immune systems (*Archives of Immunology & Therapeutic Experiments*, vol. 41, nos. 5-6, pp. 275-9, 1993). Research has linked these polypeptides to widespread biological actions that alleviate inflammation, nervous disorders, and even sleep patterns (*Trends in Neuroscience*, vol. 18, no. 3, pp. 130-6, 1995).

Another exciting aspect of the infopeptide mode of action is that it is not dose-dependent. That is, once a very small amount of an infopeptide is consumed, an increased dose does nothing more.

Help for arthritis, fibromyalgia, AIDS, and more

"Cytolog" is the name given to infopeptide products developed by a company that has been studying infopeptides since 1992. In a small-scale study, 82 percent of rheumatoid-arthritis patients experienced "good or very good" results within two to six weeks with the use of Cytolog. Subjects with osteoarthritis all reported "good or very good" responses; one patient is in complete remission. All of the patients had been taking at least one drug, and many of them had been taking up to four drugs—all to no avail.

The participants had been suffering from six to 20 years.

Cytolog helped to fight acute (and potentially lethal) diarrhea in children in Guatemala. Worldwide, between 5 and 10 million children die every year from diarrhea...making the implications of this research profound.

In another, as-yet-unpublished study, this one in Baltimore, AIDS patients showed a 50 percent reduction in symptoms in a short period of time with just 5 to 10 milliliters of Cytolog per day.

It will be months or even years before these findings appear in major medical journals, but because they are so significant, we are trying to get the word out as quickly as possible.

Doctors report incredible recoveries

Jeff Anderson, M.D., of Corte Madera, California, described his own experience with Cytolog after he contracted viral myalgic meningoen-cephalitis (a brain inflammation). He used two 5-milliliter doses per day for a week and found the results nothing short of amazing. He encountered rapid relief of inflammatory-connective-tissue pain (particularly myalgic pain and stiffness, as well as headache) within two or three minutes.

Dr. Arnold Takemoto, from Scottsdale, Arizona, stated that he thought the reports on Cytolog "too good to be true" when he first tested it clinically. He has been working with more than 500 active patients with medical problems that baffle traditional allopathic medicine. Dr. Takemoto's specialties are chronic fatigue immune-deficiency syndrome and fibromyalgia (two of the fastest-growing diseases among women), along with specialized consultation on referred patients who have stage-4 cancer. Takemoto reports that his patients are experiencing incredible results with Cytolog.

Shingles, digestive problems, joint pain:
All show dramatic improvement

Teresa E. Quinlin, M.D., of Winchester, Ohlio, has seen dramatic improvement in acute viral illnesses, including shingles. Gastritis and other digestive problems have also been quickly resolved. One woman suffering from polymyalgia rheumatica (a painful disease of the collagen tissue) had a 90 percent reduction in joint and muscle pain. Dr. Quinlin hopes to see a total remission in this case.

Are cows good enough?

Is the bovine source just as good as the human derivation? The answer is probably yes. Bovine colostrum and lactoferrin are close but not precise matches to human counterparts. Certain infopeptides from cows, however, are believed to be 100 percent identical to those found in human milk.

For those who are lactose intolerant, it's also important to recognize that milk sugars responsible for lactose intolerance and the proteins responsible for cow's-milk allergies are largely absent in colostrum.

Considering the small doses needed for effectiveness and the very small concentration of lactose remaining, the use of colostrum products should be of no concern to those with milk sensitivities.

Cytolog appears to be safe and well-tolerated when taken under a variety of circumstances and over extended periods of time. The benefits do not diminish but tend to increase over time. In fact, those who take Cytolog for three months or more relate that the benefits persist indefinitely even after they stop taking it.

We predict that you'll be hearing much more about infopeptides in the very near future. See the "Guide to Sources and Availability" on page 215.

Actions:

- Regulates the activity of the immune system
- Acts on T-cell precursors to produce helper T-cells and suppressor T-cells
- Triggers antiviral, antibacterial, and antiprotozoal functions

Benefits:

- Activates an underactive immune system, helping it fight disease-causing organisms
- Suppresses an overactive immune system, which is often seen in autoimmune diseases
- Alleviates inflammation
- Relieves myalgic pain and stiffness

CellAid:
Focusing on Skin; The Weakest Link In Your Immune System

Just when we think we've seen everything at the Health Sciences Institute, something comes across our desks that makes us take a long second look. What makes this product, CellAid, so different is the part of your body it focuses on—your skin—and how that can help you build up immunity to some of today's most deadly diseases.

When your skin is in top shape, it can help your liver, thymus, and other immune components fight illness. When it's not, you may be leaving yourself open to infection and even life-threatening microbes. Researchers have discovered that closing the skin's disease-fighting gaps, which are too frequently overlooked, may be a major way to level the playing field against infectious diseases.

Bolstering your skin can recharge your ability to fight disease

There are three main ways your skin helps fight disease. The first is with antibacterial peptides, which neutralize deadly organisms that come in contact with the skin and may protect you from bacterial invasion.[1]

Another important role of skin is to provide a home for T cells, which are the "foot soldiers" of your immune system in the fight against disease. In fact, half your circulating T cells are located in the skin's epidermis. Keeping your skin healthy helps maintain your T cells' ability to fight illness and aids the maturation process of some immune cells.

Your skin also regulates skin-cell turnover. Proper cell turnover means dead cells are being replaced by new ones at the correct rate. If the replacement process goes awry, cell replacement may become overactive or underactive. Overactive turnover means too many new cells are being made and can result in conditions like psoriasis. Underactive turnover occurs when cells are dying faster than they can be replaced. Either one of these conditions can preoccupy your immune system and prevent it from properly combating infections or other health problems.

Nutrients that target the skin and are specific to its immune system tasks may be able to strengthen your ability to fight disease, but it can be difficult to get enough through food. But now, researchers have discovered a way to use plant-based products that augment the body's cytokines. Cytokines are proteins that are part of the immune system and help prevent the spread of invading organisms.

Nourishing skin for fighting disease requires more than just beauty creams

Most skin-care products, such as emollients, wrinkle removers, and sun-blocks, temporarily improve the skin's appearance but usually don't nurture the skin's immune response. Products containing nutrients, such as vitamins A, C, and E, may help repair skin damage, but they may not boost or increase immune cells.

CellAid, a product used for the past 10 years in Europe and the Middle East has just become available in the United States. It's a three-part system containing an oral liquid and two topical creams that helps the skin (and the entire body) in its immune-system duties.

CellAid shows "complete inhibition" of a cancer-causing virus

An independent in vitro analysis conducted by University of California biochemist Kathleen S. Hall, Ph.D., found that CellAid shows "complete HPV-11 inhibition."[2] Human papilloma virus (HPV) is most frequently associated with cancers of the cervix. It is, however, also implicated in other types of cancers, especially those affecting the head and neck area. If you have HPV in your mouth, your risk of getting oral cancer is up to 4.7 times greater.[3] HPV has also been associated with cancers of the lung,[4] sinus cavity,[5] and nasal area.[6]

Increase your body's natural tumor killers

CellAid contains significant amounts of interleukin-12 (IL-12), an important tumor fighter, according to Aristo Vojdani, Ph.D., M.T., of Immunosciences Lab, who conducted an independent chemical analysis of the constituents.[7] Dr. Vojdani claims that raising your levels of this substance may increase your resistance to infectious diseases, spur the activity of your natural killer cells, and stimulate production of your T cells. Dr. Vojdani also identified a number of other types of immune reinforcers in CellAid, including IL-1a, IL-1b, IL-2, IL-4, IL-5, IL-6, IL-10, interferon-alpha and gamma, and TNF alpha (tumor necrosis factor), and TGF beta (transforming growth factor). This appears to be the first time these cytokine-like immune proteins have been extracted from a plant-based product.

Rasha Yousef Khalil, professor of immunology and head of the immuno-genetic and transplantation unit at the Ain Shams University Specialized Hospital in Cairo, found that CellAid increases the initial immune response by up to 306 percent![8]

This three-part synergistic program
may help protect you from serious diseases

To be honest, using CellAid seems a little daunting at first. And if you're someone who can't remember to take your vitamins every day, it may not be for you. Unlike other immune boosters, CellAid is a complete system that must be used together. The liquid is taken and the creams are applied every morning and evening. It is essential that all three components be used to achieve the synergistic effect.

Although this is not as quick as swallowing a few pills, it takes just a couple of minutes to go through the entire regimen.

The liquid, which has a mild licorice flavor, contains 12 active ingredients, including herbal extracts like ginger root, clove buds, cinnamon bark, and hibiscus flower. It also contains fenugreek seeds, which have anti-inflammatory properties and are shown to produce 70 percent inhibition of tumor-cell growth in animals.[9]

One teaspoonful is taken twice a day on an empty stomach 30 minutes before eating. Hold the liquid in your mouth for one minute before swallowing, allowing the cells in your mouth to absorb the nutrients and thereby get a jump-start on delivering them to your bloodstream.

The topical ointments—Skintrinsic SkinGel and Antioxidant SkinSerum—are used alternately. SkinGel contains, among other things, echinacea and panthenol. For the first three weeks, a dime-size portion of SkinGel is applied twice a day, at the same time you take the liquid. Rub in the cream gently and wait for it to absorb, which can take 10-15 minutes.

After the first three weeks, switch from SkinGel to SkinSerum. SkinSerum contains 16 ingredients, including inositol, lipoic acid, maritime pine, and quercetin. Apply the SkinSerum for one week, following the same procedure mentioned above for SkinGel.

The manufacturer suggests using CellAid for a minimum of three and up to six months to help build up your body's immune response. They also recommend taking a two-week break from the product every three months, which will allow your body to continue responding to the formulation instead of becoming used to it. After the initial six-month period, you can use CellAid three or four months throughout the year or whenever your immune system is low, such as during times of illness or stress.

One of the most important factors in supplement use is knowing whether the product is working. Some people may experience temporary immune responses in the first month they take CellAid. These responses, if they occur, are a normal sign of immune system balancing and usually go away after a week or two. Such responses may include a rise in body temperature, fatigue, or an increase of discomfort in areas of pre-existing pain or inflammation. If the response feels too strong for you, simply decrease the amount of CellAid, or stop taking it for a few days.

In some people with high blood platelet counts, high blood pressure, or hyperthyroidism, CellAid may elevate these conditions. This response is usually temporary and the body adjusts. However, if you have any of these conditions, you should be monitored by your doctor and should initially take CellAid only every two to three days (and in lesser amounts than indicated). If you are diabetic or on blood thinning medications (including regular aspirin therapy), you should have your blood monitored regularly as the medication may need adjustment. And, again, please work closely with your physician.

CellAid is not cheap. It's available from Herbaceuticals only as a complete system, so its components cannot be purchased separately. In order to follow the manufacturer's recommended three to six month treatment regime, the initial investment can be costly. Of course, if you've been battling illness and unable to strengthen your immune system enough to fight it, this could be the solution you've been seeking. For additional ordering information see the "Guide to Sources and Availability" on page on page 215.

Actions:

- Completely inhibits HPV-11, the Human pailloma Virus that is associated with cancers of the cervix, head and neck areas.
- Delivers significant amounts of interleukin-12 an important tumor fighter.

Benefits:

- Increases your resistance to infectious diseases, spurs the activity of your natural killer cells, and stimulates the production of your T cells.
- Boosts the initial immune response by up to 306%.

References
[1] Nord Med, 111(6):176-9, 1996
[2] Personal communication from Kathleen S. Hall, Ph.D., University of California, Davis, Oct. 26, 1998
[3] Oral Surg Oral Med Oral Pathol Oral Radiol Endod, 91(6):622-35, 2001
[4] Histopathology, 38(4):355-67, 2001
[5] Laryngoscope, 111(6):1,104-10, 2001
[6] Head Neck, 21(1):21-9, 1999
[7] Personal Communication from Aristo Vojdani, Ph.D., M.T., Sept. 8, 2000
[8] Personal Communication from Professor Rasha Yousef Khalil, Ain Shams University Specialized Hospital, Oct. 29, 1996
[9] Phytother Res, 15(3):257, 2001

Cancer-Free for the 21st Century

Cancer: one of the most feared diagnoses in medicine today and, unfortunately, one of the most common. Every day 3,014 Americans hear the words, "You have cancer." The good news is that the majority of them will survive it. In fact, at this moment, there are 10 million cancer survivors in this country alone. Although cancer still ends far too many lives prematurely, the death rates from some important cancers are falling. With better and earlier detection, as well as a wide range of conventional and alternative treatments, cancer is a treatable disease. More importantly, it is a preventable one.

In this section are the results of late-breaking research that confirms the roles of nutrition and natural immune-supporting substances in reducing your chances of developing this dreaded disease. You'll find chapters on powerful immunity-protecting mushroom extract, glycoalkaloids, Chinese herbs for prostate cancer, and cancer fighting graviola. Lactoferrin is also an important adjunct therapy for cancer: HSI research shows its promise as a supplement to traditional therapy. Read about lactoferrin in the immuno-support section of this book on page 7.

---— C H A 5 P T E R —---

AHCC:
Hybridized Mushroom Extract
Provides Powerful Immune Protection

Until now, unless you knew someone who could secretly mail it to you, or you were lucky enough to be part of a research study, the only way you could have access to this remarkable immune booster was to live in Japan. For the last five years in Japan, people with cancer, AIDS, and many other life-threatening illnesses—as well as healthy people who wish to stay that way—have been revving up their immune systems, destroying tumor cells, and preventing cancer and other illnesses with a powerful extract called AHCC (activated hexose correlate compound). Now, for the first time, AHCC is being made available to consumers in the United States.

AHCC is an extract of a unique hybridization of several kinds of medical mushrooms known for their immune-enhancing abilities. On their own, each mushroom has a long medical history in Japan, where their extracts are widely prescribed by physicians. But when combined into a single hybrid mushroom, the resulting active ingredient is so potent that dozens of rigorous scientific studies have now established AHCC to be one of the world's most powerful— and safe—immune stimulators.

In vitro, animal, and human studies confirm that AHCC effectively works against and, in some cases, even prevents the recurrence of liver cancer,[1] prostate cancer, ovarian cancer, multiple myeloma, breast cancer, AIDS, and other life-threatening conditions, with no dangerous side effects. In smaller doses, AHCC can also boost the immune function of healthy people, helping to prevent infections and promote wellbeing.

One reason for AHCC's success is its relatively tiny molecular size. Most mushroom extracts have a molecular weight in the hundreds of thousands of daltons[2], making them too large to be absorbed directly into human blood. But, AHCC is an ogliosaccharide with a molecular weight of just

SPECIALIZED IMMUNE CELLS AND COMPONENTS

Recent studies show that the compound AHCC significantly boosts the function of the immune system. The immune system consists of highly specialized cells and components. These cells and components find and destroy microbes, pathogens and tumor cells and are broken down as follows:

Interleukin-12 is released by macrophages in response to infection and begins the process of customizing immune system cells to suit the specific invader. It enhances the ability of Natural Killer (NK) cells to destroy microbes and cancer cells, induces interferon production, and stimulates the production of activated T cells and NK cells.

Interleukin-2 is a chemical messenger, a substance that can improve the body's response to disease. It stimulates the growth of certain disease-fighting blood cells in the immune system.

Tumor Necrosis Factor (TNF) is released by macrophages and induces fever. It kills cancer cells and causes the production of other immune components called lymphokines.

Interferon is a type of specialized protein made by human cells that fights viral infections by preventing the virus from multiplying inside cells.

Lymphocyte is a type of white blood cell that is long lived and carries memory of past infections. As they mature they eventually turn into B and T cells.

T cells are a class of lymphocytes (also called T lymphocytes) derived from the thymus that control cell-mediated immune reactions and the development of B cells. There are three fundamentally different types of T cells: helper, killer, and suppressor. Each has many subdivisions.

B cells are a type of lymphocytes normally involved in the production of antibodies to combat infection. During infections, individual B cell clones multiply and are transformed into plasma cells, which produce large amounts of antibodies against a particular antigen on a foreign microbe.

5,000 daltons, making it easily absorbed in the gut. Instead, they are simply digested without any particular clinical benefit. Once absorbed, AHCC profoundly improves immune system function—our first line of defense against infection and disease.

Many health problems, including some that were previously thought to be unrelated to the immune system, are now known to result from some degree of immune deficiency. Subtle to severe immune dysfunction can combine with other factors to cause many illnesses, including:

- Recurrent infections, such as colds, flu, and parasites
- Gum disease
- Heart disease
- Peptic ulcer
- Cancers
- Slow healing wounds
- Digestive problems
- AIDS
- Multiple sclerosis
- Auto-immune illnesses

For years, conventional medicine has tried to cope with these and other conditions as separate illnesses, often relying on invasive and potentially dangerous disease-specific drugs, surgery, and other treatments. Not only has this approach yielded only moderate success, in many cases it has created additional health problems: chemotherapy side effects, surgical complications, drug reactions, super-resistant bacteria, and other problems that in some cases may be as bad as (or worse than) the specific disease. In fact, according to the *Journal of the American Medical Association*, (vol. 279, April 1998) prescription medications kill more than 100,000 people a year, making adverse drug reactions the fourth leading cause of death in the United States.

The cutting edge in medicine today is to shift away from disease-specific interventions and to focus on the fundamental, underlying causes of health and disease: the proper functioning of interdependent body systems, such as the nervous system, the endocrine system, and the immune system.

Calling up your first line of defense

Around the clock, our immune systems literally stand between us and the rest of the world. Without it, our bodies would be overrun by all sorts of bacteria, viruses, parasites, fungi and other invaders, infections would rapidly spread, and cancer cells would proliferate. Like a highly responsive and well-coordinated army, our immune systems are composed of a variety of specialized immune cells (see the box on page 30) that identify, seek out, and destroy microbes, pathogens, and tumor cells.

First on the scene of possible trouble are the phagocytes and natural killer (NK) cells, which respond quickly to potential threats. Often referred to as the body's "front-line defense," these cells are constantly on the look out for any suspicious substances—a virus lurking in the throat, a bacterium on the skin, a toxin breathed into the lungs, or a wayward cancer cell hiding among healthy cells.

Macrophages (a type of phagocyte) destroy and digest invading particles. NK cells, on the other hand, latch onto the surface of substances or the outer membranes of cancer cells and inject a kind of chemical hand grenade (called a granule) into the interior. Once inside, the granules explode and destroy the bacteria or cancer cell within five minutes. Itself undamaged, the NK cell then moves onto its next victim. In its prime, a NK cell can take on two cancer cells at the same time, speeding up the process.

Recent research shows that as we age, our immune systems function less efficiently. In particular, the ability of our NK cells to respond quickly and effectively declines with age and illness. When NK cells lose their ability to either recognize or destroy invaders, health can deteriorate rapidly. Moderately low to dangerously low NK cell activity levels have been found in people with AIDS, cancer, immune deficiency, liver disorders, various infections, and other diseases. Because measurements of NK cell activity are closely correlated with one's chances of survival, anything that helps increase NK cell activity may help people treat, recover from, and/or prevent these illnesses.

Research finds remarkable immune system boost in multiple ways

Several scientific studies of the extract AHCC, published in respected peer-reviewed journals such as International Journal of Immunology,[3] Anti-Cancer Drugs,[4] and Society of Natural Immunity,[5] have established the health benefits and safety of AHCC more conclusively than nearly any other natural supplement. What is especially remarkable about AHCC is that it consistently and effectively boosts immune system function in the following ways:

- It stimulates cytokine (IL-2, IL-12, TNF, and INF) production, which stimulates immune function.
- It increases NK cell activity against diseased cells as much as 300 percent.
- It increases the formation of explosive granules within NK cells. The more ammunition each NK cell carries, the more invaders it can destroy.
- It increases the number and the activity of lymphocytes, specifically increasing T Cells up to 200 percent.
- It increases Interferon levels, which inhibits the replication of viruses and stimulates NK cell activity.
- It increases the formation of TNF, a group of proteins that help destroy cancer cells.

These dramatic immune effects translate into profound health benefits.

Study documents complete remission in six of 11 patients

A 1995 clinical trial reported on in the *International Journal of Immunotherapy*[6] showed that 3 grams of AHCC per day significantly lowered the level of tumor markers (substances that detect the presence of tumors) found in patients with several different types of cancer, including prostate cancer, ovarian cancer, multiple myeloma, and breast cancer. This study documented complete remissions in six of 11 patients and significant increases in NK cell activity in nine of 11 patients. T and B cell activity levels also rose considerably.

AHCC shown to prevent the recurrence of liver cancer

The latest, and most extraordinary AHCC research results were presented at the 33rd Congress of the European Society for Surgical Research in 1998, regarding the treatment of liver cancer.[7] Liver cancer was the fifth most prevalent type of cancer worldwide last year, accounting for 5.4 percent of new cancer cases yet it is fourth in terms of mortality (427,000 deaths, 8.2 percent of the total). This difference reflects the extremely poor prognosis for this cancer, with survival rates currently only at three to five percent.

In this study, 121 patients with hepatocellular carcinoma (liver cancer), who all had their tumors surgically removed, were divided into three groups. Group A (38 patients) took 3-6 grams of AHCC per day after surgery. Group B (18 patients) began taking AHCC after recurrences of their cancers were verified. Group C (the remaining 65 patients) took a placebo.

One year after surgery, blood levels of tumor markers were significantly lower in Group A (those taking AHCC right after surgery) than in Groups B and C. And after approximately three to four years (depending on when each patient entered the study), the survival rate of Group A was much higher than the survival rate of Group C (placebo).[8] Not only did many Group A patients survive longer than patients in the other two groups, many remained entirely free of liver cancer. This study strongly suggests that AHCC has a powerful preventive effect in postoperative liver cancer patients.

After hearing about these and other research results, the University of California is testing the effects of AHCC in a large clinical study of prostate cancer patients. Results are expected to be announced later this year.

No side effects reported from AHCC

Unlike conventional cancer treatments, AHCC seems to be completely non-toxic. Even after years of use at therapeutic dosage levels, toxicity tests confirmed that this natural extract caused no toxicity, adverse reactions, or unwanted side effects.[9] Experts say this is because AHCC works to enhance the activities of the immune system, rather than attack cancer cells directly as chemotherapy does.

Chemotherapy works by trying to destroy fast-growing or replicating cells. Unlike most normal, healthy cells, which grow slowly, cancer cells replicate very quickly, amassing into tumors and metastasizing (spreading) to other areas of the body. Chemotherapy is intended to poison and kill quickly replicating cells. Unfortunately, chemotherapy does not have the ability to discriminate rapidly replicating cancer cells from rapidly replicating normal, healthy cells, such as hair, nail, and stomach lining cells, which are killed off during chemotherapy. This explains why so many cancer patients endure hair loss and vomiting during chemotherapy.

AHCC causes no side effects because, rather than directly killing living cells, it stimulates the body's natural defense system to seek out and selectively destroy invading bacteria, viruses, parasites, and cancer cells.

AHCC now available in the United States

There are many immune stimulators on the market today, some backed by research documenting increases in NK cell activity. AHCC is one of the few that has shown the ability to actually promote cancer remission in human clinical trials.

With results this powerful, many people without cancer or other life-threatening illnesses, such as AIDS, also choose to take AHCC to stave off flu, herpes, and other infections, as well as to fight cancer.

After years of successful use in Japan, AHCC is now being made available in the United States as the active ingredient in a product called ImmPower. Distributed by American BioSciences, ImmPower comes in gelatin capsules containing 500mg of AHCC (proprietary blend).

"As a researcher and immunologist I feel AHCC is an absolute blessing for those fighting disease and for those who want to prevent disease. Many illnesses can be traced back to immune dysfunction and there is no doubt in my mind AHCC can enhance NK cell, T-cell and B-cell function," says Aristo Vojdani, Ph.D., M.T., associate professor of internal medicine, Drew University School of Medicine and Science and president of ImmunoSciences Lab, Inc.

ImmPower can be taken in preventive or therapeutic doses and should be discussed with your personal physician. For prevention, the recommended dose is one gram per day taken as one 500mg capsule in the morning and again at night. This dose will help increase NK cell activity and support immune system functioning for good health and general well-being. For those with cancer, AIDS, or other life-threatening conditions, the research indicates a therapeutic dose of two capsules in the morning, two at mid-day and two at night for a total of 3 grams per day to jump start NK cell activity. After three weeks, the dose can be reduced to one gram per day (one capsule in the morning and one at night), to maintain the increased NK cell activity level. To determine whether or not your NK cells are functioning properly, there is a test available. We highly recommend discussing this option with your personal physician. A four-hour 51 Chromium-release assay test (NK Cell Function Test) will determine your NK cell activity level. If you are interested in having this test done your doctor may call ImmunoSciences Lab, Inc. in Beverly Hills, California at (800) 950-4686.

See your source directory on page 215.

Actions:

- Boosts the number and activity of lymphocytes, cells that convey nourishment to and collect waste products from tissues.
- Increases Interferon, antiviral glycoprotein, levels

Benefits:

- Stimulates cytokine production leading to an increased immune functioning and amplifying the ability to prevent infections.
- Improves the functioning of Natural Killer Cells by providing increased granulation enhancing their ability to destroy invading bacteria, viruses, parasites, and fungi.
- Improves immune system function.

References

[1] H. Kitade, et al. XXXIIIrd Congress of the European Society for Surgical Research, p 74, 1998.

[2] Daltons are ultra small units of measure used to compare the weights of molecules.

[3] International Journal of Immunology XI (1), pp. 23-28, 1995.

[4] Anti-Cancer Drugs, vol. 9, pp. 343-350, 1998.

[5] Society of Natural Immunity, pp. 56, 1997.

[6] Ghoneum M., et al. International Journal of Immunotherapy, XI (1) pp 23-28, 1995.

[7] H. Kitade, et al. XXXIIIrd Congress of the European Society for Surgical Research, p 74, 1998.

[8] H. Kitade, et al. XXXIIIrd Congress of the European Society for Surgical Research, p 74, 1998.

[9] Mamdooh Ghoneum, Ph.D., Society of Natural Immunity, p 56, May 25-28, 1996.

CHAPTER 6

Glycoalkaloids:
A new non-surgical solution for skin cancer

Sooner or later, skin cancer affects nearly everyone. The removal of skin-cancer lesions is one of the most common outpatient surgeries performed today. But before you let your dermatologist schedule surgery to remove a cancerous or "suspicious" lesion, you should know about an inexpensive, all-natural product that can completely remove some skin cancers in as little as three to four weeks, without a trace of scar tissue.

You can also use this product to remove precancerous actinic keratoses (unsightly patches of scaly, sun-damaged skin that can turn cancerous at any time). Within a few weeks, any area of rough, uneven skin can be smoothed and renewed. In fact, this cream is also being used to erase wrinkles, blemishes, and age spots—(more on that in a moment.)

The results are in: you can use this therapy with confidence

In recent months, you may have read of a natural botanical extract from Australia reported to be highly effective in treating skin cancers without surgery or harsh chemical treatments. We've received many letters from members asking for more information about the mysterious "devil's apple" plant and whether it is a safe and effective alternative for treating skin cancer.

There's no doubt that chemical compounds called glycoalkaloids, derived from the devil's apple plant, can effectively remove skin-cancer lesions. An Australian study of 72 patients posted a 100% cure rate. Unfortunately, there are drawbacks to the Australian product. Although it is effective, it can be highly irritating to the skin and can take up to three months to work. Moreover, it is very difficult to obtain outside Australia.

Last year, however, a leading American research laboratory made several important advances in the formulation of glycoalkaloid cream. The researchers created a new product called SkinAnswer, which promised to be even more effective (and quicker) than the Australian prototype, and much less irritating to the skin.

And now, the first clinical trials on SkinAnswer are complete. The results have confirmed the preliminary reports beyond a doubt: It dissolves both basal cell and squamous-cell cancers in as little as three to four weeks, with absolutely no scarring. It also painlessly removes precancerous actinic keratosis lesions. Patients and doctors who have used both SkinAnswer and the earlier Australian version report that SkinAnswer seems to work more quickly and with less pain and irritation.

Selectively targets cancer cells; healthy cells are unaffected

Glycoalkaloids are produced in many fruits and vegetables as part of their defense against insects and other animals. Historically, the use of glycoalkaloid-rich plants (members of the Solanum family) in the treatment of cancer goes back to the second century.

As a treatment for skin cancer, glycoalkaloids are thought to work by exploiting structural differences between healthy and abnormal skin cells. As skin cells change from healthy to cancerous, the cell wall becomes more permeable, allowing glycoalkoloids to penetrate into abnormal cells. Once inside the cell wall, glycoalkaloids release enzymes that literally digest the cells from the inside out. Under a microscope, the cells actually appear to explode.

As the abnormal cells die, they are replaced by normal, healthy skin cells that do not absorb the glycoalkaloids and are spared their destructive effects.

DEPLETED OZONE LEVELS LEAVE YOU UNPROTECTED

This year, nearly 1 million cases of skin cancer will be diagnosed in the U.S. alone. Many scientists attribute rising skin cancer rates to the thinning of the ozone layer. Each 1% decrease in ozone translates into a 3% increase in the amount of UV-B radiation reaching the earth, which in turn translates into 10 to 15 thousand new cases of skin cancer. Experts predict that at this rate, worldwide skin cancer rates will be 26% higher in the year 2001 than they were in 1997.

EFFECTIVENESS OF SKINANSWER IN ELIMINATING SKIN LESIONS

Type of lesion	Mean treatment	Complete period recovery
Basal cell	27 days	78%
Squamous cell	30 days	100%
Keratosis	31 days	72% (28% had partial recovery)

All results were confirmed by biopsy. In the cases in which only partial recovery was achieved in the trial period, it was anticipated that continued use would eventually result in 100% remission rates.

Source: Margaret Olsen, M.D., Chief of Dermatology at Saint John's Health Center, Santa Monica, California.

In any cancer therapy, the ideal is a "targeted therapy"(one that attacks cancer cells and spares healthy ones). And it appears that SkinAnswer does precisely that. When it is applied to a cancerous lesion, you are likely to notice redness and inflammation (even a burning sensation indicating that the cancer cells are being destroyed). An ulceration, or opening in the skin, may develop as the lesion begins to slough off.

These diseased cells will quickly be replaced by healthy cells, which are unaffected by the glycoalkaloid cream. In fact, you know that the treatment is complete when the cream no longer produces a reaction, indicating that normal healthy cells have replaced all of the skin-cancer cells.

For use on squamous cell or basal-cell skin cancers, SkinAnswer is applied to the area twice a day, as directed on the package. Before reapplying, rubbing the area with a washcloth to remove dead skin layers will speed the healing process. Treated areas should be left uncovered if at all possible. (Covering the treatment area with a bandage seems to increase the amount of irritation to the skin and may actually slow the speed of treatment.)

Get rid of that "suspicious" spot before it becomes cancerous

In addition to their dramatic effect on skin-cancer lesions, glycoalkaloids can also act a natural exfoliant that can smooth virtually any rough, uneven, or raised skin condition. As Dr. Margaret Olsen, author of the recent clinical trial, noted, "This study began as a search for treatment for basal and squamous cell cancers, but evolved into a more effective treatment for actinic [sun-damage-related] keratoses."

Several of the trial participants had, in addition to diagnosed skin cancers, extensive areas of sun damage, resulting in raised, scaly patches of actinic keratosis. According to Dr. Olsen, these patients came in for treatment for one or two symptomatic lesions, had thousands of keratosis lesions. They were, as Dr. Olsen noted, "generally oblivious to the extent of their sun damage."

In addition to treating the active lesions as part of the trial, these patients also applied SkinAnswer to wide areas of sun-damaged skin. The result was easy and painless exfoliation of the keratoses, leaving smooth skin after a few weeks. These findings were confirmed by other researchers. With the ease and cost-effectiveness of SkinAnswer, there is no longer any reason to "watch and wait." Precancerous lesions can be removed immediately before the situation becomes more serious.

Other noncancerous, raised skin growths, such as moles, skin tags, and even "liver spots," can be effectively and painlessly removed by SkinAnswer's powerful exfoliating action. Although these irregularities usually pose no

---

YOU CAN STILL ENJOY THE WARM SUMMER SUN *(IN FACT, YOU SHOULD)*

There are also some benefits to moderate sun exposure. For example, direct sunlight promotes the production of Vitamin D. Among its many beneficial functions, Vitamin D aids in the absorption of calcium, which is crucial to maintaining bone mass as we grow older. Unfortunately, our bodies make less vitamin D as we age. In fact, vitamin D deficiency is epidemic among seniors.

Recent studies have shown that sufficient levels of antioxidant vitamins, like vitamin C, E, and betacarotene, act as natural sunscreens, protecting your skin from sunburns and other sun damage. (*Journal of Photochemistry and Photobiology*, vol. 41, nos. 1-2, pp. 1-10, 1997). So, take your antioxidants and enjoy a regular dose of sunlight. It will strengthen your bones and buoy your mood as well.

threat of cancer, you may wish to remove them for cosmetic reasons. Compared with elective cosmetic surgery, glykoalkaloids provide an extremely cost-effective alternative. Other treatment applications currently under investigation include acne and psoriasis.

Note: In the treatment of active lesions (basal-cell and squamous-cell cancers) with SkinAnswer, some temporary discomfort is to be expected. However, it appears to be far less uncomfortable than Efudex (commonly prescribed as a topical chemotherapy for skin cancers). One patient remarked, "If this were Efudex, I'd be screaming by now." In addition, SkinAnswer was effective on lesions that had been unsuccessfully treated with Efudex. SkinAnswer is essentially painless to use for keratoses and for other cosmetic applications.

A "face-lift in a jar?"

Dr. Allen Rosen, a prominent plastic surgeon in Bloomfield, New Jersey, began using SkinAnswer as part of a clinical trial for squamous-cell skin cancer. Like Dr. Olsen, he also found it to be highly effective in eroding noncancerous and precancerous lesions, such as keratoses. Its intense, yet gentle exfoliating action led Dr. Rosen to consider the role of glycoalkaloid creams as a treatment for fine lines and wrinkles. "Physician-administered glycolic peels are routinely used as an alternative to cosmetic surgery to rejuvenate the skin. SkinAnswer is an over-the-counter product that might be used in much the same way and with the same level of effectiveness [to reduce the effects of aging and sun exposure]. It has a gentleness that traditional peels do not have."

Dr. Rosen notes that the extent of exfoliation can be controlled through frequency of use and by covering the treatment area. He cautions against covering or bandaging the treatment area, as this can over-intensify the exfoliation effect, especially on delicate skin. Intense discomfort and/or burning may indicate a sensitivity or allergy to the product. In this case, use should be decreased or discontinued. (A slight tingling sensation when the cream is applied is normal.)

Dr. Rosen is now conducting a clinical trial on SkinAnswer as a cosmetic treatment for facial wrinkles and will have the results of that study by the end of the year. Although there is much research still to be done, he finds SkinAnswer to be "an incredibly exciting development in skin care."

It may be a year or more before the new clinical studies are published, but you or your doctor can request a set of the published glycoalkaloid research papers for $10 (including shipping) by calling 1(800) 742-7534. SkinAnswer is available through some pharmacies and by mail order. (See page 215 for details.)

Actions:

- Penetrates into cancerous cells, where it releases enzymes that digest the cells from the inside out.
- Acts as a powerful exfoliant.

Benefits:

- Provides painless, cost-effective removal of precancerous growths and skin irregularities.

Juzen-taiho-to:
Increasing Cancer Survival Rates

When we stumbled upon Energy Kampo, we assumed it must be a mild botanical designed to put a little extra pep in a person's day, maybe even ease the symptoms of chronic fatigue. But this product, which makes only the humble claim to help "maintain energy and well being," is actually one of Japan's most widely used herbal combinations that reportedly help the body cope with infections, disease, injury, and other stresses.

In Japan, this formulation of 10 herbal ingredients is called Juzen-taiho-to and is used for a wide variety of conditions. People struggling with chronic diseases (including rheumatoid arthritis, ulcerative colitis, atopic dermatitis, and chronic fatigue syndrome) take it to ease fatigue, anemia, circulatory problems, night sweats, and loss of appetite. Cancer patients take it to improve their overall condition and lessen the adverse effects of chemotherapy, radiation, and surgery.[1] It has been the subject of dozens of published studies in Asia, which have shown its potential to stimulate activity in the immune system by activating components like T-cells, lymphocytes, macrophages, spleen cells, and natural killer cells. Researchers say its immune-building properties can help people lessen the impact of lingering illness, retard the growth of cancer, and even slow the aging process.

Juzen-taiho-to proven to increase life span

Aging is caused in part by the gradual decline of T-cell activity. T-cells identify and destroy antigens (such as toxins and tumor cells) in the body, and often muster other immune responses to protect the body from disease.

One group of researchers reported that enhanced T-cell activity could even affect lifespan. Their study showed that mice fed Juzen-taiho-to lived an average of six months longer than untreated littermates.[2] On average, mice live for roughly two years; so this study showed that Juzen-taiho-to increased the average life span by 25 percent.

Treatment has potential to retard tumor growth and increase cancer survival rates

An enhanced immune system can help your body recover from any form of infection, disease, or injury. While some research and clinical practice has dealt with Juzen-taiho-to's ability to fight a range of diseases, the majority of the research has focused on the formula's potential to help cancer patients.

To our knowledge, there have not been any large-scale human trials examining the potential of Juzen-taiho-to. While researching this chapter, however, we found numerous published studies (all in Asian medical journals) documenting the formula's ability to retard tumor growth and metastases in laboratory animals.

At the Research Institute for Wakan-Yaku in Japan, researchers injected cancer cells into a group of mice, then gave them oral doses of Juzen-taiho-to (40 mg/day/mouse) for seven days. The treatment significantly inhibited tumor growth and prolonged survival compared to untreated mice.[3]

At the same institute, researchers set out to determine if Juzen-taiho-to could prevent colon cancer from metastasizing to the liver. They gave mice oral doses of Juzen-taiho-to for seven days prior to implanting tumors in their colons. The treatment produced a dose-dependent inhibition of cancer cells in the liver and significantly enhanced the subjects' survival rate compared to untreated mice. The treatment was not effective on mice that were already T-cell-deficient at the beginning of the experiment.[4]

However, in two separate studies, researchers documented how daily doses of Juzen-taiho-to caused old mice to develop more T cells.[5] (Curiously, one study showed the treatment did nothing to enhance the immune functions of younger mice.) The researchers reported that the treatment proved useful in correcting impaired T-cell activity in older mice and could be recommended to older humans. They concluded that, "such effects of [Juzen-taiho-to] may help prevent the development of diseases…in the elderly."[6]

THIS UNIQUE COMBINATION OF HERBS OFFERS A WEALTH OF HEALING POTENTIAL

Juzen-taiho-to is actually an ancient Chinese medicine, and was adopted by Japanese physicians during the Kamakura dynasty (1192-1333 AD). Following extensive clinical experience and pharmacological examination, the Japanese came to regard Juzen-taiho-to as a strengthening tonic for the ill and the elderly. The formulation contains the following 10 herbs, each of which has a long history and strong reputation for its healing properties.

Astragalus root (Astragali Radix)—An antiviral agent and general immune enhancer used in traditional Chinese medicine (TCM) to ease night sweats, fatigue, loss of appetite, and diarrhea. Reportedly, it helps counteract the immune-suppressing effects of cancer treatments like chemotherapy. It also helps lower blood pressure, improve circulation, and prevent heart disease.

Atractylodes Rhizome (Atractylodis Rhizoma)—A little-known TCM botanical grown mainly in Inner Mongolia, this thistle has been used to treat digestive problems, diarrhea, bloating, fatigue, as well as pain in the joints or extremities.

Chuangxiong (Cnidium Rhizome)—A TCM herb used to promote blood circulation and relieve pain.

Cinnamon bark (Cinnamomi Cortex)—Used in TCM to treat diarrhea, influenza, and parasitic worms. Cinnamon is currently taken to ease indigestion and stimulate appetite.

Dong quai (Angelicae Radix) —In TCM, dong quai is often taken as a menopause supplement (to relieve such conditions as such as hot flashes and vaginal dryness) and as a blood tonic (to regulate blood sugar and pressure, and to prevent blood clots and anemia). Studies have produced conflicting results on its efficacy and have suggested that it may work better in multi-herb formulas.

Panax ginseng (Ginseng Radix)—Traditionally, ginseng has been used to strengthen digestion, improve lung function, calm the spirit, and increase overall energy. Modern medical research has documented its potential to strengthen immunity against colds, flus and other infections; to stimulate the mind and foster a sense of well-being; and to help control diabetes and improve physical endurance.

Hoelen (Hoelen)—A botanical that reportedly acts as a diuretic and sedative, and a moderator of high blood sugar.

Licorice (Glycyrrhizae Radix) —Licorice has demonstrated abilities to act as an anti-inflammatory, cough suppressant, and anti-viral agent. It appears to increase blood flow in the stomach, possibly preventing ulcers. Recently, it has also been suggested as a possible treatment for chronic fatigue syndrome (CFS), since it mimics the action of adrenal hormones that are underactive in CFS patients. Licorice, however, contains glycyrrhiza, which can cause fluid retention, increased blood pressure, and loss of potassium.

Peony root (Paeoniae Radix) —Considered a blood tonic, it is used to correct imbalances in the blood, including poisoning, anemia, and poor circulation. It is not recommended for people with weakened livers.

Rehmannia root (Rehmanniae Radix)—An ancient Oriental botanical used to lower blood pressure and cholesterol, improve blood flow in the brain, and ease weakness. Some reports suggest it might even help avoid premature graying and baldness.

Source: The Natural Pharmacist (www.tnp.com), "Healthy Healing," 11th edition by Linda Page, Alternatives from Nature (www.herbsrainbear.com), Herbwalk.com, Healthphone.com, and Holistic-online.com.

Not every experiment was successful, though. Studies showed that Juzen-taiho-to alone was not effective or only slightly effective in inhibiting the growth of certain varieties of melanoma, sarcoma, and fibrosarcoma (cancers of the skin, bone, and connective tissue), leukemia and Lewis lung carcinoma.

Formula increases power, lessens side effects of chemotherapy

While no one has suggested this 10-herb formula can replace radiation, chemotherapy, or surgery, preliminary research suggests Juzen-taiho-to can increase the power of conventional cancer treatment and lessen some of its worst side effects.

At Toyama Medical and Pharmaceutical University in Japan, researchers tested the ability of Juzen-taiho-to and the cancer drug interferon alpha (IFN-alpha) to prevent renal (kidney cell) cancer from metastasizing to the lungs of laboratory mice. They found that the combination of both treatments offered much greater results for inhibiting metastasis than either treatment had alone. Furthermore, the combined treatment did not induce any weight loss—one of the negative side effects associated with IFN-alpha therapy."[7]

Other studies reported that the combination of Juzen-taiho-to and conventional cancer drugs inhibited the growth of sarcoma, melanoma, fibrosarcoma, bladder cancer, colon cancer, leukemia, and abdominal tumors more effectively than either the formula or the drug could individually."[8,9]

The combination can also ameliorate the side effects of treatment. In several studies, Japanese researchers found that mice treated orally with Juzen-taiho-to for one to two weeks before receiving conventional cancer drug treatment suffered fewer side effects. Liver and kidney toxicity was significantly reduced, and the animals didn't lose as many blood cells and platelets or as much body weight as untreated mice. Overall, their immune systems remained stronger and their survival times were longer.

Juzen-taiho-to is sold in the United States under the label Energy Kampo. Ordering information is in the Guide to Sources and Availability starting on page 215.

Actions:

- Ability to stimulate activity in the immune system by activating componets like T-cells, lymphocytes, macrophages, spleen cells, and natural killer cells.

- May retard tumor growth and metastasis.

Benefits:

- Immune-building properties can help lessen the impact of lingering illness, retard the growth of cancer, and even slow the aging process.

- Corrects impaired T-cell activity and may prevent the development of diseases in the elderly.

- Can increase the power of conventional cancer treatment and lessen some of its worst side effects.

References

[1] Bio Pharm Bull 2000; 23(6): 677-88.

[2] J Invest Dermatol 2001; 117(3): 694-701

[3] Jpn J Cancer Res 1996; 87(10): 1,039-44

[4] Jpn J Cancer Res 1998; 89(2): 206-13

[5] Mech Ageing Dev 2001; 122(3): 341-52

[6] Am J Chin Med 1999; 27(2): 191-203

[7] Anticancer Res 2000; 20(5A): 2,931-7

[8] Bio Pharm Bull 2000; 23(6): 677-88

[9] Gan To Kagaku Ryoho 1989; 16(4 Pt 2-2): 1,500-5

CHAPTER 8

Graviola:
Colon and Breast Cancer Conquered With Miracle Tree From the Amazon

Recently, we learned about an astounding cancer-fighting tree from the Amazon that has sent shock waves through the HSI network. Today, the future of cancer treatment and the chances of survival look more promising than ever. There's a healing tree that grows deep within the Amazon rain forest in South America that could literally change how you, your doctor, and possibly the rest of the world think about curing cancer. With extracts from this powerful tree, it may now be possible to…

- conquer cancer safely and effectively with an all-natural therapy that doesn't cause extreme nausea, weight loss, and hair loss
- protect your immune system and evade deadly infections
- feel strong and healthy throughout the course of treatment
- boost your energy and improve your outlook on life

Through a series of confidential communications involving a researcher from one of America's largest pharmaceutical companies, this ancient tree's anticancerous properties have recently come to light. Although not yet tested in human trials, the tree has been studied in more than 20 laboratory tests since the 1970s, where it's been shown to:

- effectively target and kill malignant cells in 12 different types of cancer, including colon, breast, prostate, lung, and pancreatic cancer
- be 10,000 times stronger in killing colon cancer cells than Adriamycin, a commonly used chemotherapeutic drug
- selectively hunt down and kill cancer cells without harming healthy cells, unlike chemotherapy

UNLOCKING THE HEALING BOUNTY WITHIN THE AMAZON...

The U.S. National Cancer Institute has identified 3,000 plants that are active against cancer cells--70 percent of which are found in the Amazon rainforest.[1] Until recently, only shaman, healers, and indigenous tribes held the key to unlocking their extraordinary secrets. Now, thanks to the unrelenting work of leading nutritional researchers, herbalists, and alternative doctors like those in the HSI network, the healing secrets of these plants, such as Graviola, are being uncovered.

In addition to promoting Graviola, Raintree Nutrition has taken the lead in making several other rainforest botanicals available to U.S. practitioners and consumers. They've combined Graviola with seven of these to create a power-packed, immune-boosting formula called N-Tense. Graviola makes up 50 percent of the N-Tense formula, which also consists of smaller amounts of the rainforest botanicals described below. These extracts have been widely used by indigenous people in South America and other tropical regions around the world to heal a wide range of ailments, including indigestion, inflammation, liver and gallbladder disorders, hepatitis, malaria, infection, respiratory problems, and more. And over the last decade, many of them have become popular among alternative physicians. But it's their cytotoxic and immune-boosting potential, as shown in studies, that makes these extracts invaluable in the fight against cancer.

BITTER MELON
(MOMORDICA CHARANTIA)

Over the last decade, most of the research on bitter melon has focused on the vegetable's anti-viral properties. But bitter melon extracts are also being closely studied for their anticancerous properties.

Five of the plant's phytochemicals have been well documented as having cytotoxic properties, meaning they've been shown to both kill and inhibit the growth of cancer cells in vitro. One recent in vitro test conducted by researchers at Seoul National University studied the cytotoxic effects of 100 plants on different cell lines in the body. According to their results, the bitter melon extract showed the "strongest" ability to kill and retard the proliferation of cancer cells.[2]

CONTINUED ON PAGE 54

So why isn't every health publication extolling the benefits of this treatment? Why hasn't it been made widely available throughout the natural-medicine community? And, if it's only half as promising as it appears to be, why isn't every oncologist at every major hospital insisting on using it on all his patients? Especially when you consider that since the early 1990s, extensive independent research—including research by one of today's leading drug companies and by the National Cancer Institute—confirms that the tree's chemical extracts attack and destroy cancer cells with lethal precision.

Graviola is 10,000 times stronger in killing colon cancer than Adriamycin, a commonly used chemotherapeutic drug.

The answer to these difficult questions can only be explained by recounting a disturbing story we recently uncovered. The story of this Amazon cancer treatment reinforces the need for groups like HSI and illustrates how easily our options for medical treatment are controlled by money and power.

News of this amazing tree was nearly lost forever

A confidential source, whose account we've been able to independently confirm, revealed that a billion-dollar drug company in the United States tried for nearly seven years to synthesize two of the tree's most powerful anticancerous chemicals. In the early 1990s, behind lock and key, this well-known drug giant began searching for a cure for cancer—while preciously guarding their opportunity to patent it and, therefore, profit from it.

Research focused on a legendary healing tree called Graviola. Parts of the tree—including the bark, leaves, roots, fruit, and fruit seeds—had been used for centuries by medicine men and native Indians in South America to treat heart disease, asthma, liver problems, and arthritis. Going on little documented scientific evidence, the company poured money and resources into testing Graviola's anticancerous properties— and they were shocked by the results. Graviola was a cancer-killing dynamo. But that's where the story of Graviola nearly ended.

The pharmaceutical company had a big problem. They'd spent years trying to isolate and create man-made duplicates of two of the tree's most powerful chemicals. But they'd hit a brick wall. They couldn't replicate the original.

ESPINHEIRA SANTA (MAYTENUS ILLICIFOLIA)

Early scientific research in the 1970s showed that this tree's leaves contain a unique group of chemicals called maytansinoids that display powerful antitumorous properties. Although testing on cancer patients revealed some significant regressions in ovarian carcinoma and some lymphomas, research was discontinued due to the toxicity reported at high dosages. In the 1990s, scientists isolated and synthesized a version of the tree's chemicals showing little to no toxicity to humans. Since then, the tree has been given a second look.

According to one recent study by a research team in Massachusetts, maytansinoid extracts were found to be "100- to 1,000-fold more cytotoxic than anticancer drugs currently in clinical use." Specifically, when combined with a special protein called an antibody that hunts down and kills foreign substances in the body, this chemical extract was found to be highly cytotoxic toward cultured colon cancer cells in vitro and showed "remarkable antitumor efficacy in vivo" (in the body).[3]

MULLACA (PHYSALIS ANGULATA)

Mullaca's recently identified steroids have garnered the most attention from the scientific community. In several in vivo animal tests and in vitro lab tests, Mullaca's steroids demonstrate powerful immune-system support.

Recent cancer studies indicate Mullaca is capable of killing several different types of malignant cells in vitro. In one study from 1992, Mullaca exhibited strong cytotoxicity against cancerous kidney cells in a test tube. The plant extract was also shown to reduce the size of cancerous tumors in mice with lymphocytic leukemia.[4]

VASSOURINHA (SCOPARIA DULCIS)

Much of the recent research on Vassourinha has centered around one powerful phytochemical called scopadulcic acid B (SDB). In a 1993 clinical study, SDB inhibited the growth of tumors in a test tube and in mice.5 Since the mid-1990s, scientists have been trying to synthesize several of Vassourinha's phytochemicals, including SDB, for mainstream use by the pharmaceutical industry.[6]

CONTINUED ON PAGE 56

And they couldn't sell the tree extract itself profitably—because federal law mandates that natural substances can't be patented. That meant the company couldn't protect its profits on the project it had poured millions of dollars and nearly seven years of research into.

As the dream of big profits evaporated, testing on Graviola came to a screeching halt

After seven frustrating years and without the promise of lucrative sales, the company shelved the project and refused to publish its findings in an independent journal. But one responsible researcher struggled with the decision. While understanding the company's goal of profits, he couldn't accept the decision to hide this unique cancer killer from the world. Following his conscience and risking his career, he contacted Raintree Nutrition, a company dedicated to harvesting plants from the Amazon.

As a result, Raintree went into high gear and began to research related studies published on Graviola. They discovered that several other teams in the United States (in addition to that of the drug company) had been testing Graviola in vitro (in test tubes). The results supported the drug company's secret findings; Graviola had been shown to kill cancer cells.

Encouraged by these early laboratory tests, Raintree hired indigenous Indian tribes in Brazil to grow and harvest the tree. They spent a year on research and development and then began offering Graviola in the United States. They also developed a new supplement called N-Tense, which contains 50 percent Graviola as well as smaller amounts of seven other cancer-killing botanical extracts. (See the "Guide to Sources and Availability" on page 215 for more information on N-Tense.)

Health Sciences Institute came across Graviola and Raintree Nutrition a few months ago while researching Chanca Piedra, a natural kidney-stone therapy from the Amazon. In the course of our working together, Raintree pointed us toward Graviola. And needless to say, our panel of experts were intrigued by the possibility of this powerful natural cure for cancer.

Graviola hunts down and destroys prostate, lung, breast, colon, and pancreatic cancers leaving healthy cells alone

For several months, we've been looking closely into the research to date on Graviola. It appears one of the first scientific references to it in the United States was by the National Cancer Institute (NCI). In 1976, the NCI included Graviola in a plant-screening program that showed its leaves and stems were effective in attacking and destroying malignant cells. But the results were part of an internal NCI report and were, for some reason, never released to the public.[1]

Since 1976, there have been several promising cancer studies on Graviola. However, the tree's extracts have yet to be tested on cancer patients. No double-blind clinical trials exist, and clinical trials are typically the benchmark mainstream doctors and journals use to judge a treatment's

---

UNLOCKING THE HEALING BOUNTY WITHIN THE AMAZON ... *continued*

MUTAMBA (GUAZUMA ULMIFOLIA)

In 1990, a team of Brazilian researchers demonstrated that leaf extracts from the Mutamba tree inhibited the growth of cancer cells in vitro by 97.3 percent. Some of the latest research on Mutamba has focused on the antioxidants found in the bark and leaves and their ability to inhibit the growth of bacteria and pathogens.

SUMA (PFAFFIA PANICULATA)

Recent studies on Suma's anticancerous properties look particularly promising. Two of Suma's phytochemicals have been shown to inhibit the growth of tumor cells in vitro, and in the year 2000 a Japanese team of researchers demonstrated that Suma inhibited lymphomas and leukemia in mice.

CAT'S CLAW (UNCARIA TOMENTOSA)

Recent studies indicate that at least six of the Cat's Claw vine's alkaloids can increase the functioning of the immune system by up to 50 percent. This has led to its use around the world by cancer and AIDS patients. Cancer patients who take Cat's Claw in conjunction with traditional cancer therapies have reported fewer side effects than typically associated with chemotherapy and radiation, such as hair loss,

---

value. Nevertheless, Graviola has been shown to kill cancer cells in vitro in at least 20 laboratory tests that our research has uncovered.

The most recent study, conducted at Catholic University of South Korea, revealed that two chemicals extracted from Graviola seeds showed "selective cytotoxicity comparable with Adriamycin" for breast and colon cancer cells. The chemicals targeted and killed malignant breast and colon cells in a test tube—comparable to the commonly used chemotherapy drug Adriamycin.[2]

Another study, published in the *Journal of Natural Products*, showed that Graviola is not only comparable to Adriamycin—but dramatically outperforms it in laboratory tests. Results showed that one chemical found in Graviola selectively killed colon cancer cells at "10,000 times the potency of Adriamycin."[3]

UNLOCKING THE HEALING BOUNTY WITHIN THE AMAZON ... *continued*

weight loss, nausea, secondary infections, and skin problems. Additionally, five of the vine's alkaloids have been shown to inhibit the growth of lymphoma and leukemic cells in vitro.[7]

Used for centuries by South American medicine men, Graviola and these other botanicals from the Amazon have only recently begun to reveal their secrets in rigorous scientific tests. And their cancer-fighting potential is undeniable. Furthermore, these extraordinary botanicals actually boost your immune system, instead of destroying it, as chemotherapy does. By taking N-Tense, you can support your overall health and mount a powerful, all-natural assault on cancer.

References

[1] Rainforest Facts found at http://www.rain-tree.com/facts.htm

[2] Anticancer Res 18(1A):119-24, 1998

[3] Proc Natl Acad Sci USA 93(16):8618-23, 1996

[4] Anticancer Res 12(3):837-43, 1992

[5] Oncology 50(2):100-3, 1993

[6] Fitoterapia (61)4:353-355, 1990

[7] Anticancer Res 18(5A):3363-8, 1998

Graviola selectively targets cancer cells leaving healthy cells untouched. Chemotherapy indiscriminately seeks and destroys all actively reproducing cells—even normal, healthy ones.

Other promising and ongoing research at Purdue University is supported by a grant from the National Cancer Institute. Purdue researchers recently found that leaves from the Graviola tree killed cancer cells "among six human-cell lines" and were especially effective against prostate and pancreatic cancer cells.[4] In a separate study, Purdue researchers showed that extracts from the Graviola leaves are extremely effective in isolating and killing lung cancer cells.[5]

Perhaps the most significant result of the study cited above from the Catholic University of South Korea, and of each of the others we've found, is that Graviola was shown to selectively target the enemy—leaving all healthy, normal cells untouched. By comparison, chemotherapy indiscriminately seeks and destroys *all* actively reproducing cells—even normal hair and stomach cells. This is what causes such often-devastating side effects as hair loss and severe nausea. In this respect, Graviola looks to be a promising alternative or supplement to mainstream treatments.

Patient reports show Graviola and N-Tense help eliminate tumors

From a clinical standpoint, Graviola still has a long way to go. Its properties have only been studied in a test tube. That's why it has yet to become widely known and accepted. The unfortunate truth is that without the promise of huge revenues from a synthesized, patented drug, it's unlikely that any pharmaceutical company will invest the hundreds of thousands (even millions) of dollars it would take to conduct the double-blind, placebo-controlled studies on humans. This is the underlying challenge to substantiating most nutritional therapies. Fortunately, Graviola is a natural substance, so we don't have to wait around for the drug companies. And, thanks to one researcher with a conscience, Raintree Nutrition bravely took the initiative in making this promising cure available.

Only a relative handful of doctors and patients in the United States have been using Graviola and the Graviola-rich botanical supplement N-Tense to fight cancer. Still, according to Raintree Nutrition, the combined therapy has produced some incredible results.

One such case history involved an executive at a high-tech company in Texas. Daryl S. came across Raintree when exploring alternative treatments to cure his prostate cancer. A sonogram and biopsy confirmed that Daryl had more than 20 tumors in his prostate. One doctor recommended surgery. But Daryl thought a cure using this common conventional treatment would come at too great a cost. He didn't want to suffer from impotence and incontinence for the rest of his life.

Instead, he agreed to a far less invasive round of hormonal therapy (to shrink the size of his prostate) and began a rigorous supplement regimen that centered around the Graviola-rich supplement N-Tense.

Within two months, Daryl's PSA level had dropped from 4.1 to 0.00. A sonogram and several other gamma-ray tests later confirmed that all the malignant tumors inside his prostate had disappeared.

Seven years of silence broken

We are continuing to work with Raintree and others conducting ongoing

---

GRAVIOLA FIGHTS MORE THAN CANCER

While the research on Graviola has focused on its cancer-fighting effect, the plant has been used for centuries by medicine men in South America to treat an astonishing number of ailments, including:

hypertension	diarrhea	dysentery
influenza	nausea	palpitations
rashes	dyspepsia	nervousness
neuralgia	ulcers	insomnia
arthritis	ringworm	fever
rheumatism	scurvy	boils
high blood pressure	malaria	muscle spasm

research on Graviola as more scientific and anecdotal evidence comes to light. However, after seven years of silence and hidden research, we felt it irresponsible not to bring this to you now.

Grown and harvested by indigenous people in Brazil, Graviola is available in limited supply in the United States and distributed only through Raintree Nutrition. But now, you can be among a select few in the entire country to benefit from Graviola. You are strongly encouraged to consult with your doctor before beginning any new therapy, especially when treating cancer.

You can make tea out of the Graviola leaves, obtain the herb alone in capsule form, or benefit from the power of Graviola combined with seven other immune-boosting herbs in Raintree Nutrition's N-Tense capsules. (See the sidebar on page 46 for more details on N-Tense.)

Graviola leaves are available through Raintree Nutrition. Each capsule contains 700 milligrams. Based on South American traditional therapies, it's recommended you take one to five grams a day. As a dietary supplement, N-Tense should be taken at 6 to 8 capsules daily.

Graviola and N-Tense are completely natural substances with no side effects apart from possible mild gastrointestinal upset at high dosages (in excess of 5 grams) if taken on an empty stomach.

Despite the mounting collection of laboratory tests and anecdotal reports about this cancer-fighting dynamo, Graviola may always remain an underground therapy!

Graviola has yet to be clinically tested on animals or humans. And because Graviola is a natural product, it can't be patented. Without the promise of exclusive sales and high profitability, it will likely never again draw the attention of a major drug company or research lab. So we may never see a double-blind clinical study on the tree that's reported to help defeat cancer.

But there's no doubt about it—the early laboratory tests and anecdotal reports about Graviola are very exciting. And if you've been diagnosed with cancer, you and your doctor should look at all the available treatment options. Graviola may just provide the help you've been looking for that could make all the difference in beating cancer.

Raintree Nutrition can supply you with more information on Graviola and N-Tense. See the "Guide to Sources and Availability" on page 215 for ordering and contact information.

Action:
- Selectively targets cancer cells leaving healthy cells unharmed.
- Protects the immune system from deadly infections.

Benefit:
- Effective in attacking and destroying malignant cancer cells.
- Boosts energy levels and improves mood.
- Safely targets cancer cells without the typical side effects caused by chemotherapy.

References
[1] Unpublished data, national Cancer Institute. Anon: Nat Cancer Ist Central Files—(1976) from Napralert Files, University of Illinois, 1995

[2] Bioorg Med Chem 8(1):285-90, 2000

[3] J Nat Prod 59(2):100-108, 1996

[4] Phtochemistry 49(2):565-71, 1998

[5] J Nat Prod 58(6):902-908, 1995

Body Oxygen:
This Rejuvenation Supplement
May Kill Cancer Cells

Since last year, we've been investigating Body Oxygen, a German product that has a strong reputation as a cell rejuvenator. It has been used in Europe for over 30 years to increase energy and carries endorsements from numerous professional athletes. However, over the years, German oncologists have also claimed that Body Oxygen may kill cancer cells—and many of them use it to do just that. While there are no controlled clinical trials to prove this, the theory on which it is founded is gaining acceptance in the scientific community. We've looked at the available research and now report our findings to you.

DNA damage is the first step in the disease process

Inside the nucleus of each cell is chromosomal DNA, which has been the focus of most DNA research. However, DNA is also located in each cell's mitochondria (mtDNA). The mitochondria are tiny powerplants that process the nutrients and oxygen that feed the cell (a process known as respiration). When mitochondrial respiration decreases or is impaired, it causes aging, which, in turn, contributes to the progress of degenerative diseases.[1] In the past 13 years, researchers have identified over 100 mtDNA-associated human diseases.[2]

Getting older also lowers mitochondrial function. As you age, the number of mitochondria you have naturally decreases, so there are fewer of them to carry on the work. And the ones that remain don't perform as efficiently or effectively as they did when you were younger. The combination of these two events means your cells are receiving less oxygen, which further increases the opportunities for degeneration through oxygen deprivation. This reduced activity can cause mitochondrial diseases, such as neurodegenerative illnesses, which affect muscle tissue and the brain. Illnesses sometimes associated with mitochondrial dysfunction include chronic fatigue syndrome (CFS), dementia, cardiomyopathy, and kidney and glandular disorders.

When mitochondrial activity is reduced, it hampers activity and performance much the same way that lung dysfunctions, such as asthma and emphysema, can limit how much oxygen you take into your lungs. The less oxygen you breathe in affects energy, brain function, and a number of other important bodily systems. Likewise, cell respiration is fundamental to energy production—and the mitochondria are responsible for most of it.

Most nutritional supplements never reach— or benefit—your mitochondria

Probably the most effective way to maintain proper cell functioning is to increase the number of mitochondria and keep each one functioning at its peak. Researchers believe this can be done through nutritional supplementation. But finding the right supplement—along with an effective way to deliver it—has baffled scientists.

To be effective, the nutrients must have the right "key" to unlock the membrane "door" that surrounds each mitochondria. In many cases, supplements that could help the mitochondria never make it in. They're simply absorbed by the digestive system and excreted. But even if the nutrients pass through the membrane, they have to be of the right structure in order to be used by the mitochondria—or they'll be removed by the digestive process without ever having nourished the cell.

Dr. Siegfried Wolz, a German physician, discovered a solution to both these problems. Dr. Wolz decided to use beet juice—shown to destroy cancerous tumors—as his primary mitochondrial nutrient. To deliver the beet juice, he used the findings of another German physician, Dr. Herbst, who discovered in 1843 that orally administered yeast cells could permeate the mitochondrial membrane.[3] Dr. Wolz combined these two concepts to form Body Oxygen, in which yeast cells are nourished with beet juice and other beneficial nutrients.

Adding even a small number of mitochondria could significantly increase cell life

Since it has been shown that a reduced number of mitochondria can decrease their effectiveness, an increase in respiration is believed to offer additional cell protection from damage and aging.[4] Recent research in the United States seems to support this. According to scientists at Harvard Medical School, laboratory experiments have shown that adding just 5 percent more mitochondria to mouse ovaries can cut the death rate by nearly 50 percent. This is significant, since mouse ovaries have a particularly high death rate.[5]

According to research by Dr. Wolz, the high level of nutrients available in Body Oxygen can increase the amount of mitochondria by up to 25 percent. Because the walls of the yeast cells are thin, the nutrients are quickly dispersed into the mitochondria and easily used by them.[6]

Over 20,000 cancer patients have benefited from Body Oxygen

While we know of no published supporting clinical trials, doctors in Europe have reported remarkable results with Body Oxygen. In 1997, at the World Congress for High Technology Medicine in Lucerne, Switzerland, Portuguese clinician Dr. Serge Jurasunas presented a lecture regarding the effect of Body Oxygen in treating over 20,000 cancer patients. According to Dr. Jurasunas, Body Oxygen appears to increase cellular respiration (oxygenation) as much as 1,500 percent if taken three times a day for a year. Increased cellular respiration indicates that more mitochondria are functioning at a higher capacity.

Specializing in metabolic medicine—a discipline that focuses on helping the body defend against disease—Dr. Jurasunas recommends that Body Oxygen be taken on a regular basis…and not just during illness. He believes regular use helps ward off disease before it gets a foothold.

This claim was borne out in two German studies in which patients treated with Body Oxygen experienced a "significant increase" in respiration by raising the oxygen content of their cells[7]—an indication that mitochondrial degeneration may have been thwarted.

If you decide Body Oxygen is right for you

Body Oxygen is sold in liquid form and packaged in glass vials. Based on our experience at the Institute's headquarters in Baltimore, we strongly suggest that you mix Body Oxygen with juice, because the product has an overpowering flavor.

Two formulations are available: the original formula, which contains royal jelly, and a sports formula supplemented with coenzyme Q10. Both formulations are made with active yeast cells, citrus juices, wheat germ oil, and wheat germ extract in addition to other beneficial components.

Whether you have cancer or just want to delay the aging process, Body Oxygen may be the solution you need. While the absence of independent published research keeps us from making a full recommendation, Body Oxygen is used widely by European oncologists...many of whom have touted its powerful effects against cancer. These experiences cannot be ignored.

See the "Guide to Sources and Availability" on page 215 for more information on Body Oxygen.

Note: Body Oxygen contains a form of baker's yeast, so those with a sensitivity should avoid the product.

Actions:

- Triggers a significant increase in mitochondrial respiration fighting illnesses including chronic fatigue, dementia, kidney and glandular disorders.

- Effectively passes through the membrane surrounding the mitochondria providing it with the nutrition necessary to feed the cell.

- Uses an all natural proven cancer fighter, beet juice, to destroy cancerous tumors.

Benefit:

- Raises the oxygen content in cells to help fight illness and ward off potential disease.

- Through increased cellular respiration offers additional cell protection against damage and degenerative disease.

References

[1] Novartis Found Symp, 235:247-63, 200; Ann N Y Acad Sci, 908:199-207, 2000

[2] Mol Genet Metab, 71(3):481-95, 2000

[3] Successful Biological Control of Cancer by Combat Against the Causes, P.G. Seeger and S. Wolz, 1990, Neuwieder Verlagsgesellschaft mbH, p. 79

[4] Ann Clin Lab Sci, 31(1):25-67, 2001

[5] Nature, 403(6,769):500-1, 2000

[6] Health Professional, 101:1-3, 1996

[7] Successful Biological Control of Cancer by Combat Against the Causes, P.G. Seeger and S. Wolz, 1990, Neuwieder Verlagsgesellschaft mbH, p. 35

A Strong Heart for the Next Century

One in every 2.4 Americans dies from heart disease. Even though "only" one in every four Americans today has any of the symptoms—chest pain, high blood pressure, or exertion pain...almost every man and woman in America has some degree of heart disease. The cholesterol-lowering drugs you're currently taking may not be doing enough to protect the health of your heart and cardiovascular system—in fact, cholesterol is not the enemy the medical establishment once thought it was! Take steps now to boost your circulation, lower your homocysteine levels, and harness the power of an amazing "entrainment" technique for your heart. See also the chapter on Larreastat (page 117) for another way to naturally fortify your heart.

CHAPTER 10

T. arjuna:
Angina, heart disease, high cholesterol, atherosclerosis—they can all be improved with an Ayurvedic herb.

Once in a blue moon, we uncover a supplement that does so many things, it's hard even for us to believe it's real. Such is the case with arjuna. The Terminalia arjuna tree is found throughout India, and its bark has been pulverized and used for heart conditions for over 2,700 years. Researchers are now investigating other diseases that may benefit from this Indian herb, but it's already a well-proven cardiovascular "cure."

If you're under a doctor's care or taking prescription drugs for any cardiovascular condition, you should consult with a practitioner before supplementing with arjuna. Because the herb is so potent and effective, the combination of arjuna and drugs may cause too sudden or too severe an effect.

Lower LDL cholesterol by at least 25 percent

Although vitamin E has been shown time and again to be an effective supplement for controlling cholesterol levels, the antioxidant capacity of arjuna outperformed the vitamin in a recent randomized placebo-controlled trial in India. After only 30 days of supplementation with arjuna, the test group decreased their average LDL ("bad") cholesterol levels by 25.6 percent with a corresponding 12.7 percent drop in total cholesterol. The groups receiving either the placebo or 400 IU of vitamin E had no significant change in either measurement.[1]

In a study conducted at SMS Medical College in India, scientists gave 500 mg of arjuna per day to a group of rabbits suffering from high blood-fat levels. After 60 days of therapy with the herb, the rabbits' average total cholesterol dropped from 574 to 217 and their LDL levels dropped from 493 to 162.[2] A group of rabbits receiving only 100 mg of arjuna also experienced lower cholesterol levels, although the drop in cholesterol levels was not as significant.[3]

Reduce angina attacks <u>without</u> the side effects of drugs

More than 6.2 million Americans suffer from angina (chest pain) due to an insufficient supply of blood to the heart. While nitroglycerin is a drug often prescribed for this condition, its effectiveness is reduced with each use. Arjuna, however, can continue to relieve angina regardless of how long it's used.

Researchers at Kasturba Medical College in Mangalore, India, tested arjuna against ISMN (Isosorbide Mononitrate), a nitroglycerin-based drug commonly prescribed for stable angina. While ISMN was effective over a 12-week period, it didn't perform as well as arjuna. The arjuna group had a 30 percent reduction of angina attacks, while the group taking ISMN had a 27 percent reduction. While this is not a significant difference, the performance of arjuna is considerable when you take into account the possible side effects of ISMN—lightheadedness, dizziness, a rapid pulse rate, and blurred vision. Scientists found none of these side effects with the group taking the herb.[4] And, of course, arjuna can be used without fear that it'll stop working when you need it most.

Another study found that 15 stable angina sufferers taking arjuna for three months experienced a 50 percent reduction in angina episodes. A treadmill test administered before and after the subjects took the herb showed that angina symptoms were significantly delayed after supplementation. Subjects also reduced their systolic blood-pressure levels, had a marked decrease in their body-mass indexes—which indicates weight loss—and experienced an increase in HDL ("good") cholesterol levels. The researchers concluded that treating stable angina patients with arjuna was an effective way to relieve symptoms.[5]

Patients with congestive heart failure improve to moderate levels in just two weeks

The New York Heart Association has developed a classification system that helps doctors determine the appropriate treatment depending on the severity of a patient's condition. Classes I and II are mild, class III is moderate, and class IV is severe and sufferers are completely incapacitated. In a recent double-blind, crossover, placebo-controlled study, 12 class IV patients with refractory chronic congestive heart failure received arjuna for two weeks in addition to traditional medication. The placebo term of the trial included only traditional medication. During the short treatment with the herb, the patients were reclassified as class III patients due to improvements in a number of cardiac factors. The results were so impressive that during a later third phase of the study, the same patients continued supplementing with arjuna for 20-28 months in addition to conventional medications. Their conditions continued to improve, and they were able to tolerate additional physical effort.[6]

Protect yourself from ischemic heart disease

If heart disease runs in your family and you'd like to take preventive measures, arjuna may do the trick. Scientists gave laboratory rats a supplement containing the herb for 60 days, and after that time gave them isoproterenol, a synthetic chemical that causes an irreversible destruction of heart tissue. Researchers found that pretreating the subjects with arjuna offered "significant cardioprotection." They also found that there was a remarkable

---

LOWER YOUR BLOOD PRESSURE...JUST ENOUGH

One of the many risks associated with medications for hypertension is that of lowering blood-pressure levels too much. Too-low blood pressure can be hazardous to your health, and use of these medications must be monitored carefully because of this risk. Symptoms of too-low blood pressure include dizziness, fainting, weakness, and fatigue. Hypertension medications also come with the possibility of more serious side effects, including heart palpitations, pulmonary edema (fluid collection in the lungs), breathing difficulties, and chest pain. Terminalia arjuna has not been demonstrated to have the same harmful effects as harsh drugs,[15] nor has it been shown to lower blood pressure excessively in tests conducted on laboratory animals.[16,17]

reduction in the loss of high-energy phosphate (HEP) stores,[7] a protective factor against ischemia. (Ischemia is a reduction in the supply of oxygen to an organ.)

Keep your arteries flowing free and clear

If the cholesterol circulating in your bloodstream isn't removed on a regular basis, it can deposit on the walls of your arteries. While this happens to everyone to a certain extent, thicker cholesterol deposits reduce the volume of blood flowing through your vascular system and decrease the oxygen reaching your organs. Blood vessels with significant deposits become inflexible and hard, which is why atherosclerosis is also called "hardening of the arteries." This can cause a deterioration of tissues and organs. Your arteries also deteriorate from the accumulation of cholesterol. If left untreated, atherosclerosis can kill you. But arjuna has been shown to turn around this life-threatening condition.

In an animal study, rabbits were fed a cholesterol-rich diet to create atherosclerosis and then divided into three groups to compare the effects of cholesterol- lowering supplements. One group of rabbits was treated with arjuna while the other two groups were supplemented with pharmaceuticals proven to lower cholesterol levels. In a comparison of all three groups, arjuna was pronounced as "the most potent hypolipidimic agent" and proved to induce "partial inhibition of rabbit atheroma."[8] Both these findings indicate that arjuna may help prevent the buildup of fat deposits in your arteries and possibly correct the deadly effects of atherosclerosis.

The same herb may fight cancer as readily as bacterial infections

One of the unique benefits of herbal therapies is their adaptogenic property. Many times, a single herb can conquer diseases and medical disorders with seemingly different origins and mechanisms. (Drug therapy is much more targeted and thus limited.) Doctors prescribe antibiotics for bacterial infections and must use completely different types of drugs to fight cancer. Although bacteria and cancer seem to start and spread by different means, arjuna has been shown to successfully fight both types of illnesses.

According to the Entomology Research Institute of Loyola College in India, E. coli, which is a dangerous food-borne pathogen, is no match for arjuna. Researchers tested 34 traditional tribal plants of India and found that arjuna had "significant antibacterial activity" against E. coli as well as the bacteria responsible for pneumonia, cystitis (a bladder infection), and pyelonephritis (a kidney infection).[9]

Salmonella typhimurium is the culprit behind paratyphoid fever, which is a milder form of typhoid fever, as well as salmonella gastroenteritis, a type of food poisoning. But researchers found that ellagic acid, one of the constituents of arjuna, is quite effective against it and stops it from mutating, thus preventing the spread of disease.[10]

While antibacterial drugs have not been proven to work against cancer, it appears arjuna can live up to this double duty—and without the damaging effects of chemotherapeutic drugs.

Many of the side effects of prescription drugs, especially those used to treat cancer, may damage organs or have a serious negative impact on general health. But according to studies at the University College of Medical Sciences and SMS Medical College, both in India, researchers have not found liver or renal damage in either human or animal test subjects receiving arjuna.[11,12]

While no one drug or therapy works against all types of cancers, arjuna may help fill the gap for some forms of the disease. According to scientists at the Department of Botanical Sciences at Guru Nanak Dev University in India, arjuna has cancer-fighting properties and may be a promising agent for stopping cell mutation[13]—believed to be one of the first steps in cancer development. By preventing this initial process, arjuna may cut off one of the most common routes used to convert normal cells to cancerous ones.

In research conducted by the National Institute of Bioscience and Human Technology in Japan, even osteosarcoma, a type of malignant bone tumor, was found to be no match for arjuna. By inhibiting the growth of osteosarcoma cells, arjuna may be able to prevent the growth and spread of this type of cancer.[14]

T. arjuna is not only effective—it's inexpensive!

T. arjuna is available from Himalaya USA under its "Singles" brand of products. It sells the herb under the name of "Arjuna – Cardiac Tonic." See the "Guide to Sources and Availability" on page 215 for ordering information.

Actions:

- Controls LDL "bad" cholesterol levels warding off potential deterioration of tissues, organs, and arteries.

- Relieves angina pain and episodes caused by insufficient supply of blood to the heart without the possible troubling side effects of standard nitroglycerin-based drugs.

Benefits:

- Provides significant protection against destruction of heart tissue.

- Has significant antibacterial and cancer fighting properties.

References

[1] J Assoc Physicians India, 49:231-5, 2001

[2] J Ethnopharmacol, 55(3):165-9, 1997

[3] ibid.

[4] J Assoc Physicians India, 42(4):287-9, 1994

[5] Int J Cardiol, 49(3):191-9, 1995

[6] Int J Cardiol, 49(3):191-9, 1995

[7] Indian HJ Physiol Pharmacol, 42(1):101-6, 1998

[8] Int J Cardiol, 67(2):119-24, 1998

[9] J Ethnopharmacol, 62(2):173-82, 1998

[10] Indian J Exp Biol, 35(5):478-82, 1997

[11] J Assoc Physicians India, 42(4):287-9, 1994

[12] J Ethnopharmacol, 55(3):165-9, 1997

[13] J Environ Pathol Toxicol Oncol, 20(1):9-14, 2001

[14] In Vitro Cell Dev Biol Anim, 36(8):544-7, 2000

[15] J Assoc Physicians India, 42(4):287-9, 1994

[16] Indian Drugs, 29:144-9, 1992

[17] Phytotherapy Research, 11:424-7, 1997

Grapefruit Pectin:
Powerful, Proven Treatment Against Heart Disease

In 1994, Dan O'Connell, a 65-year-old retired manager from London, England, was out running as part of his regular exercise program. He'd always tried to keep fit and healthy and had completed several marathons in his time. It was on this particular run, however, that he collapsed with excruciating pains in his chest. He was rushed to the emergency room, where tests revealed that he had blockages in three of the main coronary arteries. He also had raised blood- cholesterol levels. Dan underwent a triple bypass operation and recovered well. However, his fears returned a few months later when further tests showed the arteries had become blocked again.

If you've suffered from heart disease (or know someone who has), you'll know just how frightened he was. However, Dan found a solution that's now available to you.

Atheroslerosis may be killing you...slowly

The most common cause of heart problems is atherosclerosis—the clogging of the arteries that supply the heart muscle with blood. Atherosclerosis occurs when fat, cholesterol, and substances like calcium and cellular waste collect in the tears along the walls of arteries (usually after the inside walls of the artery have been damaged in some way).

The fatty tissue builds up and will ultimately restrict blood flow to the heart muscle causing chest pain and, eventually, a heart attack. One of the biggest risk factors for heart disease is a high level of homocysteine, which we've covered at length in the past. Another is high cholesterol-levels, especially high levels of the "bad" cholesterol known as low-density lipid cholesterol (LDL). The Western diet is rich in saturated fats, and LDL levels can become high—raising the chance of a heart attack or a stroke by 60 percent.

Just changing your diet isn't always enough

For more than two decades, doctors have urged us to give up smoking, follow a healthier diet, and exercise more—and yet heart disease remains the nation's biggest killer. Even after his triple bypass, Dan discovered that his ordeal was far from over: "I spent the next year going in and out of the hospital for tests and procedures," he says. "Finally I decided to see what I could do to help myself." He began to follow a low-fat dietary regime, eating plenty of oily fish—known to be rich in heart-protective fats.

Frustratingly, however, the change in diet had little impact on his cholesterol levels. He knew he needed extra help. And new research reveals that help is available.

Grapefruit pectin lowers LDL cholesterol by 25-30 percent in just four weeks

Grapefruit pulp—which contains a substance called pectin—can help in the fight against heart disease. Not only can grapefruit pectin lower LDL levels, but it also appears to help reverse existing atherosclerosis and arterial-wall damage.

In the 1970s, Dr. James Cerda, a gastroenterologist at the University Hospital in Gainesville, Florida, started experimenting on reducing plaque build up in the arteries of animals by testing various types of food fibers. He used pigs because they have a similar circulatory system to humans.

The pigs were given a diet containing 40 percent saturated fats and, within a year, their cholesterol levels had risen twelve-fold. During the following nine months, half were given bran-type fibers alongside their high-fat diet, while others received various fruit pectins. The scientists were astonished to discover that in animals fed with grapefruit pectin, the plaque levels were reduced by as much as 60 percent—*even though the pigs remained on a high-fat diet.*[1]

Human trials showed similarly exciting results. In one study, patients found their LDL was lowered by 11 percent—even if they made no other changes to their lifestyle or diet.

A report in the health journal *Clinical Cardiology* concluded: "This study has shown that daily dietary supplementation of 15 grams of grapefruit pectin significantly lowered plasma cholesterol and improved the ratio of LDLC to HDLC in hypercholesterolemia patients who are unable or unwilling to follow a low-risk diet."[2]

For those willing to make dietary and lifestyle changes, such as exercising regularly and avoiding high-cholesterol foods, the results were even better. A study of more than 200 patients showed that pectin lowered LDL cholesterol between 25-30 percent in just four weeks.

Grapefruit pectin inhibits arterial plaque and lowers "bad" cholesterol

Grapefruit pectin is a water-soluble fiber, which is more effectively absorbed than other dietary fibers. Pancreatic enzymes digest protein in the small intestines, releasing the water-soluble fibers, which pass into the large intestine. Here, bacteria break down the water-soluble fiber into short-chain fatty acids. The fatty acids lower LDL cholesterol and interfere with the plaque formation in arteries.

However, few of us are likely to eat two grapefruits, rind and all, per day—the amount needed to get therapeutic results. And raw pectin is a slimy, sticky mess—nothing you'd want to eat. So Dr. Cerda and his team mixed citrus pectin and guar gum with a protein (such as egg white or soy) to make the substance both more palatable and more easily processed in the gut. The result was ProFibe, which can be mixed with beverages or foods like oatmeal, cereal, and sauces. Most people tolerate it well, although a few might experience increased flatulence.

ProFibe is "as good, if not better" than prescription cholesterol-lowering medication

ProFibe is all natural; a tablespoon of it contains the equivalent pectin of two grapefruits. In fact, it's one of the few cutting-edge health supplements approved by the FDA under the GRAS (Generally Recognized As Safe) ruling. While you should not stop taking prescribed medication without your doctor's approval, many people find that they can reduce their drug intake when used in conjunction with ProFibe. In fact, in some cases it may be possible—in consultation with your practitioner—to stop taking the drug altogether. (Have your cholesterol levels measured before taking ProFibe, so you can determine its effect.)

"ProFibe is not a medicine," says Dr. Cerda, "and it lacks the risks of side-effects that occur with cholesterol-lowering drugs. ProFibe is as good, if not better than any prescription cholesterol-lowering medication now on the market. We urge people to eat abundant fruits and vegetables; it's certainly healthy to do so. But to achieve a therapeutic effect for people with high cholesterol, I don't think they can consume enough fiber in their normal diet to therapeutically lower their cholesterol without a product like ProFibe." See page 215 for ordering information.

Actions:

- Lowers low-density lipid "bad" cholesterol reducing the chances of suffering a heart attack caused by atherosclerosis or clogging of the arteries.
- Reverses arterial-wall damage and existing plaque formation in arteries.

Benefit:

- High fiber water-soluble supplement that is very effectively absorbed by the body.

References

[1] Circulation, 89:1247-1255, 1994

[2] Clinical Cardiology, 11:589-594, 1988

Perilla Oil:
A New Way to Protect Your
Heart, Brain, and Joints

Although many health experts are telling us that we have too much fat in our diet, evidence suggests that most of us are actually deficient in essential fatty acids, especially Omega-3 fatty acids. The most up-to-date research shows that by increasing our consumption of these essential vitamin-type fats, we can lower our rates of heart disease, reduce inflammation in our joints, enhance immune response against cancer, and promote healthy brain function.

The modern diet is notably lacking in Omega-3 EFAs (see box on page 74). Up until now, those wanting to supplement their diets with Omega-3 EFAs had only two choices: fish oil and flaxseed oil. Unfortunately, both of these can have mild to severe digestive side effects, ranging from an unpleasant taste in the mouth to noxious burping, nausea, and diarrhea. Finally, there is a better option.

Protect your heart (and more) with the oil of the beefsteak plant

Perilla oil is derived from the Perilla frutescens, common in East Asian countries and sometimes known as the beefsteak plant. The oil is over 50 percent pure alpha-linolenic acid, the essential Omega-3 fatty acid. Supplemen-tation with perilla oil delivers all of the benefits of Omega-3 EFAs, and in some cases appears to be even more powerful than fish or flaxseed oil. But perhaps most importantly, it is free of the digestive side effects that many people suffer with the traditional sources of Omega-3 fatty acids.

Here is a brief summary of the research to date on perilla oil.

Perilla oil protects against strokes,
heart attacks and heart disease

An elevated clotting factor, or platelet-activating factor (PAF) can lead to blood clots that cause heart attacks and strokes. Perilla oil has been shown to lower PAF by 50 percent in rats, compared with safflower oil, which is low in Omega-3 fatty acids.[1] Perilla oil was more powerful than fish oil in its ability to reduce PAF, and did not increase the risk of brain hemorrhage (a concern that has been associated with excessive consumption of fish oils).[2]

Over-production of a substance called thromboxane A2 is another significant cause of blood clot formation. After only seven days, the administration of perilla oil reduced the production of thromboxane A2 in diabetic rats.[3] In a third study, perilla oil was found to be very effective in reducing blood cholesterol, exerting a significant cholesterol-reducing

EATING YOUR WAY TO A HEALTHIER HEART

In addition to supplementing with Omega-3 EFAs, your dietary choices (particularly the types of fat you eat) can make a big difference in your risk of developing or dying of heart disease. But unlike what you may have been led to believe, it's not necessary to reduce fat consumption in order to reduce your risk of heart disease. In fact, in one recent study, researchers concluded that replacing unhealthy fats such as margarine and shortening with healthy sources of fats‹such as olive oil, avocado, nuts, and coldwater fish—was more effective in preventing coronary disease than reducing total fat intake.[9]

Are you confused about which types of fats are healthy and which should be avoided? Here's an easy way to tell:

Saturated fats are those that are solid at room temperature. They are found in meat, dairy products, palm and palm kernel oils, cocoa butter, and coconut oil. Numerous epidemiological analyses have observed that increased consumption of saturated fat is linked to increased incidence of heart disease and cancer. While some scientists, such as Dr. Robert Atkins, have argued that saturated fat have been unfairly maligned for their role in the development of heart disease, most nutritionists advise that saturated fat be kept to 10 percent or less of your total daily calories.

effect after only seven days.[4]

Cancer formation inhibited

Japanese researchers tested the ability of perilla oil to suppress the risk of colon cancer in rats. At the end of the experiment, the rate of colon cancer in those rats who received 12 percent of their daily calories from perilla oil was less than half the rate of cancer in rats who ate the same amount of safflower oil (which is low in Omega-3 fatty acids). The researchers concluded that "a relatively small fraction of perilla oil, 25 percent of total dietary fat, may provide an appreciable beneficial effect in lowering the risk of colon cancer."[5] A second study found that perilla oil significantly reduced the rate of breast and colon tumors and kidney cancer.[6]

EATING YOUR WAY TO A HEALTHY HEART ... *continued*

Monounsaturated oils are those that are liquid at room temperature but become cloudy or solid when refrigerated. They include olive oil, canola oil, and avocado. Studies have shown that cultures that get the majority of their fat calories from monounsaturated fats have lower incidence of all types of cardiovascular disease and many kinds of cancer. Health and nutrition experts now recommend that the majority of one's dietary fat intake be from monounsaturated oils.

Polyunsaturated oils remain liquid even when chilled. They are important because they supply the essential fatty acids. The most commonly used vegetable oils, such as those made from corn, peanut, and soybeans are high in Omega-6 EFAs. Sources of Omega-3 fats include deep-sea (coldwater) fish such as salmon, herring, cod, mackerel, and sardines, and flaxseed (also known as linseed).

Most of us get adequate Omega-6 from our diets, but unless you are eating coldwater fish four or five times a week, or chewing a tablespoon of raw flax seed daily, you will most likely benefit from an additional Omega-3 EFA supplement. Perilla oil appears to be the most inexpensive and best-tolerated source of these valuable compounds.

Perilla oil protects neurons and brain function

Laboratory rats were fed diets containing either perilla oil or safflower oil for two generations. The second generation performed significantly worse in their ability to learn new information based on trial and error. The brains of the rats were then compared and it was found that the rats eating safflower oil had 30 percent less synaptic development than the rats eating perilla oil.[7] This fascinating study suggests that the type of fat in our diet has a dramatic impact on brain development and intelligence. (Subsequent research showed that the inferior brain development in the mice given safflower oil was quickly reversed by adding perilla oil to their diets.)

Inflammatory bowel disease alleviated

Past research has shown that fish oil can be very beneficial in treating inflammatory bowel conditions such as Crohn's disease and colitis. However, many patients find it difficult to take the required dosage of fish oil due to the digestive problems it can cause. Perilla oil offers a useful alternative, having been shown to protect the mucosal lining of the intestine and reduce markers of inflammation and allergic reactivity common to these conditions.[8]

Other proven benefits of perilla oil

In addition to the benefits noted above, perilla oil has also been shown to regulate blood sugar and glucose metabolism, reduce allergic hyper-reactivity, lower high blood pressure, and protect against retinal damage. It even appears to inhibit the production of body fat in subjects consuming a high-fat diet.

Perilla oil may help with diabetes, allergies, high blood pressure and vision loss.

As you can see, perilla oil has been the subject of extensive scientific research. As a source of Omega-3 fatty acids, it is far cheaper than fish or flax oil, which may explain its popularity among lab scientists working on a tight research budget. And yet, it remains virtually unknown outside of the laboratory, most likely for purely commercial reasons. Unlike fish and flax oil, perilla oil was not picked up and developed as a retail product until very recently, when a nutritional supplement company recognized its overlooked potential and invested in retail production and distribution. For the first time, you now have access to this superior option.

Supplementing with perilla oil: dosage recommendations

Since its recent introduction to the public marketplace, many health-conscious consumers have replaced their fish or flax oil supplements with perilla oil, finding it both cheaper and easier to 'stomach.' Even more importantly, those who simply couldn't tolerate the digestive side effects of fish or flax oil finally have an effective alternative.

The oil is packaged in 1,000 mg gel capsules, each providing 550 mg of alpha-linolenic acid. A daily intake of three to six capsules is recommended. See the "Guide to Sources and Availability" on page 164 for ordering information. For best results, do not take perilla oil or any nutritional oils together with fiber supplements or high-fiber foods as these can interfere with optimal absorption.

How to avoid the most dangerous fat of all

Modern food processing has created an unnatural kind of fat called Trans-fats, made when unsaturated oils are artificially hydrogenated in order to increase stability and shelf life. Virtually all packaged foods, including cake mixes, crackers, breakfast cereals, and mayonnaise are made with artificially hydrogenated fats. Trans fats are also created when unsaturated fats are heated to high temperatures, as in deep fat frying.

Although they are technically unsaturated fats, trans fats behave like saturated fats by clogging arteries and increasing the susceptibility of cholesterol to oxidize. Sadly, when the American Heart Association advised Americans to give up butter in favor of "heart-healthy" margarine, they were guiding people out of the frying pan right into the fire. The hydrogenated fats in most margarines have now been shown to be far more damaging to the heart and arteries than the naturally-saturated fats in butter.

Your best bet? Become a vigilant label-reader. If you see the words "hydrogenated" or "partially hydrogenated" you can be sure that the product contains trans fats. There is good news however. As those on the vanguard of nutritional health spread the word about the dangers of trans fats, some manufacturers have begun to respond with products made without hydrogenated fats. As you and other health-conscious consumers vote with your dollars, more are sure to follow.

Actions:

- Lowers platelet-activating factor to reduce the incidents of heart attack and stroke producing blood clots.
- Effectively reduces the production of thromboxane A2 a significant factor in blood clot formation.
- Reduces blood cholesterol levels.
- Regulates blood sugar and protects against retinal damage.
- Lowers high blood pressure.

Benefits:

- Significantly lowers the risk of certain cancers including colon, breast, and kidney cancers.
- Dramatically effects brain development and intelligence and the ability to learn new information.
- Has protective effects on the mucosal lining of the intestine and is beneficial in treating inflammatory bowel conditions such as Crohn's disease and colitis by reducing inflammation and allergic reactivity

References

[1] Oh-Hashi, K. Journal of Lipid Mediators and Cell Signaling vol. 17, no. 3, pp. 207-20, 1997

[2] Oh-Hashi, K. Biol Pharm Bull vol. 21, no. 6, pp. 558-64, 1998

[3] Jkeda, A. Nutrition vol. 11, no. 5, pp. 450-455, 1995

[4] Ihara, M. Comp Biochem Physiol B Biochem Mol Biol vol. 121, no. 2, pp. 223-31, 1998

[5] Narisawa, T. Cancer vol. 73, no. 8, pp. 2069-75, 1994

[6] Hirose, M. Carcinogenesis vol. 11, no. 5, pp. 731-735, 1990

[7] Yoshida, S. Journal of Neurochemistry vol. 68, no. 3, pp. 1261-1268, 1997

[8] Ohtsuka, Y. Pediatric Research vol. 42, no. 6, pp. 835-839, 1997

[9] Hu, F.B. N Engl J Med vol. 337, no. 21, pp. 1491-9, 1997

New Solutions for Autoimmune Diseases

Nature supplies us with many potent and nontoxic solutions to the illnesses and conditions that we struggle with every day. If you are among the millions who live with arthritis, herpes, or osteoporosis....and have felt let down by the "solutions" that traditional medicine has to offer—you'll find both help and hope in the pages that follow. Go beyond traditional painkillers that just mask the pain and discover natural products that can halt bone loss, grow new cartilage, control the debilitating pain of arthritis, and put an end to herpes breakouts.

See the chapter on infopeptides (page 15) for another important breakthrough that can ease the pain and discomfort of arthritis and protect against osteoporosis.

CHAPTER 13

Thymic Formula:
Reverse Hepatitis, Rheumatoid Arthritis, and More

When rumors spread that a small-town doctor was curing patients of "incurable" hepatitis infections, Dr. Michael Rosen, then a medical correspondent for an Atlanta, Georgia, television station, went to Savannah to investigate. Although he originally planned an exposé on "quack" medicine, Dr. Rosen ended up filming an enthusiastic multipart report on Dr. Carson Burgstiner and his breakthrough method for treating so-called "incurable" diseases. Outside the local viewing area, however, Dr. Burgstiner's discovery remains largely unknown.

What caused Dr. Rosen's unexpected conversion? An impressive body of evidence in the form of Burgstiner's patients and their stories. In his own clinical experience, Dr. Burgstiner had witnessed the following:

- 84 cases of hepatitis B arrested
- 34 cases of hepatitis C arrested
- 28 cases of rheumatoid arthritis arrested
- 12 cases of systemic lupus in remission
- 10 cases of multiple sclerosis arrested
- 12 cases of psoriasis arrested

Whatever other therapies were employed, Dr. Burgstiner's treatment protocol featured the same "magic bullet" in every case. He had, over years of experimentation and analysis, identified a specific combination of nutrients, including extract of thymic glandular tissues, that appeared to stimulate his patients' malfunctioning immune systems and reverse even supposedly incurable conditions. The news spread from one cured patient to the next, and a steady stream of hopeful patients began trickling into Savannah to see Dr. Burgstiner.

The most impressive case history in Burgstiner's files may be his own

Burgstiner was a board-certified obstetrician-gynecologist, a past president of the Medical Association of Georgia, and a fellow of several prestigious medical associations. In 1983, He contracted hepatitis B when he punctured his finger while operating on an infected patient. The acute infection progressed to chronic illness, and Dr. Burgstiner, then a carrier of the blood-borne virus, was forced to limit his practice to nonsurgical procedures.

After seven years, Burgstiner was still sick and was frustrated at his body's inability to heal itself. His search for answers led him to focus on the role of the thymus gland in controlling the immune system. Unique among all the glands of the human body, the thymus reaches its maximum size in childhood, when it weighs up to 2 ounces. In early adulthood, the thymus begins to shrink; it eventually stops functioning altogether and withers to a few grams of shriveled tissue.

Recalling the medical principle of using glandular extracts to supplement underfunctioning glands like the thyroid and pancreas, Dr. Burgstiner reasoned that supplementing with thymus extract might restore his malfunctioning immune system. As he explained: "If your thyroid dries up, we give you thyroid. If your pancreas dries up, we give you insulin. If your ovaries dry up, we give you female hormones. However, when the thymus gland dries up, no one treats that as a medical condition, even though every doctor and nurse is taught that the thymus gland controls the immune system."

As HSI panelist Dr. Michael Rosenbaum explains in his book, **Super Supplements** (with Dominick Bosco, Signet, pp. 65, 83, 1989);

> *"Glandular extracts were among the original cornerstones of medicine, and were first used many thousands of years ago. Most ancient cultures, from the Egyptians, to the Hindus, to the Greeks, used glandular therapy. Among the glandular supplements, thymus substance is the most important. You*

want all the possible rejuvenation of the thymus gland that you can get, because the thymus gland is the major controlling gland of the immune system."

Dr. Burgstiner purchased thymic extract and a vitamin-mineral complex from a local health-food store and began taking them. Six weeks later, after seven years of chronic infection, his blood test for the hepatitis virus was negative. Amazed, he reported his results to the authorities. The Centers for Disease Control in Atlanta, the Massachusetts General Hospital in Boston, and the Scripps Institute in California all confirmed his test results, proclaiming him to have undergone a "spontaneous remission." Dr. Burgstiner's surgical privileges were restored.

REPORTS FROM GRATEFUL PATIENTS

"I had hepatitis C, and Thymic Formula cleared up my liver-function tests. I think I can live forever with this liver. My disease has been cured."

—Tony P.

"I have multiple sclerosis. My symptoms cleared up completely after beginning Thymic Formula."

—Pat M.

"I had hepatitis B and was given no hope. Two months after beginning Thymic Formula, my blood work showed no hepatitis B virus in my system. Without a shadow of a doubt, the Thymic Formula saved my life."

—Cynthia F.

"I had lupus and could not get out of bed. My kidneys became involved, and I was spilling blood and protein in my urine. Five days after beginning Thymic Formula, my energy level was normal and my kidneys cleared up."

—Sharon B.

Source: Thymic Extract: Hidden Hope to Good Health? a series of investigative reports for WAGA-FOX 5 in Atlanta, Georgia, by Michael J. Rosen, M.D.

The balance of Dr. Burgstiner's career was dedicated to the research, refinement, and documentation of the near-miraculous results he and scores of patients experienced using this thymic protocol. An independent laboratory tested the supplements and confirmed that they produced marked increases (up to 700 percent) in immune-system activity, as measured by the levels of thymic hormones in the blood.

Specific nutrients provide key activating agents

Further research established that the thymic extract alone, without the vitamin and mineral formula, did not have the same effect. Dr. Burgstiner theorized that the nutrients provided key activating agents for the natural synthesis of immune factors. Patients were dispatched to the health-food store with a shopping list for the various nutrients and instructions for the complicated regimen. Over the following years, Dr. Burgstiner fine-tuned his protocol, searching for ways to maximize its effectiveness.

Ultimately, he joined forces with a manufacturer to produce what he felt would be the most effective combination of nutrients, minimizing the expense and inconvenience for his patients. The final formulation included thymic factors and other glandular extracts, antioxidants, amino acids, enzymes, herbs, and minerals. (The only complaint ever registered by his

---

WHAT'S IN BURGSTINER'S THYMIC FORMULA?

- Thymus enzymatic polypeptide fractions (containing thymosin, thymopoietin, and Thymic Humoral Factor)

- Spray/freeze-dried raw glandular extracts (including spleen, lymph, bone marrow, and pituitary extracts)

- A complete vitamin and mineral complex (including vitamins A, C, D, E, B-complex, and 10 trace and essential minerals)

- A synergistic blend of herbs, phytonutrients, amino acids, and digestive enzymes (including echinacea, bromelain, inositol, and bioflavonoids)

- Whole-food extracts (including alfalfa leaf, wheat germ, apple pectin, acidophilus, and kelp)

---

patients was that the pills are somewhat large.)

Dr. Burgstiner's practice, once primarily obstetrics and gynecology, was transformed into a practice treating patients with a wide variety of immune-related conditions. Burgstiner felt that his thymic formula produced an immune-regulating effect—that is, in hyperimmune conditions, such as rheumatoid arthritis and multiple sclerosis, it would turn the overactive immune response down. In hypoimmune conditions like cancer, it would turn the immune response up.

Some of Dr. Burgstiner's colleagues are now recommending his thymic formula to their own patients. Susan Kolb, M.D., reports as follows: "I put all my patients on [Burgstiner's] Thymic Formula before and after surgery. They feel much better, recover quicker, and have fewer symptoms. They have increased energy levels, fewer muscular aches, and lower infection rates."

HSI panelist Ann Louise Gittleman, M.S., C.N.S., is also quite impressed with the formula: "I have found Burgstiner's Thymic Formula to be very helpful, particularly for my readers who needed special nutritional support for hepatitis C and other immune-related disorders. In my own research, I have found the glandular extracts to represent the true fountain of youth."

There are, however, many in the conventional medical community who question Burgstiner's theory. Some argue that it is normal for the thymus to stop functioning, simply because it is no longer needed. As Dr. Burgstiner's case files swelled with miraculous cures and remissions, the next step was to pursue large-scale, double-blind trials that would document his results to the satisfaction of the skeptics.

Unfortunately, Dr. Burgstiner died before he was able to see his theory proven and fully recognized. But the formula he created survives him, and the momentum of his incredible discovery continues. The National Institute of Health and the Centers for Disease Control have both expressed interest in investigating Dr. Burgstiner's Thymic Formula. Trials are planned or under way at the University of Alabama-Birmingham and Nova Southeastern University.

Meanwhile, as Dr. Burgstiner told Dr. Rosen, to wait for the research to be complete would mean that many would miss the opportunity to get well. Dr. Rosen, originally expecting to debunk Dr. Burgstiner's claims, has become a champion of the formula. As he commented in his report, "Is thymic extract a hidden hope for good health, or are Dr. Burgstiner's many patient testimonials the result of a placebo effect? I interviewed patients from diverse backgrounds and geographic locales, with a variety of different illnesses, all of whom have reached the same conclusion: If this is a placebo effect, it is an amazing one!"

Dr. Burgstiner's Thymic Formula continues to be manufactured and distributed from his home state of Georgia. All of the individual components in the formula (see box) have been completely evaluated for safety and meet FDA standards. Although most of the constituents—including the thymic extract—can be found in health-food stores, as single nutrients and in various combinations, Burgstiner's extensive work with his formula demonstrated that its potent effect relies on this particular combination and dosage.

The formula provides excellent and multifaceted nutritional support when taken as a daily vitamin-mineral-herbal supplement. For this purpose, the recommended dosage is six tablets per day. The therapeutic, immune-enhancing protocol used in most of the cases cited above calls for 12 tablets a day. Before adding the Thymic Formula to your current supplement regimen or medications, however, please consult your personal physician for advice.

Dr. Burgstiner's patients report that, in general, they experienced a significant improvement within 30 days. Dr. Rosen will soon be publishing a book about Dr. Burgstiner and his remarkable story.

For purchasing information, see the "Guide to Sources and Availability" on page 215.

Action:

- Provides nutritional support for the natural synthesis of immune factors

Benefits:

- Stimulates malfunctioning immune systems
- Treats a wide variety of immune-related conditions
- Faster recovery from surgery
- Increased energy levels
- Lowers infection rates

14

Shark-Cartilage Therapy:
Help Your Body Create NEW Cartilage

You have probably been led to believe that arthritis is a disease of the joints, that it is an inevitable part of the aging process, that there is fundamentally no cure. Don't believe it. Alternative doctors and researchers associated with the Health Sciences Institute have identified several underlying causes-causes your doctor may not even know to look for-that may be the source of much, if not all, of your arthritis pain. Although healing is a gradual process, pain relief can be immediate.

America's No. 1 Crippling Disease

According to the Arthritis Foundation, 40 million Americans suffer from arthritis. That's one out of every seven people of all ages. By the time you reach 60, your chances of having arthritis are close to 100 percent. In fact, arthritis is one of the most prevalent chronic health problems and the No.1 cause of limitation of movement in the United States. When you consider these statistics, it might appear to be an inevitable part of aging.

If you've tried conventional medicine, you know the truth: Drug therapy doesn't free you from pain and doesn't help to slow down your disease. What you may not know is that all conventional arthritis drugs from NSAIDs—nonsteroidal anti-inflammatories—to steroids carry serious risks to your health, both immediate and long-term.

The good news is that you no longer have to settle for conventional therapy. We've learned about a revolutionary treatment for joint care that relieves pain, can be used safely over the long term, and may actually help prevent joint problems.

Research suggests that it not only relieves pain and restores flexibility but may actually help cartilage regrow—something that, until now was believed impossible! This is no small feat. Unlike your liver or your heart, which can recover from devastating trauma, cartilage cannot heal itself. Once it's gone—it's gone (or so we thought).

A warning to all men and women over 35:
You are losing your cartilage, little by little

Over time, the cartilage between your joints wears thin. Most doctors consider this wear and tear normal and inevitable. By the time you turn 35, you can be sure some measurable change in the shape of your cartilage has occurred. Almost everyone suffers from degenerative changes by that age. If you're over 55, your doctor probably expects to discover at least some symptoms of osteoarthritis.

There are two kinds of arthritis:
you do NOT have to suffer from either

Rheumatoid arthritis is a chronic, inflammatory disorder that causes stiffness, deformity, and pain in joints and muscles (usually those of hands and feet, particularly the knuckle and toe joints.) Your joints gradually become inflamed and swollen, leading to the destruction of tissue and, in severe cases, deformity.

Unlike osteoarthritis, which progresses steadily over time, rheumatoid arthritis is a waxing/waning condition. You could have a single attack, or you might suffer several episodes that could leave you increasingly disabled. Rheumatoid arthritis is also associated with damage to the lungs, heart, nerves, and eyes. It's seen mostly in those between the ages of 40 and 60, but it can also affect children and teen-agers. Three times more women than men are afflicted. The causes are not fully understood, but it's considered an autoimmune problem: Immune-system defenders attack the joint tissues as if they were threats to your body.

Osteoarthritis is very different. It's the gradual wearing away of cartilage in your joints, generally considered a process of aging. As cartilage wears thin, your joint mobility decreases. Eventually, cartilage wears through completely. Whenever you flex your joints, your bones rub against one another, causing inflammation of the synovial tissues, which cushion the joints. Movement becomes difficult and painful.

The cause? If you ask mainstream doctors, most will tell you the cause is unknown. That's the traditional stance of the Arthritis Foundation and the orthodox medical community. The standard solution? Drugs: over-the-counter pain relievers, anti-inflammatory drugs, NSAIDs, cortisone-type drugs (steroids), gold salts, and even experimental cytotoxic (cell-killing) drugs.

NSAIDs are by far the most common therapy for arthritis. If you use NSAIDs, such as ibuprofen (Motrin), naproxen (Naprosyn), oxaprozin (Daypro), nabumetone (Relafen), or diclofenac (Voltaren), you should be aware that every year almost 25,000 people using these drugs suffer serious gastrointestinal side effects, including bleeding, ulceration, and perforation.

NSAIDs also interact with blood-pressure medicine. New evidence shows their long-term use can cause liver and kidney damage. They also may accelerate the destructive nature of arthritis. These effects can occur at any time, with or without warning symptoms. Your risk increases with longer use or higher dosages.

Then there are steroids (powerful drugs that present a host of serious health risks.) To quote former Orioles baseball pitcher Jim Palmer, "Cortisone is a miracle drug...for a week!" By suppressing your immune-system response, steroids lessen swelling, soreness, and allergic reactions. In some cases, they give your body a chance to heal itself, but in the case of arthritis, they provide little more than a temporary fix.

> **WARNING:** Steroids are strong medicines and can have very serious side effects. Since they suppress your immune system, they can lower your resistance to infections and make them harder to treat. Steroids are broad-spectrum, which means they scatter their immune-suppressing effects throughout your body (from your liver to your central nervous system). Side effects of short-term use include frequent urination, mental depression, and sudden blindness. Side effects from long-term use can include insomnia, an increase in hair growth on the body and face, an irregular heartbeat, shortness of breath, and sudden death.

Even with all of these risks, neither NSAIDs nor steroids alter the arthritis process itself. And if they don't work, surgery is usually the final option: removal of badly inflamed joint synovia, joint realignment and reconstruction, tendon repair, joint fusion, or artificial joint replacement.

Rebuilding cartilage

Yes, it is possible to rebuild cartilage. When HSI first made this statement two years ago, it wasn't just controversial, it was unthinkable. Two years later, with the well-documented successes of cartilage-building substances like glucosamine and chondroitin, HSI's "audacious" assertion is now generally accepted in alternative-medicine circles.

But there's still more to the story. Glucosamine-based products fill the shelves at drugstores and health-food stores, but there are newer cartilage-regenerating products not yet on the market that promise to be even more effective than the first generation of glucosamine products. We've uncovered a breakthrough product that has not yet been publicized or widely marketed, but that you should know about immediately.

Relief from cartilage damage

Glucosamine is a nutrient found in very small amounts in food; it is also made by the cartilage cells of your body. Glucosamine plays an integral role in stimulating the production of connective tissue and new cartilage growth essential to the repair of arthritis damage. Chondroitin is another major cartilage builder and is found in bovine, shark, and whale cartilage.

As glucosamine and chondroitin formulas began filtering onto store shelves, researchers at Lane Laboratories began wondering. You see, Lane processes an ingestible form of shark cartilage, called BeneFin, that contains naturally occurring glucosamine and chondroitin and has been used successfully in the treatment of certain types of cancer for years.

When scientists at Lane studied the research findings on glucosamine and chondroitin in the treatment of arthritis, they began to wonder if shark cartilage might benefit arthritis sufferers in a way that the chemically processed versions could not. Their rationale was a simple one: If arthritis sufferer's respond somewhat to glucosamine and chondroitin, would they receive an even greater benefit from the substances as they occur in nature, in the form of shark cartilage?

HSI panelist Dr. Martin Milner uses BeneFin shark cartilage extensively as a natural cancer therapy and has noted its dramatic effect on the arthritis symptoms of his patients. According to Dr. Milner, shark cartilage offers effective, naturally occurring constituents not provided by glucosamine or chondroitin supplements alone, including the following:

- Angiogenic-inhibiting proteins, substances that prevent additional blood-vessel invasion of the joints in rheumatoid arthritis (Chondroitin and glucosamine have no known effect on rheumatoid arthritis.)

- Naturally occurring glucosamine and chondroitin for the treatment of osteoarthritis, forms your body can more easily assimilate
- Collagen, which has a body of evidence supporting its efficacy in treating arthritis
- Calcium and phosphorus (15% and 7% respectively by weight), both of which are important for maintaining bone health and recommended by the FDA to fight osteoporosis

A more efficient delivery system

Recently, shark-cartilage therapy has made an exciting new advance. Typically, shark cartilage is administered orally, in a powdered form. However, it appears that shark cartilage can also be absorbed directly through the skin, delivering the substance directly to the desired location, with all of its constituents intact and with a minimum of fuss.

Apply it directly to your joints

Lane Labs has extended this line of research to the creation of an odorless shark cartilage cream designed especially for the targeted treatment of arthritis pain and inflammation. The new product is called BeneJoint, and it is unique among topical arthritis creams. It combines the restorative power of shark cartilage with the pain-relieving compound capsaicin.

Capsaicin is a natural substance derived from cayenne pepper. It works by depleting "substance P," a chemical messenger in nerve cells that transmits pain signals. BeneJoint is the only product that combines the analgesic action of capsaicin with the cartilage-building substances in shark cartilage.

"I've had arthritis in my lumbar spine for a couple of years. I had X-rays taken, and I went to a specialist who told me I have a lot of spurs. The pain gets worse all the time. I tried Mineral Ice, but it really never helped much. I've done exercises—you name it, I've tried it. I work for Lane Labs, and people there asked if I would like to try a sample of BeneJoint for my arthritis. After only three or four days, it was really

helping me—I could bend down without feeling pain! I was so impressed with the product that I told many of my mother's friends who have arthritis about it, and they're anxious to try it too. I'm hoping this will help a lot of people."

—Regina F., Fairlawn, NJ

Because BeneJoint delivers a natural source of glucosamine and chondroitin directly to the joints, this cream may be used in conjunction with other nutrient-based arthritis therapies for maximal benefit. See page 215 for sources.

Actions:
- Acts as an anti-inflammatory
- Acts as an antiantiogenic
- Inhibits enzymes that destroy cartilage-cell proteins
- Depletes "substance P," a chemical messenger in nerve cells that transmits pain signals

Benefits:
- Delivers a natural source of glucosamine, chondroitin, and collagen directly to the joints in forms the body can more easily assimilate
- Prevents additional blood-vessel invasion of the joints in rheumatoid arthritis
- Improves the body's ability to rebuild cartilage
- Increases natural lubrication of the joints
- Reduces joint pain and inflammation
- Reduces synovitis, an inflammation of the lining of the joints

Wobenzyme:
German Enzyme Therapy Targets Autoimmune Disorders

In autoimmune diseases like rheumatoid arthritis, lupus, and MS, the immune system goes "haywire." Instead of serving its normal protective function, it produces abnormally high levels of antibodies called circulating immune complexes (CICs). In a healthy person, the pancreas naturally produces enzymes that break down CICs so they can pass through the kidneys for excretion. But in people with compromised immune systems, CICs begin to accumulate in the body's soft tissue and organs—causing serious inflammation and, in extreme cases, organ failure.

If you suffer from an autoimmune disorder, you can clear your system of excess CICs by supplementing your body's stockpile of enzymes. This can lead to a dramatic reduction in inflammation and many of your most debilitating symptoms.

Enzymes initiate and support virtually all your body's chemical processes

Enzymes are proteins that act as powerful catalysts throughout your body. Vital organs like your liver, kidneys, spleen, and pancreas depend on enzymes to function properly. They've also been found to be natural anti-inflammatories and to play a major role in regulating your immune and digestive systems.

The pancreas is the hub of your body's enzyme activity. When not assisting in digestion, these enzymes are free to travel directly to the blood stream—seeking out the lurking CICs. They then attach to the CICs and are flushed out of the body through the kidneys. Researchers have found that enzyme supplementation can increase the number of excess CICs evacuated from the blood.[1]

Germany—the birthplace of naturopathic medicine—has led the research on enzymes and autoimmune diseases. During the past two decades, they've focused on the oral supplement called Wobenzyme which contains several important pancreatic enzymes, such as Pancreatin, Trypsin, and Chymotripsin. Produced by a German company called Mucos Pharma GmBH, Wobenzyme is actually the leading over-the-counter drug in Germany and is used primarily to treat injury and inflammation. Unfortunately, because the majority of the published research is in German, it hasn't received the attention it deserves in the United States. And, while the research we've examined is limited due to the same challenge, we were able to find some very encouraging studies.

Wobenzyme reduces rheumatoid arthritis symptoms in 62 percent of patients tested

Rheumatoid arthritis (RA) is one of the most common autoimmune disorders in the U.S. Although few experts can agree on exactly what triggers RA, we do know that for some reason the immune system attacks the body—and begins to produce high levels of CICs that, in RA patients, cause debilitating joint inflammation and serious pain. Over time, the joint tissue is weakened and eventually destroyed.

All RA patients [receiving Wobenzyme] showed an improvement of morning stiffness and nearly a quarter of patients reduced their NSAID doses by 50 to 75 percent.

Many RA therapies such as non-steroidal anti-inflammatory drugs (NSAIDs) or corticosteroids reduce inflammation and pain, but are laden with serious side effects and do nothing to address the underlying problems with your immune system.

Studies have shown that Wobenzyme can prevent RA flare-ups and help to lower levels of CICs.[2] In one German study published in Zeitschr. F. Rheumatologie in which patients took eight Wobenzyme tablets four times daily, sixty-two percent of patients showed improvement in symptoms.[3]

In another study, researchers at the Ukrainian Rheumatology Center in Kiev tested Wobenzyme on 78 patients with severe RA who were using other traditional drugs. Patients showed a <u>decrease in CIC concentrations</u> <u>of up to 42 percent</u>. All RA patients showed <u>an improvement of morning</u> <u>stiffness and nearly a quarter of patients reduced their NSAID doses by 50</u> <u>to 75 percent</u>.[4]

Lupus sufferers experience a marked decrease in crippling symptoms

Though a far less common condition, lupus is perhaps one of the most complex and difficult to treat autoimmune diseases. With symptoms that range from swollen limbs to hair loss to organ failure in serious cases, lupus is one of the great mysteries of modern medicine.

In one report presented at a 1996 Russian oral enzyme symposium, 18 lupus patients between the ages of 18 and 46 with kidney disease, severe inflammation, and immobility were given Wobenzyme. Compared to patients not given the supplement, Wobenzyme patients experienced a marked decrease in inflammation, tendency to hemorrhage, and circulation of CICs. More than 25 percent of patients were able to reduce their dose of voltaren or prednisolone, two common drugs used to treat lupus.[5]

Wobenzyme substantially improves MS symptoms in one third of patients tested

Enzyme therapy also provides new hope in treating multiple sclerosis (MS). MS is a disorder of the central nervous system that's manifested through inflammation of nervous tissue in the brain and along the spinal cord. And like other autoimmune diseases, MS is generally treated with high dosages of corticosteroids and prednisolone. Wobenzyme's widely accepted anti-inflammatory properties have led a number of doctors throughout eastern Europe to test it on their MS patients.

Dr. Ulf Baumhackl, chief of the Neurological Department at the hospital in St. Pölten, Austria, studied the effects of enzymes on his MS patients over a period of two years. In the study, Dr. Baumhackl reported that his patients demonstrated substantially better improvement in symptoms compared to those who had been treated with cortisone and/or cytostatics.[6]

German doctor Christina Neuhofer has looked at the effects of

Wobenzyme on 150 of her MS patients. She found that <u>30 percent of her patients with chronic MS experienced a substantial improvement in symptoms. When enzyme therapy began between episodic intervals, the patients either remained free of recurrences or the periods of remission lasted substantially longer.</u>[8]

Restore your body's natural enzymatic defense against the damage of excess CICs

It should be noted that Wobenzyme, like most natural substances, works slowly to restore your natural defenses and heal your body from the inside out. It may be several weeks before you notice a sustained reduction in swelling and other symptoms.

Also, bear in mind that enzymes do effect digestion. Gas, bloating, diarrhea, and constipation are all possible when first starting enzyme supplementation. So, it's important to start slowly. After a few weeks, your body will adjust and any side effects should subside. And, as always, before considering a new therapy, it's important to consult with your doctor— especially if you suffer from any type of autoimmune disease.

Wobenzyme is available without a prescription. It's recommended you take three tablets, two times a day at least 45 minutes before meals or 2 hours after. During flare-ups of joint inflammation, take five tablets twice daily.

> **Caution**: Wobenzyme consists mainly of proteolytic enzymes, which are known to break down and dissolve particles in the blood. Therefore, if you're taking Warfarin or any other type of blood thinner, you should **not** try Wobenzyme.

If you suffer from an autoimmune disease, you know how few effective treatments there are in both mainstream and alternative medicine. Wobenzyme's success in improving these conditions makes it a promising new option for you to consider.

See page 215 for ordering information.

Actions:

- Lowers the levels of circulating immune complexes preventing them from building up in the body's soft tissues and organs leading to inflammation and even organ failure.
- Causes a marked decrease in inflammation and the tendency to hemorrhage in lupus sufferers.

Benefits:

- Anti-inflammatory properties reduce the joint-inflammation and severe pain associated with rheumatoid arthritis.
- Improves the symptoms of multiple sclerosis by reducing the inflammation of nervous tissue in the brain and along the spinal cord.

References

[1] Nature-und Ganzheitsmedizin 1:108,1998

[2] Ganzheitsmedizin 1:108,1998

[3] Zeitschr. F. Rheumatologie 44:51, 1985

[4] Compendium of Results from Clinical Studies with Oral Enzyme Therapy, presented at Second Russian Symposium, St. Petersburg, Russia, 1996

[5] Ibid.

[6] Significant New Help for Multiple Sclerosis found at http:freedompressonline.com/top_articles/ms_wobenzyme.htm

[7] Material published by Freedom Press available at www.freedompressonline.com/oralenzymes.htm

[8] Ecomed 1997:113-124

16 CHAPTER

Myco+:
Fighting Off Autoimmune Disorder Causing Microbes

Multiple sclerosis, rheumatoid arthritis, Lou Gehrig's disease, and lupus are insidious diseases that have stymied mainstream medicine for over a century. But growing research into stealth-like microbes may hold the key to offering patients the hope they've been searching for. These microbes now appear to be a common link among chronic and autoimmune disorders. We've uncovered an enormous amount of research linking these infections to some of today's most menacing illnesses.

Although mainstream researchers and physicians are starting to address mycoplasmal infections, they're concentrating on pharmaceutical therapies that, more often than not, do more harm than good. These treatments frequently take a year or longer, relief is usually temporary, and relapses are quite common.

What the mainstream therapies fail to address is that these infections are devastating to the immune system. The last thing your body needs when fighting these illnesses is to have to fight off the additional degenerative effects of antibiotics. This is where a complementary approach can prevail.

Stealth pathogens may be stealing nutrients from your cells

The reason mycoplasmas are hard to control and eliminate is that they have plasma membranes instead of cell walls, which allows them to hide or conceal their presence. And, even when they are detected, identification can be difficult, because mycoplasmas can change their appearance and structure depending on where they are in your body.

The plasma membrane coating around each mycoplasma is sticky, which allows the cell to adhere to another cell. Once attached to another cell, mycoplasmas start a parasitic relationship[1] and feed on the nutrients and waste products of normal cells to nurture their own growth. Scientists believe this type of "feeding" makes it possible for mycoplasmas to camouflage their existence, which is why it took more than 65 years for scientists to link their existence to human diseases.

High cholesterol levels and mycoplasmas put you at greater risk

One of the essential nutrients mycoplasmas require is cholesterol. This is unique, as there's no other known microorganism that must have this fat for growth. This adds another level of concern for people who suffer from mycoplasmal infections and also have elevated serum-cholesterol levels. Recent research indicates that greater quantities of cholesterol in the blood may increase plaque formation if mycoplasmas are present in the blood-stream. Scientists also think the concentration of cholesterol in arterial plaques may provide a nurturing environment for mycoplasma cells and could lead to ruptured arterial plaques, which can be fatal.[2]

Mycoplasmas put out the "welcome" mat for other disease-causing microbes

As mycoplasma colonies grow, they can compromise organs and alter their functions. Because the cells' nutrients are constantly being depleted, they're more vulnerable to mutation, damage, and invasion by other microorganisms. When other microbes work in concert with mycoplasmas, they can have a synergistic effect and make it easy for other diseases to develop or aggravate whatever disorder has already been established. Overlapping infections by different mycoplasmas and other bacteria, fungi, and viruses can cause symptoms that will change from one person to the next. This makes diagnosis of specific chronic and autoimmune diseases tricky.

When mycoplasmas are outside the natural habitat of the gut, such as in blood vessels and joints, they can grow uninhibited because the natural flora of the gut isn't controlling their expansion. This gives mycoplasmas the freedom to colonize organs and eventually destroy systems. It's believed that growth probably occurs when the immune system is weak, such as during times of illness or stress or when you're poorly nourished.

How do you know if you're at risk?

Special microscopes are used to identify mycoplasmas in blood samples, but that doesn't guarantee detection. Even if blood tests indicate the presence of mycoplasma cells, your doctor may not take action if your disorder doesn't fit a predetermined list of symptoms usually associated with a certain strain of mycoplasma.

Many people suffering from mycoplasma-associated diseases have several of the following symptoms,[3] which may be present all the time or may come and go:

- chronic fatigue
- depression
- joint pain or reduced mobility, including rheumatoid arthritis
- headaches, vision problems, or light sensitivity
- cognitive problems
- muscle spasms or burning muscles
- dizziness or balance disturbance
- stuttering or difficulty speaking
- breathing problems, cardiac problems, or chest pain or pressure
- flatulence, bloating, or diarrhea
- lack of bladder control or frequent urination
- stomach cramps, nausea, or vomiting
- sinus pain or nasal congestion
- impotence, loss of libido, or menstrual or genital pain
- sore throat, tinnitus, or hearing loss
- skin rashes, frequent sores or infections, or yeast infections
- coughing heavily or frequent thick saliva clearing
- allergies, chemical sensitivities, or dry or itchy eyes
- night sweats

The size of a colony increases and decreases depending on a variety of factors and conditions, such as the strength of your immune system, and that can affect the varying number of symptoms. Also, some people have multiple strains of mycoplasmas, since an immune system weakened by one strain seems to make it easier for other strains to establish themselves. This could account for symptoms that don't necessarily fit the established stereotype of a disease.

Pain seems to play a major role in chronic and autoimmune disorders, as evidenced by the many pain-related symptoms listed above. This isn't coincidental, as new research shows that growth of a mycoplasma colony can cause an abnormal sensitivity to substance P,[4] which is the neurotransmitter responsible for sending pain messages to the brain.

Nutritional supplements are the foundation of a full recovery

According to noted mycoplasma researcher Gary L. Nicolson, Ph.D., of the Institute for Molecular Medicine in California, "nutritional and vitamin deficiencies must be corrected" because a "fully functional immune system may be essential to overcoming these infections, and supplements and immune enhancers appear to be effective in helping patients recover."[5]

Dr. Nicolson has found that high dosages of the following supplements will help increase your nutritional profile during recovery:[6] vitamins B, C, and E; minerals, especially zinc, magnesium, chromium, and selenium; amino acids, especially L-cysteine, L-tyrosine, L-carnitine, and malic acid; coenzyme Q10; bioflavonoids and biotin; Beta-carotene; folic acid; flaxseed oil; intestinal flora replacer, including one containing fructoologosaccharides (FOS).

Dr. Nicolson suggests that you take sublingual tablets or oral sprays rather than pills to optimize absorption.

Other products suggested by Dr. Nicolson are olive leaf extract and milk proteins. While he mentions whey as an acceptable milk protein, lactoferrin may be as effective—possibly more so. Many have used this milk protein to bolster their weak immune systems. See Chapter 2 for more information on lactoferrin.

In addition to Dr. Nicolson's recommendations, you'll need to start a treatment plan that kills established mycoplasmas and other microbes while preventing future growths.

Mainstream's "cure" may _cause_ mycoplasmal infections

Mainstream treatment of chronic and autoimmune disorders usually revolves around multiple cycles of numerous synthetic antibiotics. Because mycoplasma cells grow very slowly, long-term treatment of a year or more is the norm. But this type of therapy can backfire. The longer mycoplasmas are exposed to conventional antibiotics, the more resistant they become and the greater their ability to evade detection and destruction by your immune system.

Prescription antibiotics can suppress your immune system, which slows your recovery and could make it easier for mycoplasmas to gain a foothold in the future. Some antibiotics, such as penicillin, may even increase symptoms of mycoplasma-related diseases. Additionally, these microbes compromise absorption of nutrients, which can leave you malnourished.

Botanical solutions may reduce recovery time substantially

Another drawback of most drugs is that they are very limited in the types of microbe they eradicate, which is one of the reasons you have to switch from one type to another. Botanical formulations tend to be more apt to kill many different strains and types of mic-robes. By simultaneously tackling many of them, you may be able to significantly shorten your treatment time.

Also, a botanical-based solution can do the job with fewer side effects than antibiotics, they're not as harsh on the immune system, and they normally don't cause antibiotic resistance. Such is the case with Myco+ from Raintree Nutrition, a U.S.-based company that researches and harvests medicinal botanicals from the Amazon. Raintree Nutrition is the same company that brought graviola, an anticancer botanical, to our attention. (See Chapter 8 for more information on Graviola)

Powerful botanicals "search and destroy" mycoplasmal infections

The constituents of Myco+ are derived from rain forest plants that have been traditionally used to control infectious, life-threatening diseases. The ingredients include extracts of mullaca, Brazilian peppertree, anamu, clavilla, macela, fedegoso, and uva ursi. Besides destroying mycoplasmas, Myco+ has been used to kill many other unrelated bacteria and viruses that may be disease co-factors or aggravate symptoms in chronic and autoimmune diseases, such as Candida albicans.

Although Myco+ is a plant-based antimicrobial agent, it's similar to antibiotics in that it indiscriminately kills all microorganisms—including friendly intestinal bacteria, which help limit mycoplasmal growth. Supplementing with a probiotic while undergoing treatment for mycoplasmal infections is highly recommended by Dr. Nicolson.

If you suspect you have a mycoplasma-induced disease, have your doctor order a PCR test (Polymerase Chain Reaction). While expensive, it'll be covered by insurance so long as it's ordered by your physician.

Feeling worse could mean you're getting better

While feeling better is usually a sign of recovery, not feeling better could also mean you're improving. If your illness isn't caused by a mycoplasma infection, then treatment with a mycoplasma-specific therapy probably won't affect your symptoms, and you'd likely see no improvement (hence the need to test first to see if mycoplasmas are your problem).

If you feel a little light-headed or dizzy after starting treatment, you may be experiencing a significant die-off of mycoplasma cells. Referred to as the Herxheimer reaction, this is due to the large numbers of toxins from dying cells, which your liver must process.

If you find the die-off to be a bit overwhelming, you may want to temporarily reduce the amount of Myco+ you're taking. After the die-off symptoms subside, you can go back to the recommended regimen.

Of course, you should work with your doctor when treating serious illness. If you suffer from any type of chronic condition or autoimmune disorder, especially if it's multiple sclerosis, rheumatoid arthritis, Lou Gehrig's disease or lupus, and haven't been tested for mycoplasmas, talk to your doctor again or seek another opinion from a physician experienced in this area.

(To find a physician experienced in alternative and complementary therapies, call ACAM at (949) 583-7666.)

Please turn to the "Guide to Sources and Availability" on page 215.

Note: This article made extensive use of the excellent *Why Arthritis? Searching for the Cause and the Cure of Rheumatoid Disease*, Harold W. Clark, Ph.D., Axelrod Publishing of Tampa Bay, 1997. Unfortunately, the book is now out of print.

Actions:

- Corrects nutritional and vitamin deficiencies allowing the immune system to function at top capacity to overcome infections.

- Destroys a number of bacteria and viruses that may be unrelated to the initial mycoplasmas but aggravate the symptoms in chronic and autoimmune diseases

Benefit:

- Significantly shortens recovery time from a variety of microbe infections by simultaneously fighting many of them.

References

1. J Microbiol Methods, 44(3):217-23, 2001
2. Braz J Med Biol Res, 33(9):1,023-6, 2000
3. Biomed Therapy, 16:266-271, 1998
4. Am J Physiol Lung Cell Mol Physiol , 280(2):L286-97, 2001
5. J Chronic Fatigue Syndr, 6(3/4):23-39, 2000
6. CFIDS Chronicle, 12(3):19-21, 1999

C H A P T E R

Larreastat:
Relief for Victims of Herpes and Rheumatoid Arthritis

In one of the most exciting developments of the decade, researchers recently released their findings on a new, natural product that has been shown to be 99.7 percent effective in the relief of symptoms brought on by the herpes viruses.

If you think that this good news applies only to a few, you may be surprised to learn that, according to recent estimates, up to 99 percent of the population may be infected with one or more of the many herpes viruses. (The most well-known is the virus that causes chicken pox.) These viruses can lie dormant for years before exhibiting any symptoms, and unsuspecting carriers can easily infect others.

When triggered by stress, infections, or diseases like cancer, herpes viruses can manifest themselves as cold sores, genital lesions, chicken pox, and shingles. Various strains have also been linked to mononucleosis, chronic fatigue syndrome, and Kaposi's sarcoma, a deadly type of skin cancer frequently, but not exclusively, affecting people with AIDS.

In addition, there is a growing body of evidence that a herpes virus called cytomegalovirus (CMV) plays a causal role in cardiovascular disease.

About 75 percent of Americans over 60 carry CMV, with no observable symptoms. But if the virus is "turned on," it appears to play a role in the clogging of artery walls.[1] Possible triggers include balloon angioplasty and heart-transplant surgery.

And in another startling development, scientists have linked the Simplex I virus with Alzheimer's disease.[2] Apparently, the Simplex I virus can lodge in brain tissue and replicate at a very low level. Although the replication is too subtle to cause acute disease symptoms, it is enough to activate the immune system. It is possible that the resulting inflammatory reaction, over years, may eventually lead to Alzheimer's disease.

And so it was for good reason that researchers in Arizona were elated at the results of studies, confirmed by independent clinical tests, showing that a new "botaniceutical" product derived from the Larrea bush could cripple these insidious viruses without side effects of any kind. By contrast, side effects of acyclovir (Zorivax), the drug commonly prescribed to manage herpes symptoms, include headaches, seizures, coma, nausea, vomiting, and diarrhea. More importantly, prolonged or repeated use of acyclovir can actually encourage the proliferation of drug-resistant strains of the herpes virus.

An ancient desert bush yields this remarkable healing agent

This new preparation is made from an ancient desert bush, Larrea tridentata, used medicinally for centuries by Native Americans as well as early European settlers of the southwestern United States. According to Native American legend, it was the first plant created at the beginning of the world. Scientists have in fact validated that these shrubs are among the oldest living plants on earth, some plants dating back to over 12,000 years ago.

Traditionally, Larrea was used to treat infections, snakebite, burns, rheumatism, bronchitis, colds and viruses, and digestive disorders. The phenomenon of an all-purpose natural panacea is not a new one to Health Sciences Institute members. A wide range of effective applications is the hallmark of a natural remedy. These do not work through a single, isolated action, as do our modern pharmaceuticals, but through the varied and synergistic actions of myriad phytochemical compounds.

Clearly, the Larrea shrub, also known in the Southwest as the creosote bush and to herbalists as chaparral, is a potent natural healer. Listed in the Pharmacopoeia of the United States from 1842 to 1942, chaparral was widely used to treat acne, eczema, venereal and urinary infections, and even certain types of cancer, particularly leukemia.[2] In the 1960s, promising research on the antitumor properties of one of chapparal's chief constituents was abandoned when long-term use in lab animals suggested toxicity.[3] In the early 1990s, a few cases of hepatitis were tied to use of the herb and the FDA requested a voluntary ban on products containing raw chapparal. (Scientists later determined the cases to be unrelated to chapparal use.)[4]

As we have noted before, the fact that something is natural does not

---

DRAMATIC RELIEF FROM HERPES SYMPTOMS

The new Larrea product is formulated both as a topical lotion that can be applied directly to herpes lesions and as a nutritional supplement that can be used to help avert impending outbreaks or to speed healing. Here are only a few of the dozens of successful outcomes confirmed in recent clinical trials:

- A woman suffering from recurrent oral herpes previously used acyclovir with only mixed results. After a single application of the Larrea preparation, lesions were completely healed in 12 hours. Pain and swelling were relieved immediately.

- A 90-year-old woman had Kaposi's sarcoma lesions that covered her body from head to toe. Lesions on her lower extremities were so advanced that one toe had already been amputated. Acyclovir was used without success. After three weeks of treatment twice daily with Larreastat lotion, the lesions on her arm, face, and feet had completely cleared.

- A clinic in Philadelphia treated numerous patients with severe herpes simplex 1 and 2 and zoster (shingles) with both the Larreastat lotion and capsules. They report a 100 percent success rate, usually within 24-48 hours. The clinicians also report success using the lotion to avert impending outbreaks, which are usually signaled by a tingling sensation.

- A woman with oral herpes typically had outbreaks lasting three to seven days. When she applied the lotion to a new blister, the pain, swelling, and blistering were gone in one day.

- Shingles sufferers who were treated with Larreastat reported complete relief within minutes. In dozens of case histories reviewed, one phrase appeared repeatedly: "complete resolution of the episode within 24 hours." No side effects were reported by any subjects.

mean that it is necessarily harmless. Herbs can be extremely potent, as any student of herbal medicine can attest, and it is possible for an herb to have a toxic effect. Nonetheless, one group of scientists refused to abandon the healing potential of chaparral and continued to search for a way to isolate the beneficial properties of the Larrea bush.

After a decade of research, it appears they have succeeded. Researchers identified a matrix of natural chemicals that appear to be responsible for Larrea's medicinal qualities. Through a proprietary process, they have purified, concentrated, and solubilized these phytochemicals, documented their bio-logical activity, and thoroughly tested them for toxicity of any kind. The oxidative components of the raw plant believed to be responsible for any toxicity have been eliminated. The result is a natural product that exploits all of the healing potential attributed for centuries to this desert shrub but, according to extensive testing, is safe. Even at doses five times the equivalent human dose, test animals remained in excellent health. Enzyme studies on liver and kidney functions showed no ill effects.

The herpes/rheumatoid-arthritis connection

Many herpes viruses hide out in nerve tissue. People who have shingles often feel a burning pain in their nerves before the shingles appear. This is because the zoster virus that causes shingles starts replicating in the nerves before it actually breaks through to the skin.

But researchers have recently learned that a certain group of herpes viruses can hide in the connective tissue. This group of viruses, called the gamma-herpes viruses, includes Epstein-Barr and HHV-8. It is theorized that these gamma viruses may be a hidden cause of rheumatoid arthritis and other connective tissue disorders.

The good news about rheumatoid-arthritis relief

Although the remarkable results of this new product for herpes sufferers are stealing the headlines, there have been equally dramatic reports of relief for rheumatoid-arthritis sufferers. An 18-year-old patient suffering from juvenile rheumatoid arthritis for seven years got only minimum relief from even high doses of prescription anti-inflammatories. Upon rising in the morning, the patient was so stiff that he could not walk down the stairs. After using Larreastat capsules for only two weeks, this young man is now playing basketball and holding a full-time summer job.

A 70-year-old California woman with chronic rheumatoid arthritis and long-standing pain and immobility in her knee joint reported over 90 percent relief from pain and swelling and could walk normally again after using Larreastat capsules for two weeks. Numerous other patients of collaborating physicians report dramatic improvements.

How can this preparation be so effective for such seemingly unrelated conditions as herpes and rheumatoid arthritis? For the same reason that the Larrea plant has been used successfully for centuries for a wide range of conditions. Larrea is rich in a powerful antioxidant lignan called nordihy-droguaiaretic acid (NDGA), as well as several other chemically related lignans. Lignans are phytochemicals that show significant antioxidant, anti-inflammatory, antiviral, and antimicrobial properties. In fact, before the modern food industry developed cheaper, synthetic preservatives, NDGA was widely used as a food preservative. It prevents the oxidation of fats and oils in foods, thereby inhibiting the growth of a wide variety of bacteria, yeast, and fungi.

Clearly, Larrea's strong antiviral action makes it a useful weapon against the herpes viruses. But NDGA has also been shown to inhibit 5-lipoxygenase, an enzyme involved in the biochemical process known as the inflammatory cascade. This suggests why Larrea has such a dramatic impact on the symptoms of rheumatoid arthritis, a chronic inflammation caused by the overactivity of the inflammatory cascade in the body.

Furthermore, Larrea is a source of over two-dozen flavonoid compounds, many of which are not found in any other known dietary source. These chemicals, which work synergistically with other antioxidant vitamins, especially vitamin C, provide further antioxidant, anti-inflammatory, and antiviral properties. Flavonoids also work to strengthen capillaries, enhancing the transport of nutrients to the tissues of the body.

Because Larreastat products have shown such remarkable ability against diseases for which there are currently so few effective treatments, they represent an important new botanaceutical development. See the "Guide to Sources and Availability," page 215.

Actions:
- Inhibits a critical enzyme in the inflammation process
- Prevents oxidative damage
- Strengthens capillaries

Benefits:
- Alleviates pain and inflammation
- Inhibits the growth of viruses, bacteria, yeast, and fungi
- Enhances the transport of nutrients

References
[1] NIETO Javier, er al., "CMV infection as a risk factor for carotid intimal-medial thickening," Circulation vol. 94, no5, 1996, pp. 922-7;S.E. Epstein, et. al., "The role of infection in restenosis and atherosclerosis, Lancet, col. 348, Suppl. 1, 1996, pp13-17

[2] Andrew Chavallier, The Encyclopedia of Medicinal Plants, vol. 21, 1997, p 224.

[3] Varrro Tyler, Ph.D., The Honest Herbal, 1993, p. 87.

[4] Michael Castleman, "Herbal Healthwatch," Herb Quarterly, Spring 1996, p. 6

V

Brain Power and Mental Health

Now there's no need to fear the loss of your cognitive abilities as you age—in this section of *Underground Cures*, you'll read about amazing brain boosters like DHA and phosphatidylserene. These substances fight the effects of Alzheimer's Disease and the "mental decline" that can come with aging, such as trouble concentrating, a tendency to forget things, prolonged depression, and difficulty in recalling newly learned information.

CHAPTER 18

Phosphatidylserine:
The One True Smart Pill

Can't remember where you put the car keys? Having trouble absorbing new information—even if it's as simple as a phone number or an appointment? Can't remember if you've already "told that story before?"

Symptoms of "mental decline"—which include trouble concentrating, a tendency to forget things, prolonged depression, and difficulty in recalling newly learned information—start as early as age 50 and become pronounced and outwardly.

As frightening, embarrassing, and frustrating as these symptoms are, it's no wonder the hot new item on the alternative-medicine market these days is the "smart pill." Walk into any health-food store, and you'll find dozens of herbal brain-health supplement programs. These formulas are almost guaranteed to contain significant amounts of herbs like ginseng, which has demonstrated the ability to improve endurance-and Ginkgo biloba, which has the unparalleled ability to fight peripheral vascular disease. Ginkgo not only frees up blood flow to the brain but also protects your delicate brain cells from free-radical damage.

Both herbs are well-established in the alternative-medicine community as treatments for depression and all-around 'mental fog.' In Europe, Ginkgo biloba is routinely prescribed in a standardized, concentrated form to help the elderly reverse many conditions related to problems of circulation, such as tinnitus (ringing in the ears), confusion, dizziness, headaches, and memory loss.

Both of these exceptional herbs have been proven in hundreds of cultures around the world, in study after study, to have significant brain-enhancing benefits.

But the one thing these products cannot do is improve your actual brain mechanisms: the delicate cellular relationships that are responsible for everything from recognition and recall to mood and outlook.

In other words, these popular smart pills may enhance the circulation to your brain or augment your mood-regulating hormones, but they simply do not improve the function of the brain itself. Such a substance would truly be a miracle—real-life smart pill.

Can you improve the inner workings of your brain? In a word, yes.

There is a naturally derived substance that can literally prevent and reverse the "normal" mental decline that comes with age. It can in fact, do all of the following:

- boost your ability to learn
- improve your ability to remember NEW information
- improve your visual memory
- improve your memorization skills

According to some researchers, this powerful nutrient may be able to reverse more than a decade's worth of mental decline!

It's called phosphatidylserine (PS). PS—an essential fatty acid your body produces naturally in limited amounts—keeps your brain active and alert, starting on the cellular level.

First, it "influences fluidity" of the brain-cell membrane. By facilitating the delivery of nutrients to the brain cells, as well as the cells' ability to receive the nutrients, PS effectively feeds your brain.

Second, it activates the nerve cells and nerve-transmitter production. This means it helps regulate and stimulate the instantaneous "flashes" of information and your ability to react to that information. It even gives you more brain circuits with which to communicate by actually increasing the number of neurotransmitter receptor sites.

Third, as shown in tests with rats, PS blocks the decline of nerve growth factor, which seems to occur naturally as we age.

Fourth, PS has been shown to have antioxidant properties, which means it protects your brain cells from the damage done by free radicals.

Of all the organs in your body, your brain is the most vulnerable to attack by free radicals. Free radicals are the nasty, ravenous molecules that eat away—literally—at the core of your good health. Like an apple that turns brown and rots in the open air—so the delicate tissues of your vital organs decay—ravaged by free radicals oxidizing your cells.

Simply put, PS protects and RENEWS your brain—at any age

Although your body does produce PS in limited amounts, as you age, you produce less and less. If you want to keep your brain functioning optimally, it is critical that you replenish your levels of PS regularly. Though certain foods contain this critical nutrient, the concentrations are not high enough to raise your PS levels. The best way to replenish your PS stores is through daily supplementation.

How to go back in time 12 "brain-age" years

When you replenish your PS levels, you not only boost your brain power-you may actually reverse your brain age!

Just consider the results of one study of 149 people, age 50 or older, who had "normal" age-related memory loss. Some study participants took 100 mg of PS three times a day for 12 weeks; the others, unknown to them, took placebos. By the end of the experiment, the people taking PS benefited from a 15 percent improvement in learning and other memory tasks, with the greatest benefit coming to those with the greatest impairment. Plus, these significant benefits continued for up to four weeks after stopping PS.

Clinical psychologist Thomas Crook, one of the study's authors, said the study suggests that PS "may reverse approximately 12 years of decline." (*Neurology*, vol. 41, no. 5, 1991.)

In another 12-week study, 51 people (average age: 71) took PS supplements and improved their short-term memory. They could better recall names and the locations of misplaced objects. They remembered more details of recent events and could concentrate more intently. (*Psychopharmacology Bulletin*, vol. 28, 1992.)

"Vigilance and concentration"

In other studies, PS showed great promise for those with Alzheimer's disease, Parkinson's disease, and circulation diseases (arteriosclerotic cerebrovascular disease). In particular, those with cerebrovascular disease experienced improvements linked to "vigilance, concentration, and motor reaction" (Ransmayr et al., double-blind trial., 1978).

Plus, PS may also help alleviate depression (Maggioni et al., 1990, double-blind trial, 1990), as well as significantly lower the production of a stress hormone called cortisol.

PS may one day be as widely taken as vitamins C and E, as more and more researchers discover how critical it is to good mental functioning. There are many PS products on the market, and we've reviewed many of them. One we recommend is Brain Power Plus, which includes optimal amounts of the nutrients PS, Acetyl-L-carnitine, DHA, Ginkgo biloba, Panax ginseng, and Siberian ginseng. Brain Power Plus also contains red-date extract, which is used in traditional Chinese medicine to enhance the activity of ginseng; schizandra, a powerful antioxidant that assists with mental clarity and increases your body's level of the detoxifying enzyme glutathione; and the traditional Indian "brain tonic" gotu kolu, which is used in Ayurvedic medicine to improve mental agility and reduce anxiety and depression. See the "Guide to Sources and Availability" on page 215 for the source of Brain Power Plus.

Actions:

- Activates nerve cells and neurotransmitter production
- Influences cell-membrane fluidity and facilitates delivery of nutrients to brain cells
- Blocks the decline of nerve growth factor
- Acts as an antioxidant

Benefits:

- Helps keep the brain active and alert
- Boosts your ability to learn information
- Improves visual memory
- Helps in alleviating depression

CHAPTER 19

Galantamine:
Keep your Brain Alive, Active, and Alert–
With a Proven Flower Extract

Alzheimer's disease.

The term is enough to send chills up anyone's spine. However, among those few "in the know," memory loss isn't as intimidating as it may seem and Alzheimer's disease (AD) may no longer mean a road to irreversible decline. Breaking research now shows there's a natural alternative to AD drugs that not only overcomes their limitations, but, with or without AD, may also take your memory, cognitive functions, and learning to all-new levels.

Since President Reagan's family went public with his condition, the need for more effective treatments for AD has finally come to the forefront. Over 4 million American families have been struck with the disease, and nearly 50 percent of those over age 85 will develop symptoms.

While researchers now have a deeper understanding of the brain and of behavioral changes characterizing the disease, Alzheimer's remains shrouded in mystery. And while the three FDA-approved drugs on the market (Cognex®, Aricept®, and Exelon®) provide temporary relief of some symptoms of AD, they have a number of possible side effects (liver damage, seizures, and depression, for example) and lose their effectiveness within a year.[1] Now, there's an alternative.

New research uncovers the key to stopping Alzheimer's disease

In Alzheimer's patients, chemicals in the brain, called neurotransmitters, go haywire. Neurotransmitters aid communication among brain cells and help electrical impulses jump the tiny gaps (called synapses) between nerves.

In the 1970s, researchers discovered that people with Alzheimer's disease have low levels of a key neurotransmitter called acetylcholine (a-see-tull-

KOH-leen). Not only does acetylcholine help brain cells communicate, but it also plays a vital role in memory, learning, and other cognitive functions. In advanced AD patients, acetylcholine levels plunge by 90 percent. At that point, even the personality is affected.

Acetylcholine is produced in an area of the brain called the basal forebrain. Unfortunately, these cells naturally deteriorate with age and are among the first damaged in the early stages of Alzheimer's disease. When these brain cells die, acetylcholine levels drop dramatically—affecting a patient's memory and capacity for learning.

The problem is compounded in AD patients when an enzyme called cholinesterase is introduced. Cholinesterase cleans up unused acetylcholine in the brain by breaking it down into its component parts. In a healthy person, this is a natural process. But in AD patients, it can add insult to injury and cripple an already impaired memory by further reducing already-low levels of acetylcholine.

The current medications for AD, known as "cholinesterase inhibitors," work primarily by stopping the damage of cholinesterase to optimize the levels of acetylcholine. Aside from the harsh side effects, however, their biggest downfall is that their effects last only a short time.

Does the snowdrop plant hold the key beyond the temporary relief of drugs?

Working with researchers at Life Enhancement Products, a pioneering nutritional development and research company, we've uncovered dozens of recent clinical trials on a natural flower extract that surpasses the effectiveness

---

SIDE EFFECTS OF PRESCRIPTION DRUGS FOR ALZHEIMER'S DISEASE

The following list represents some of the more significant side effects of Cognex, Aricept, and Exelon: liver toxicity, gastric problems, high or low blood pressure, dizziness, fainting, increased heart rate, shortness of breath, seizures and tremors, aggression, irritability, confusion, nervousness, crying, restlessness, cataracts and blurred vision, loss of bowel control, and mental depression.

---

of prescription drugs.

Galantamine, an extract from the snowdrop flower, daffodil, spider lily, and other plants, has been traditionally used in Eastern Europe to treat a variety of minor ailments. Current research shows its greatest promise is its ability to bring the progress of AD to a virtual standstill and rejuvenate cognitive function.

Like prescription drugs, galantamine blocks the action of cholinesterase—allowing for greater levels of acetylcholine—and boosts the production of new acetylcholine neurotransmitters in the brain.[2]

Furthermore, animal studies have found that galantamine does something else no other drug currently being prescribed can do: It stimulates acetylcholine receptors, called nicotinic receptors, in the brain—over an extended period of time. In AD patients, these receptors wear out and the brain isn't able to transport acetylcholine from one cell to another. In addition, when nicotinic receptors are healthy and active, they're thought to inhibit the formation of beta-amyloid plaque deposits, a hard, waxy substance that results from tissue degeneration and is often found in the brains of AD patients.[3] While the current AD drugs initially help stimulate the nicotinic receptors as well, the effect isn't long-lasting. Nicotinic receptors appear to become desensitized to most drugs over time—often within a year—thus making them ineffective in this respect. Unlike AD drugs, galantamine stimulates nicotinic receptors without appearing to cause desensitization when used for an extended period of time.[4]

Increase memory and cognitive function—and keep it

Scientists in Auckland, New Zealand, found that AD patients in several studies (with 285 to 978 patients taking 24 milligrams of galantamine per day for three to six months) achieved significant improvements in cognitive symptoms and daily living activities as compared to a placebo-treated control group. They also found that galantamine delayed the development of behavioral disturbances and psychiatric symptoms. After 12 months of treatment, patients using galantamine maintained their cognitive and functional abilities.[5]

Researchers in Belgium conducted a study with 3,000 AD patients enrolled in one of five randomized, controlled, double-blind groups. Various levels of galantamine were tested (16, 24, and 32 milligrams per day) against placebos, and in every study the galantamine-treated patients maintained their cognitive abilities while the placebo-treated subjects experienced significant deterioration.

PARKINSON'S DISEASE AND MULTIPLE SCLEROSIS VICTIMS MAY BENEFIT FROM GALANTAMINE

Alzheimer's disease is just one example of a medical condition that involves acetylcholine uptake. Because galantamine has shown so much promise over long-term use in AD patients, researchers are looking into other medical conditions that might benefit from a cholinesterase inhibitor—although not all the symptoms of illness may improve or be affected by galantamine. The prescription drug Aricept, for example, has been prescribed for multiple sclerosis patients to help with short-term memory problems, but it hasn't shown any signs of stopping the progress of the disease. Since galantamine is also a cholinesterase inhibitor, it might work as well or better—especially if you need to take the drug over a long period of time. Following is a list of some medical conditions affected by acetylcholine uptake and that may benefit from galantamine:

- Parkinson's disease
- multiple sclerosis
- myasthenia gravis (an autoimmune attack on acetylcholine receptors)
- post-polio syndrome (fatigue and muscle deterioration decades after a polio attack)
- impotence
- jet lag
- neuritis and neuralgia (acute pain and/or inflammation of the nerves)
- muscle fatigue
- attention deficit disorder

And the recent developments regarding its potential to go beyond AD make galantamine a truly cutting-edge therapy to be considered for all.

Prior to entering each of the five studies, patients were evaluated according to the cognition portion of the Alzheimer Disease Assessment Scale. Each subject's performance was assessed in 11 areas measuring memory and orientation. A score of zero meant the patient made no errors, while a top score of 70 meant he suffered from profound dementia. Results from the patient evaluations showed that moderately severe AD patients treated with galantamine had a seven-point advantage over similarly afflicted subjects in the placebo groups. Researchers found that the optimum dosage of galantamine was 24 milligrams per day. Groups treated with 32 milligrams demonstrated no additional improvement in their cognitive abilities.[6]

In another multicenter, double-blind trial conducted last year, galantamine delayed the progress of the disease throughout a full-year study. Conducted at the University of Rochester Medical Center, 636 patients with mild to moderate AD were given galantamine or a placebo for six months. At the end of the period, patients taking galantamine experienced improved cognitive function in relation to the placebo group. Patients taking 24 milligrams of galantamine improved by 3.8 points. Additionally, based on clinician and caregiver interviews, the galantamine group performed significantly better in the completion of daily activities and exhibited fewer behavioral disturbances. Moreover, the benefits of galantamine are long-lasting. Baseline cognitive scores and daily function continued to be high when retested at 12 months for patients taking 24 milligrams of galantamine.[7]

Not only that, but researchers have also determined that galantamine regulates the release of the neurotransmitters glutamate, gamma-aminbutyric acid, and serotonin—all of which play a vital part in proper memory function.[8]

Galantamine fights mental deterioration and increases memory and cognitive abilities— even in Alzheimer's victims

A series of comprehensive clinical trials just released in February has unveiled some exciting new potential for galantamine, not only for treatment but also for prevention and overall cognitive function.

Researchers once thought AD patients who inherited two copies of the apolipoprotein E gene (APOE genotype) believed to cause AD wouldn't benefit as much from cholinesterase inhibitors as other AD sufferers. In four international placebo-controlled clinical trials lasting from three to 12 months, researchers at the Janssen Research Foundation in Belgium studied 1,528 AD subjects with two copies of the APOE genotype and tested the efficacy of galantamine. While those with two copies of the specific gene had an earlier onset of AD symptoms, they received equal benefit from galantamine supplementation as compared with those who had AD from other gene types. So regardless of the genetic origin of AD, galantamine improved cognitive abilities and capacity to handle normal day-to-day activities.[9]

In addition to forgetting things and not being able to draw on previous learning experiences, AD patients have an impaired ability to learn new tasks. In recent animal tests, researchers found that galantamine modifies the nicotinic receptors so there's an increased release in the amount of acetylcholine in addition to acting as an acetylcholinesterase inhibitor. Scientists concluded that daily administration of galantamine over a period of 10 days results in an increase of conditions that are known to augment learning opportunities in AD patients.[10]

Put all these characteristics together, and the overall result for AD patients—as dozens of clinical trials prove—is that the disease slows dramatically and the victim's memory can stabilize and even improve. The latest studies add to the growing body of evidence on the preventative potential of galantamine and its ability to rejuvenate your overall learning and performance.

Rescue your brain—cell by cell—starting today

The proof of galantamine's effectiveness in treating AD is so impressive that it's already being put to use around the world. Under the market name Reminyl®, it has been used widely in 15 European countries since October 2000. It was only recently formulated by the drug companies, and in 1999 the manufacturer submitted Reminyl to the FDA for approval; the FDA sanctioned it for use in AD patients the beginning of March 2001.

But approval by the FDA is only the first step on a long path to getting help for the patient. According to the National Academy of Sciences'

Institute of Medicine, important research discoveries can take as long as 17 years before information about them filters down to doctors and hospitals. And even if your doctor knows about a supplement or drug, your HMO or insurance company might not approve it because of the expense. Or they may feel you don't have sufficient need for a particular drug. Regardless of the potential benefits, mountains of red tape and bureaucratic nonsense might prevent you from getting the products you need.

The good news is you don't have to wait. While the pharmaceutical giants, insurance companies, and HMOs fight to get their extracts packaged, marketed, and distributed, you can protect your memory and intellect and put a stop to the advance of AD with the natural form of galantamine.

Thanks to the diligence of researchers and formulators at Life Enhancement Products, you can benefit from galantamine extract today. It's currently available in a formula called GalantaMind®, which combines the optimum dosage of galantamine (24 milligrams per day, based on clinical trials) with vitamin B5 and choline, both of which help enhance the production of acetylcholine and prevent the removal of the unused neurotransmitter. Galantamine does have a few minor side effects: nausea, vomiting, and diarrhea. However, they can be significantly reduced and even eliminated by taking smaller initial dosages and working up to the full dosage over a week's time.

The mountain of evidence on the benefits of galantamine for Alzheimer's patients is undeniable. Anyone battling this difficult disease should consider it. See page 215 the "Guide to Sources and Availability" for more information.

Actions:

- Blocks the production of the enzyme cholinesterase which breaks down acetylcholine an essential neurotransmitter.

- Boosts the production of new acetylcholine neurotransmitters the chemicals essential to communication among brain cells.

- Stimulates the nicotinic receptors in the brain that allow for the transport of neurotransmitters from one cell to another.

- Halts tissue degeneration by promoting healthy and active acetylcholine receptors and depressing the formation of beta-amyloid plaque deposits.

Benefits:

- Elevates memory capacity, rejuvenates cognitive functions, and increases learning abilities.

- Helps to maintain cognitive and functional abilities and delays the progress of Alzheimer's disease.

- Reverses symptoms in a variety of other conditions that are affected by acetylcholine uptake including Parkinson's disease, multiple sclerosis, myasthenia gravis, muscle fatigue, impotence, and attention deficit disorder

References

[1] Dement Geriatr Cogn Disord, 11 Suppl 1:11-18, 2000

[2] Behav Brain Res; 113(1-2):11-19, 2000

[3] The Newsletter of the Memory Disorders Project at Rutgers-Newark, Winter 2001

[4] Dement Geriatr Cogn Disord, 11 Suppl 1:11-18, 2000

[5] Drugs; 60(5):1095-1122, 2000

[6] Dement Geriatr Cogn Disord, 11 Suppl 1:19-27, 2000

[7] Neurology; 54(12)2269-76, 2000

[8] National Institute on Aging

[9] Dement Geriatr Cogn Disord, 12:69-77, 2001

[10] Behav Brain Res, 113(1-2):11-19, 2000

Inositol:
Nutrient therapy for Alzheimer's disease, Depression, and Anxiety

Inositol, a lesser-known B-vitamin, has recently come into the limelight as a surprising new superstar in a variety of psychiatric and neurological disorders, including Alzheimer's disease, depression, anxiety, obsessive-compulsive disorder, and panic disorder.

Inositol is commonly found in foods that contain other B vitamins, like lecithin, brewer's yeast, liver, wheat germ, and whole grains. As HSI panelist Elson Haas, M.D. explains in **Staying Healthy with Nutrition** (Celestial Arts, 1992, p. 136), "The body can produce its own inositol from glucose, so it is not really essential. We have high stores of inositol; its concentration in the body is second highest of the B vitamins, surpassed only by niacin."

With no real danger of deficiency, the importance of inositol might easily be overlooked. But recent research reveals that inositol in therapeutic amounts has led to dramatic results in a number of double-blind, placebo-controlled studies:

> **Alzheimer's disease.** A small trial evaluated the effects of 6000 mg a day of inositol on sufferers of Alzheimer's disease. After only one month, those using inositol showed significant improvement in language and orientation, as compared to the control (placebo) group. Researchers intend to study larger doses and longer trial periods (*Neuro-psychopharm. Biological Psychiatry*, vol. 20, pp. 729-735, 1996).

> **Obsessive-Compulsive Disorder (OCD).** Based on a six-week study, researchers concluded that inositol was effective in managing OCD and other serotonin-related disorders. Subjects taking 18 grams a day of inositol showed significant improvement in OCD

symptoms. These were patients who had not responded to treatment with pharmaceutical antidepressants (selective serotonin reuptake inhibitors, or SSRIs) or had been disturbed by side effects. (*American Journal of Psychiatry*, vol. 153, pp. 1219-1221, 1996).

Panic disorder. Researchers noted a decrease in frequency and severity of panic attacks among patients using 12 grams of inositol a day for four weeks. No significant side effects were noted. (*American Journal of Psychiatry*, vol. 152, pp. 1084-1086, 1995).

Depression. Subjects taking 12 grams a day of inositol displayed significant improvement on the Hamilton Depression Rating Scale after one month, as compared to the control group. (*American Journal of Psychiatry*, vol. 152, pp. 792-794, 1995).

Inositol is found in large amounts in brain tissue and plays an important role in nerve-cell communication. One of its functions is as a "secondary messenger" or backup system for the regulation of serotonin levels in the brain. This helps to explain why therapeutic amounts of inositol appear to help those individuals whose conditions don't respond to SSRIs like Prozac. It also represents an alternative for those who suffer unpleasant side effects (such as nausea, headache, insomnia, and a reduced sex drive) from SSRIs.

A typical multivitamin formula might include only 50 mg of inositol, if it includes any at all. But the research suggests that dosages of up to 18 grams (or 18,000 mg) are indicated for some conditions. Some researchers believe that even higher amounts could increase the benefits. (Inositol is considered to be perfectly safe, with no toxic dosage.)

Taking this amount of inositol in capsule form is a tall order especially if you have difficulty in swallowing pills. (There is also the question of bioavailability.) Inositol is also available in a powdered form that can be stirred into water or juice, although you may have trouble controlling the exact amount unless you have a pharmaceutical scale.

A third option is a new effervescent formulation of powdered inositol, which is packaged in premeasured 4-gram packets. Effervescent delivery systems for vitamins and other nutrients are very popular in Europe and Asia. This method eliminates the question of whether capsules are fully dissolving in your stomach and is believed to produce a more sustained release of nutrients into the blood stream.

Powdered and capsule forms of inositol are readily available from health-food stores or through mail-order sources. The effervescent formulation is not yet available through retail outlets, but can be ordered from the source listed on page 215.

Actions:

- Regulates serotonin levels in the brain
- Plays important role in nerve cell communication

Benefits:

- Appears to help conditions that don't respond to SSRIs
- No unpleasant side effects including nausea, headaches, insomnia, and a reduced sex drive
- Improves language and orientation in Alzheimer's patients
- Manages OCD symptoms
- Decrease frequency and severity of panic attacks
- Relieves depression

21

Citrudex:
End Severe Exhaustion and Mental Fatigue in Just Two Weeks

We're excited to bring you the exclusive report on a product that's just becoming available in the United States. Manufactured and marketed in Europe for over 20 years, this natural energy booster has helped thousands of people end their muscle fatigue and increase performance.

The product is called Citrudex™ (marketed under the name Stimol™ in Europe). It's a combination of the amino acid citrulline and malate, an apple derivative that has been shown to enhance the work of the amino acid.[1] European doctors have been using citrulline malate (CM) for over 20 years to help patients overcome physical and mental fatigue and exhaustion, but it has yet to be exported to the U.S. until now. After reviewing the research, clinical trials, and amazing success in helping patients overcome severe mental and physical exhaustion as well as reversing dementia, we knew Citrudex needed to reported on.

Reduce toxic by-products in your tissue and move freely again

Most people are familiar with lactic acid, which is a normal by-product of muscle use that increases when you exercise or exert yourself physically. When lactic acid builds up, your muscles feel sore and tender. Your body removes excess lactic acid and that's why the soreness disappears after a while. As you get older, your body's ability to remove lactic acid slows down which means you'll feel muscle soreness a bit longer than usual.

Removing the build up of lactic acid has been the focus of much of the research and product development to date. There are a lot of performance products already on the market that address this roadblock to exercise and physical exertion.

However, there's another by-product of muscle use that can also build to excessive levels—and can cause a lot more damage to your health than high levels of lactic acid: Ammonia. And the products that fight lactic acid, may not have any effect on ammonia levels. A build up of ammonia can result in serious consequences, including extreme fatigue and dementia.[2]

Besides being produced through physical activity, ammonia is also a normal by-product of protein digestion, but your liver's urea cycle is usually pretty efficient at handling additional ammonia. But as you age, your liver's capacity for processing ammonia diminishes and too much could remain in your tissues. When it isn't removed quickly, it reaches levels that can make you so weak that even simple tasks become impossible. As the extra ammonia stays in your system for longer periods of time, it can wreak havoc with other functions and your organs. High ammonia levels inhibit the synapses that allow your brain and spinal cord to communicate with your muscles, blood vessels, glands, and organs. If you could find a way to give your urea cycle a boost, you could reduce the damage caused by an excess of ammonia. This is where citrulline comes into play.

The amino acid citrulline helps in the removal of wastes. When your urea cycle or your liver isn't functioning efficiently, it could be due to low levels of citrulline. It's considered a nonessential amino acid, which means you don't have to get it from food because your body manufactures it. But the amount your body makes decreases with age, and some people have never made enough to adequately control any significant increase in ammonia. And in some people, it drops so much that they constantly have too much ammonia surrounding their tissues. Studies have found that supplementing with citrulline malate can help.

CM reduces fatigue by 200 percent

The Regional Teaching Hospital Centre in Nimes, France, conducted a 12-day randomized, double-blind, placebo-controlled trial (unpublished) with 41 patients age 70 to 100 to see if CM could substantially relieve a variety of symptoms normally associated with aging and/or mental impairment. By the fifth day of treatment, patients taking CM had clinically detectable improvements. A higher level of conscious awareness was one of the initial improvements, and some CM patients said they "felt better." Subjects were evaluated for 13 different factors, including memory of recent events, depression, emotional stability, motivation and initiative, fatigue, sleep, and tinnitus. After the trial was over, **patients taking CM had a 200 percent greater improvement when compared to the placebo group.** Furthermore, the researchers found that CM worked much faster and considered the supplement to be safer than traditional prescription drugs, since it doesn't have harsh side effects.

In a placebo-controlled study at the Hôspital Général de Montpellier in France, researchers evaluated 36 patients age 65 and older on overall severity of muscle weakness, impaired general condition, anorexia, muscle fatigue, and anxiety. After taking citrulline malate for 12 days, patients were re-evaluated. Those taking CM had a **56 percent greater improvement over the placebo-treated subjects** when compared with their physical and mental fatigue prior to the study.[3]

In another French study, scientists tested 10 normally sedentary men given either a placebo or CM before working out on stationary bicycles. During the 30-minute cool-down period following the exercise, **the men whom had taken CM showed a 61 percent lower level of nitrogen than those given the placebo.**[4] By lowering your nitrogen levels, your muscles recover faster, potentially reducing feelings of weakness and exhaustion.

Incapacitated patients show incredible improvement

One of the most remarkable trials with citrulline malate involves patients suffering from a variety of illnesses, including kidney failure, Parkinson's disease, insulin-dependent diabetes, aspirin-induced hemorrhagic gastritis, rheumatoid arthritis, angina, and hypertension. But they all had one thing in common—age-related dementia.

Thirty subjects age 64 to 96 were treated with CM for 12 days. By the third day, many patients showed improvement. And almost everyone who could benefit from CM treatment had measurable improvement by the fifth day.

One 74-year-old male patient had suffered two strokes and was bedridden. **After treatment with CM, his improvement was so great that he was able to leave the hospital** and return to a nursing home.

An 85-year-old woman suffering from angina and muscular and arthritis pain, had severe muscle weakness and was unable to participate in daily activities. She had **such significant improvement after CM treatment that she was able to return to her routine activities**. Her newfound energy was maintained for two months after supplementation stopped. It appears that in some individuals, CM supplementation may have a lasting and permanent effect that doesn't require continued treatment.

One of the most amazing recoveries in this study concerned an 82-year-old insulin-dependent man with chronic bronchitis. He'd suffered an influenza attack that resulted in a state of confusional decompensation (his heart wasn't supplying enough blood to his brain). The researcher describes the man's recovery: "During the 12 days of the trial, the patient passed from the picture of slovenly dementia with perpetual soiling to that of predementia, at the same time jovial and perplexed, of agreeable aspect and florid complexion."

Reviewing the entire study, the **change in muscle strength was almost a 76 percent improvement for CM-treated patients** when compared with muscle weakness before treatment. Feelings of **mental and physical exhaustion also improved**. The researchers used several criteria to measure this, including "vivacity of spirit" (improved 38 percent), mood (improved 28 percent), and motivation (improved 27 percent).[5]

Be among the first in the U.S. to benefit from the rejuvenating effects of CM

Although American doctors have used citrulline for hospitalized patients experiencing extremely high blood levels of ammonia that could lead to permanent brain damage or serious impairment, there is no indication that they've used this amino acid to relieve chronic exhaustion or fatigue. Biocodex recommends you take 2 capsules 3 times a day. See page 215 for additional ordering information.

It doesn't matter how fatigued you are, CM might be the key to rejuvenating your physical and mental wellbeing…and it could be mere days away.

Caution: If you have Multiple Sclerosis, check with your physician before using Citrudex.

Actions:

- Boosts low levels of the amino acid citrulline that is essential to the proper functioning of your liver and urea cycle.
- Reduces nitrogen levels allowing muscles to recover from exercise more quickly and reducing feelings of exhaustion and weakness.
- Enhances the liver's ability to process excess ammonia that can inhibit the synapses that allow the brain and spinal cord to communicate with your muscles, blood, vessels, glands, and organs.

Benefits:

- Relieves a variety of symptoms associated with aging and/or mental impairment including short-term memory loss, depression, emotional instability, fatigue, sleeplessness, and tinnitus.
- Improves quality of life for those suffering from age-related dementia.

References

[1] Sem Hôp Paris; 66(9):477-81, 1990

[2] Sem Hôp Paris; 66(9):477-81, 1990

[3] Marseille Medical; 272(1), 1982

[4] Sem Hôp Paris; 66(9):477-81, 1990

[5] Le Revue de Gériatrie; 7(9), 1982

[6] Crit Care Med; 28(9):3248-8, 2000

[7] Methods and Findings, 22(7), 2000

Super Sex for as Long as You Want

Although perhaps rarely discussed, even between the closest of couples, and almost never by the medical establishment, loss of libido is one of the most disturbing effects of aging. Even the American Medical Association's Encyclopedia of Medicine defines libido (sex drive) as something that can be expected to fade with age. But satisfactory and exciting sexual vigor can be maintained into old age, and this section highlights three breakthrough products that can help without the risks and unknowns of Viagra.

V-Power:
Promote Your Sexual Health

For many men, as they age, maintaining prime sexual function is a primary concern. To do this, you first need a healthy heart and cardiovascular condition. In the heart-health section of this book, you can read about how nutritional supplements can help keep your arteries youthful and flexible. But you also need to have powerful, local circulation...plenty of blood flowing strongly into your penis. And there are ways to increase both general and local circulation—without risking your life with drugs like Viagra.

There are dozens of herbs reputed to be sexual stimulants, but two in particular have been proven in modern, scientific trials to increase blood flow to the penis.

Coleus forskohlii is an herb from India that dilates the arteries going to your penis, increasing blood supply to the region. It also blocks a certain enzyme that is known to suppress your ability to form an erection. This effective and targeted approach to impotence has been the model for pharmaceutical impotence drugs. But the all-natural original has one important advantage: It is perfectly safe, and it even promotes healthy blood-pressure levels.

Muira Puama (also known as Amazon Potency Wood) is another natural substance proven to enhance sexual function. A study by French researchers found that more than 50% of men suffering from erectile dysfunction reported improvement when using it.

Poor circulation is at the root of many sexual problems, and it is relatively easy to address by using natural substances like Forskohlin, and Muira Puama. But circulation is only the beginning of the story. Often, when

CONTINUED ON PAGE 154

KEEPING THE PROSTATE HEALTHY

One of the more common health complaints for middle-aged and older men is a prostate problem. Sooner or later, it seems that prostate difficulties inevitably interfere with men's quality of life. At least six out of 10 men over the age of 50 have "significant" enlargement of the prostate, the doughnut-shaped gland that surrounds the urethra at the base of the penis.

The condition comes about when cells in the prostate begin to multiply too quickly, causing the prostate to swell, sometimes pressing on or pinching off the urethra. Benign prostatic hyperplasia, or BPH can cause pain and tenderness, painful or frequent urination, and can increase your risk of a prostatic disease like prostatitis (infection of the prostate gland) or even prostate cancer. And it can throw a wet blanket over even the healthiest sex life.

The prevention of prostatic disease is of primary importance. At all costs, you want to avoid prostate surgery, which can leave you permanently impotent and incontinent. But there is no reason to suffer a diminished quality of life or even occasional discomfort.

Prostate health can be easily enhanced and protected with simple nutritional measures. You may be familiar with saw palmetto, an herb that is commonly used to reduce swelling and inflammation of the prostate gland.

Saw palmetto works by blocking the action of an enzyme called 5-alpha-reductase. This leads to a reduction in the levels of dihydrotestosterone (DHT), a hormone that promotes growth of prostate tissue. It works by the same mechanism as synthetic pharmaceutical drugs for BPH—only better and with fewer side effects.

Other tried and true herbs for prostate health include:

Pygeum africanum is a powerful, natural anti-inflammatory that helps to reduce swelling of the prostate gland. Like saw palmetto, Pygeum has a well-established track record against BPH. In fact, French doctors regularly prescribe it for their patients suffering from BPH instead of pharmaceutical drugs.

Stinging nettle possesses strong anti-inflammatory properties and also helps regulate sex-hormone levels in the prostate. Studies show that it can reduce the size of a swollen prostate by over 50 percent.

Recent research has led to new breakthroughs in the natural approach to prostate health. Scientists have uncovered two new power nutrients that substantially reduce the risk of malignant growth in the prostate.

A recent study at the Harvard Medical School found that men with increased consumption of tomatoes and tomato products had a significantly lower risk of prostate cancer. Subsequent research isolated an antioxidant called lycopene as the active plant chemical responsible for this protective effect.

The other breakthrough finally solved the mystery of why prostate difficulties are almost unheard of in Japan. Those who consume soy on a daily basis cut their risk of prostate cancer by almost 70 percent over those who eat it only once a week or less. (This is not the first time that soy has been revealed as a cancer preventive food: Other research has demonstrated lower rates of colorectal, breast, lung, and gastric cancer among soy eaters.)

Scientists have established that naturally occurring chemicals called isoflavones are responsible for soy's powerful cancer protective effects. The most well-researched of the soy isoflavones is called genistein: It's been shown to selectively kill cancer cells and prevent the formation of blood vessels that support tumor growth. Soy also has weak hormonal effects and helps to balance hormonal imbalances.

circulatory problems that cause impotence are corrected, another underlying problem surfaces: a diminished sex drive, or lack of desire for sex. And that's something you won't hear about from the folks promoting Viagra, because Viagra can't do a thing to enhance a reduced libido.

Testosterone—fueling the fire

A lagging libido, or a reduced desire for sex, is the second most common form of sexual dysfunction and is usually the result of low testosterone levels. According to some estimates, as many as 20 percent of men over 50 have testosterone levels below the normal range.

As we age, testosterone levels tend to decrease, but their decline is hastened in our modern society by the high amounts of estrogenlike chemicals in our environment. Pesticides, plastics, and other industrial chemicals pose a hidden threat to the modern male by throwing the body's hormones—especially sex hormones—out of balance.

In recent years, testosterone-replacement therapy has become popular, and testosterone "precursors" like androstenedione have become widely available over-the-counter. But these solutions—especially when attempted without a doctor's supervision—are not without risk. Although they may temporarily increase your sex drive, they may also inadvertently feed prostate-cancer growth or cause other health problems. They also do not tend to result in permanent improvement in sexual function.

Instead, we turn again to the wisdom of traditional Asian and Indian medicine. It is no coincidence that in these cultures men regularly marry and father children well into their 70s and 80s. For centuries, these cultures have used herbs to safely and naturally balance sex hormones and increase testosterone production, without any of the hazards of hormone therapy.

Three scientifically proven power herbs give the most significant boost to a sagging sex drive:

Tribulus terrestis is traditionally used in Ayurvedic (Indian) medicine as a male tonic—to improve the health of the **prostate, penis,** and urinary tract. More recent studies show that it **leads to** a significant increase (up to 30%) in testosterone levels in as **little**

as five days. Men report that Tribulus not only steps up sex drive but also increases stamina and endurance; it's helpful in the bedroom as well as the in the gym or on the job.

Epimedium grandiflorum is used in Chinese medicine to combat

VIAGRA: DOES IT WORK? IS IT SAFE?

Viagra helps impotent men achieve erections by causing tiny blood vessels in the penis to relax, allowing blood to flow in and cause an erection. It does work—about half the time. But it's not safe. According to reports filed with the Food and Drug Administration, the drug has been linked to heart attacks and can be fatal when combined with common heart medication like nitrates (used for angina pain). If you have any kind of cardiac disorder or other risk factor or are taking cardiac medications, you should not be taking Viagra.

Viagra can also damage your vision, reducing your retinal function by up to 50% for several hours after use...and possibly permanently. It can cause extreme light sensitivity and cause a pronounced blue tint in your field of vision. The American Academy of Ophthalmology has issued warnings about the serious risks of Viagra.

More importantly, in order for Viagra to work for you, you must suffer from erectile dysfunction due only to insufficient blood flow to the penis. If you wake up in the morning with an erection but rarely have the energy or drive for sex, then Viagra is almost sure to disappoint.

And if you are simply looking for a sex aid to enhance your pleasure, you're looking in the wrong place. If you can already achieve and maintain an erection, Viagra is not going to enhance your performance or staying power.

Viagra does one thing and one thing only—it causes blood to flow to, and stay, in the penis. It does NOT:

- Enhance your desire
- Heighten your enjoyment
- Give you the mental energy and alertness to perform optimally
- Supply the physical vigor and stamina that fuels good sex

impotence and infertility. Clinical research has shown that it acts directly on the testes and prostate gland, increasing sperm production, and stimulates the sensory nerves that can trigger sexual desire.

Ginseng has long been revered for its potency and libido-enhancing powers. Panax ginseng has been found to increase sperm production and raise testosterone levels and is considered one of the most potent herbal libido enhancers.

These herbs, along with the circulation-enhancing herbs discussed earlier are best used together for the most reliable results. When using herbs in combination, however, it is important to adjust the amounts accordingly. Because each enhances the action of the others, you can get the maximum benefit from smaller amounts than you might use if you were taking them individually.

HSI researchers have uncovered a libido and potency formula called V-Power that includes all five of these powerful herbs—along with several other supporting nutrients—in the amounts found to be most effective in enhancing circulation, performance, and desire. V-Power is available from the source listed on page 215.

Actions:
- Increases blood flow to the penis
- Balances sex hormones and increases testosterone production

Benefit:
- Safe, natural sexual stimulant

23

Maca:
Staple of the Andean Diet Can Improve Stamina, Sexual Function, Fertility and More.

Hidden in the high altitudes of the Andean Mountains in Peru is one of the world's oldest, and perhaps most powerful, sexual stimulants—maca. A staple of the Andean diet and culture, the maca-plant root has been used for centuries to improve stamina, sexual function, fertility, and more. A new study shows it may prove to be a safe, but powerful, alternative to Viagra.

On the Junin Plateau, where maca thrives, the altitude ranges from 11,000 to 14,500 feet, and the extremes of heat and cold, high winds, and rocky soil prohibit the growth of most crops. But residents of the region, dating as far back as the Incan Indians, have known and celebrated the effects of this simple, hardy plant. Now, as its powerful effects have become more publicized and celebrated by local governments, scientists are finally taking a good look at this herbal aphrodisiac.

New research proves maca's ancient powers

Maca is an annual, cruciferous plant, from the same family as radishes, cauliflower, and cabbage. Its botanical name is Lepidium meyenii, and while it is sometimes referred to as Peruvian ginseng, it is no relation to the ginseng plant. But, as is the case with ginseng, science is beginning to prove that it can increase stamina and performance.

Little lab research had been done on maca—until now. Recent studies conducted by scientist at PureWorld Botanicals, in conjunction with Shenyang Medical College and Liaoning College in China and the Chinese Academy of Preventative Medicine, demonstrate maca's effects on libido and sexual function. In several studies examining its effects on mice and rats, the researchers found that it significantly increased the number of times the mice had sexual intercourse and improved the erections of rats with erectile dysfunction.[1]

Boosted libido—in just one day!

In the first study, male mice were randomly divided into three groups: two experimental groups and one control group. Each experimental group received a different formula of maca extract (M-01 or M-02), provided twice daily at a dosage of 40 mg per gram of body weight. The control group received a regular granulated feed. After 21 days of this regimen, the mice were placed in cages with female mice. During the subsequent three-hour period, the frequency of sex among the M-01 mice was 2.9 times that of the control group, while the M-02 mice had 4.1 times more sexual encounters than the control group.

The second study further confirmed these findings, in a shorter time span. Male mice were randomly divided into two groups of 10. One group received regular feed, while the other received about 96 grams of the M-01 maca formula—for just one day. That same day, five female mice were put in each male's cage. The next morning, vaginal smears from each female mouse were examined for the presence of sperm. The number of sperm-positive females in the maca group was 2 1/2 times higher than in the control group.

Maca can help with erectile dysfunction

With confirmation that maca increased libido, the researchers then sought to learn if it could help those suffering from erectile dysfunction. A group of 90 rats was divided into experimental and control groups. In each group, there were an equal number of normal rats, testosterone-treated rats, and castrated rats. The castrated rats in the experimental group were divided into smaller groups to receive varying dosages of the different maca formulas (M-01 and M-02), while the control-group rats received a regular diet.

After 20 days, researchers used an electric pulse to stimulate each rat's penis. They measured the amount of time between the initial stimulus and the achievement of a full erection. The findings showed that castrated rats treated with certain dosages of the maca formulas achieved erection rates similar to or better than those of normal rats and those treated with testosterone.

What is the magic in maca?

There are still many unanswered questions about how maca works, but the body of knowledge is growing. It seems to be an *adaptogen*, meaning it helps to restore balance and normalize bodily functions compromised by stress, in this case caused by hormone levels. Hormonal secretion is controlled by the hypothalamus in the brain and the pituitary gland, by their sending messages to the organs and glands that secrete hormones, such as the ovaries, testes, adrenal glands, pancreas, and thyroid. By stimulating the pituitary and the hypothalamus, maca can provide a needed stimulus to jump-start the process and restore the body's hormonal balance.

Maca is about 59 percent carbohydrate, 10 percent protein, and 9 percent fiber. Linoleic, palmitic, and oleic acids make up the 2.2 percent of the fat found in maca. It is a good source of iron, magnesium, calcium, potassium, and iodine and contains valuable plant sterols.[2] Maca also contains compounds called isothiocyanates, which are thought to play a role in regulating hormone secretion and enhancing libido. The calcium and magnesium in maca may benefit the female endocrine system, as may the iodine, through its impact on the thyroid gland.

Newly discovered compounds are key to maca's powers

But several recently discovered compounds might provide the true explanation for maca's powers. Dr. Qun Yi Zheng of PureWorld Botanicals revealed the presence of several new compounds in maca, including the long-chain fatty amides macaenes and macamides.[3] These newly discovered compounds seem to be the key to maca's effectiveness, based on the results of the studies discussed above. Of the two different formulations of maca fed to the experimental mice, the M-02 formula contained more macaenes and macamides. The mice that were fed the stronger concentration of the compounds showed more dramatic results than those fed the weaker extract. This suggests that these compounds play a crucial role in maca's sexual impact.

Dr. Zheng's discovery of macaenes and macamides, as well as the results of the clinical study on the effects of maca on the sexual activity of mice and rats, appeared in the April 2000 issue of the peer-reviewed medical journal *Urology*. Dr. Zheng is very excited about having his work included in this prestigious publication. "This is the first time, worldwide, that a study on the effects of maca has been accepted by a peer-reviewed journal," said Dr. Zheng. "We are very pleased with the response we are getting to our research."

Alleviates problems for men and women

While maca's ability to affect sexual dysfunction in men may receive the most attention, it is far from its only reported use. Maca's ability to correct hormone imbalances may impact a wide range of disorders that affect both men and women.

For men, the results are fairly straightforward. A lack of testosterone in men can cause decreased libido and sexual dysfunction. Maca can stimulate the production of more testosterone, boosting libido and improving sexual performance.

For women, the regulation of hormones may relieve a whole host of troublesome symptoms. In menopausal women, maca can help even out the estrogen and progesterone levels, relieving such symptoms as fatigue, night sweats, dizziness, and palpitations. It may also help reduce vaginal dryness. Maca has also been used as a natural fertility aid for centuries.

Aside from the gender-specific benefits, maca has also been reported to improve overall physical performance, stamina, energy, and concentration. And some experts say that even children may benefit from maca's effect on concentration. Peruvian natives report its effectiveness against a wide range of maladies, including rheumatism, respiratory disorders, constipation, anemia, and depression.

Powerful results without dangerous side effects

Remember, maca is a food. An entire culture of people has been relying on it as a staple of their diet for centuries, without any discernable side effects. Clinical studies have supported these observations. Toxicity studies at Product Safety Labs in East Brunswick, New Jersey, showed that maca has no toxicity and no negative pharmacological effects.[4]

If you do decide to give maca a try, note that some experts recommend alternating periods on and off of maca to maximize results. For example, you might alternately take it for 90 days and then stop for 30 days. There are no reported problems with withdrawal during the off periods.

Dosage recommendations vary, depending on the formula you take and its concentration. But it is virtually impossible to take too much maca— the Peruvians have been eating it for nearly every meal for centuries. It can be taken as a tablet or as a powder, which can be added to blender smoothies and other drinks.

MacaPure™ is a standardized, concentrated, powdered extract of maca produced by PureWorld Botanicals under the direction of Dr. Zheng. The formula contains 0.6 percent macamides and macaenes. The recommended dosage for MacaPure is at least one 450-mg capsule twice daily. Because maca is such an exciting breakthrough and fortunately, very affordable, it is already available in your local health-food store. When looking for maca products be sure to check the label's ingredients for MacaPure to insure that you are receiving the highest quality maca product.

Actions:

- Stimulates the pituitary and the hypothalamus to help restore the body's hormonal balance and normalize bodily functions compromised by stress.

- Reverses sexual dysfunction in men by stimulating the production of testosterone.

- Levels off progesterone and estrogen levels in menopausal women to alleviate troubling menopausal symptoms such as night sweats, dizziness, vaginal dryness, and palpitations.

Benefits:

- Enhances stamina, sexual function, and fertility.

- Recharges the libido and regulates hormone secretions with isothiocyanates compounds.

References

[1] Zheng, Q., et al. "Effect of Lipidic Extract From Lepidium Meyenii on Sexual Behavior in Mice and Rats"

[2] Food Chemistry, 493:47-49, 1994

[3] Zheng, et al

[4] Natural Foods Merchandiser, p. 46, February 2000

CHAPTER 24

Red Deer Antler Velvet:
Animallike Results

An ancient scroll recommends deer antler for 52 different diseases. Today, it has been scientifically proven to strengthen muscle contractions, improve nerve impulses, regulate blood pressure, and treat arthritis.

Deer antler velvet sounds like the kind of ingredient that should go into the cauldron right after "eye of newt" and just before "toe of frog." At first impression, the uninformed might be tempted to put the users of antler products on the "far out" nutritional fringe. And yet this substance has a credible history of effective use in Chinese herbal medicine that goes back at least two millennia, and it continues to be widely used in China, Korea, Japan, and Russia.

What is antler velvet?

We think of the antler as an inert growth of material with no biological activity. This is more or less true, but the velvet is an entirely different kind of tissue than the actual antler material itself.

Male deer grow a new set of antlers every year. Unlike most mammalian tissue, which contains an internal circulatory system to provide blood and nutrients, the blood flow to new antlers is on the outside of the antlers. The velvet is a fuzzy membrane that contains and distributes this external supply of blood and nutrients to support the new antler's growth. And this growth rate is extremely rapid: on a large male, a 20-pound set of antlers can grow in three to four months. The velvet falls off as mating season approaches, and the fully mineralized antlers become the inert structures we perceive them to be.

So the antler velvet, in sharp contrast to the antlers themselves, is a tissue of extremely high and specialized bioactivity. It is rich with precursors for growth hormone, leutinizing hormone (the hormone stimulating testosterone synthesis), and prostaglandins. It contains elements that could be effective against cancer and arthritis, similar to those found in shark cartilage.

How does it work?

It's not surprising that several modes of action are at work with such a complicated substance. Some of the therapeutic properties of red deer antler velvet appear to be similar to those of cartilage. Of particular interest, however, is the relatively high level of insulinlike growth factor found in deer antler.

Growth hormones have an anabolic effect. That is, they cause tissue to grow and cause stored energy (fat) to be consumed. This is in contrast to hormones that are catabolic, causing tissue to break down and release energy—an endocrinological dichotomy that is reminiscent of the yin and yang of Chinese medicine.

Insulin, the hormone released by the pancreas to help metabolize sugar, is also anabolic. Some of the effects of growth hormone are similar to those of insulin, but others are in conflict. Growth hormone can impair glucose uptake in cells by suppressing the action of insulin receptors, while at the same time causing fatty acids to be released from fatty tissue.

A receptor is a special part of a cell, usually a protein in the cell membrane. It is "tuned in" to respond to the presence of a particular hormone and then

---

WHAT IS RED DEER ANTLER USED FOR?

In Korea and Japan, red deer antler velvet is commonly used to:
- increase blood production in the treatment of anemia
- modulate the immune system
- treat infertility in women
- treat impotence in men
- improve blood circulation in patients with heart disease
- improve muscle tone and glandular functions
- increase lung efficiency
- increase muscular strength and nerve function

---

initiate a process within the cell-like a radio receiver that only gets one station. In the case of insulinlike growth hormone, the hormone "looks" enough like insulin to jam the receiver, preventing regular "insulin signals" from getting through.

The net effect of the two actions (the suppression of insulin reception and the release of stored fat) is to encourage cells to consume fat rather than sugar or other carbohydrates, with obvious benefits for both body-builders and weight watchers.

Growth hormone also has an important role in immunity. The real nuts and bolts of immunity take place at the cell-membrane level, where specialized proteins "float" in the thin fatty membrane, controlling what goes in and what goes out. For at least part of the day, it's critical to maintain a protein-building (anabolic) environment: If you can build protein, you can strengthen your immune system; if you are consuming protein to maintain blood sugar or other crucial physiological functions, immunity gradually degrades. So the daily production of growth hormone is enormously important, especially as we age.

Unfortunately, growth-hormone production falls off very quickly as we leave our teen years. Between the ages of 20 and 23, daytime growth-hormone levels begin to drop. And by the time we reach age 30, even the growth-hormone release in response to vigorous exercise is greatly reduced.

Much of the action of growth hormone is carried out through secondary hormones called somatomedins. These hormones are manufactured in the liver in response to growth hormone, and the two main somatomedins promote bone growth, collagen synthesis, and the stimulation of tissue growth.

In an older individual with very low growth-hormone production, a natural dietary source of these hormones has been shown to produce the same anabolic effects found in a much younger individual. This is probably the best way to account for the reported rejuvenating properties of deer antler velvet. In addition to the beneficial growth hormones, the following substances are also found in red deer antler velvet:

- prostaglandins, which help control a wide range of physiological functions, including reduction of inflammation especially important to athletes and arthritis sufferers

- velvatins, which include a nucleoside demonstrated to have value in cancer therapy and AIDS treatment. Nucleosides are the building blocks of DNA and RNA, the masters of cellular function
- pantocrine, shown in a 1974 Russian study by Dr. Arcady Koltun to increase athletic performance
- N-acetyl-glucosamine sulfate, for wound healing
- chondroitin sulfate, which, along with glucosamine, is an effective agent against arthritis. (Chondroitin sulfate in particular has been claimed to reverse atherosclerosis and dramatically improve circulation)

Traditional Chinese medicine calls for its use to treat impotence and infertility, frequent urination, cold extremities, lower back and knee pain, loss of hearing, tinnitus (ringing in the ears), and dizziness.

Future uses are likely to include treatment of a wide range of degenerative diseases, especially arthritis. It continues to show great promise as a natural source of growth-hormone precursors, useful for achieving both athletic and weight-reduction goals.

Data and research, published and otherwise

Despite its long history of medicinal use, authoritative studies on the use of this product are scarce. But there are a few exceptions. Research from 1989 (by Dr. Ivan Kinia) shows that constituents of deer antler velvet are anti-inflammatory.

A Russian study (Dr. Taneyvia, 1964) claims to demonstrate that young men score better on intelligence tests after using velvet deer antler.

In Japan, a 1988 report by Dr. Wang showed that red deer antler increases the number of blood components related to the immune system.

In New Zealand, studies at the Invermay Research Center indicate that antler extracts improve cell growth and have antitumor and antiviral properties.

And in China, researchers at the Chinese Academy of Medical Sciences in Beijing found that nutrients in deer antler increased the number of cell replications by a factor of three, from about 60 to 180.

Is it only for males?

Both male and female hormones are found in deer antler velvet. It is equally beneficial for both sexes.

Animal friendliness

In modern times, many antler products are regarded as "elite" natural remedies (partly due to their scarcity and expense but also because of the uncomfortable opposition between the concern for endangered species and the interest in natural healing).

In the case of deer antler velvet, modern harvesting methods do not affect wild populations and do not destroy any animals. In fact, no pain or stress to the deer is evident even when the antler itself is removed, suggesting that this could be a useful "animal-friendly" alternative for obtaining nutritional substances that are difficult to get from other sources. (Other parts of the antler are also used as nutritional supplements. The antler, however, is the only appendage that can be regenerated by advanced mammals.)

See the "Guide to Sources and Availability" on page 215 for the source of red deer antler velvet.

Actions:

- Impairs glucose uptake in cells by suppressing the action of insulin receptors

- Causes fatty acids to be released from fatty tissues

- Helps maintain a protein-building (anabolic) environment

- Promotes the manufacture of somatomedins (secondary growth hormones) in the liver

Benefits:

- Encourages cells to consume fat rather than sugar or other carbohydrates

- Helps strengthen the immune system

- Stimulates bone growth, collagen synthesis, and tissue growth

Powerful Pain-Relief Solutions

Like most people living with pain caused by arthritis, injury, migraines or surgery, you have probably tried everything to bring some relief, reluctant to become dependent on painkillers or barbiturates to get through the day. The products in this section are natural, nontoxic, nonaddictive solutions discovered by the Health Sciences Institute.

CHAPTER 25

Pain Away:
Eliminate Chronic Pain In Seconds...
and Keep it Away Forever

Backache...sore muscles...aching joints...sprains...strains. As we get older, it seems as if pain becomes a constant companion. Just getting out of a chair can become challenging, let alone enjoying simple pleasures like gardening and strolling through the park. Taking aspirin helps, but it can eventually tear up your stomach. And prescription drugs have side effects that only compound the underlying problem. About 50 percent of the population is suffering—not from occasional aches but from chronic, unrelenting pain.[1]

Chronic pain is an invitation to illness

Pain is considered chronic when it goes unrelieved for three months. And allowing it to continue can compromise your immune system. The connection between pain relief and immune system defense is still being researched. But according to scientists at the Johns Hopkins University (JHU) School of Nursing in Baltimore, preventing or relieving pain appears to bolster the body's immune response. Researchers found that relieving pain associated with cancer surgery may increase the body's power to fight off subsequent life-threatening conditions. Since anesthesia is known to compromise your natural immune system, the JHU scientists wanted to see if relieving surgical pain could help bolster immune response. When they inoculated rats with lung-cancer tumors and then performed surgery on them, the group receiving pain relievers had a 65 percent greater reduction in lung tumors than did those in a control group.[2]

Most medical schools don't teach pain relief

Mainstream medicine is finally becoming aware of the need to relieve pain. Hospitals now have pain-management teams. Palliative care—a relatively new medical specialty—was developed to address pain relief. Pain centers are also opening across the country as more and more people look for relief. But they all concentrate on mainstream "cures"—drugs and surgery, which are rife with uncomfortable and even life-threatening side effects.

Unfortunately, doctors aren't receiving much training in medical school about pain intervention. According to a recent survey of oncology surgeons, 90 percent of respondents said they received 10 hours or less of medical-school education on palliative care and 79 percent said they received no more than 10 hours of instruction in palliative care during their surgical residency.[3]

Healed injuries can continue to transmit pain signals to your brain

Effective pain management is a complex issue, because your body responds with all its defenses to protect and heal an injury. When you injure yourself, your body sends protective fluids, such as histamine, bradykinin, prostaglandin, and substance P, to surround and heal the area. But they can also irritate the injury, especially substance P, which makes the nerve fibers in the injured area more sensitive or receptive to pain. Substance P also plays an important role in persistent inflammation[4] and is the neurotransmitter in your spinal cord that sends pain signals to the brain. That's when you become conscious of pain.

Pharmaceutical pain relievers work by temporarily interrupting the pain cycle, but they don't block the future production of substance P. Once a drug wears off, the production of substance P starts all over again, transmitting the pain signal to your brain. But you can relieve chronic pain by stopping the signal from occurring in the first place and preventing substance P from being released. As a result, your brain never receives the pain signal from your spinal cord.

Another problem associated with chronic pain is referred to as the "snow-ball effect." This is the result of pain caused by injury and inflammation, which in turn causes distress and, as a result, continued pain and inflam-mation. This cyclic pattern snowballs and results in discomfort even after the original injury has been healed.

A UNIQUE HERBAL BLEND DELIVERS INCREASED PAIN RELIEF

Most of the ingredients in Pain Away have been used for centuries as effective pain-fighting agents. You'll recognize some of them, but others may be new to you. Combined, the ingredients have a synergistic effect that enhances their ability to relieve pain and, in many cases, keep it from ever returning.

Arnica. Used both internally and externally as a homeopathic remedy, arnica has an excellent reputation as an anti-inflammatory[8] topical ointment for bruises and sprains. It has been used for hundreds of years to soothe aching muscles and reduce pain and inflammation associated with sprains and bruises. It's one of the oldest and most important drug plants.[9] Aside from these applications, the German Commission E (the herbal regulatory agency for Germany) has approved arnica for inflammation caused by insect bites and for superficial phlebitis (vein inflammation).[10]

Calendula. This flower has a long-standing reputation as a pain reliever and anti-inflammatory agent[11] and has been used in the development of medicated wound dressings[12] for serious wounds.

Cayenne. Capsaicin is the painkilling constituent of cayenne, which is derived from hot peppers. Cayenne's properties are unique and able to accomplish something no other pain reliever can: It inhibits the production of substance P, which helps reduce future sensitivity to pain,[13,14] by confusing the affected nerves. According to the *PDR for Herbal Medicines*, cayenne is used to relieve pain associated with muscular tension, rheumatism, arthritis, chronic lumbago, and muscle spasms.[15] An article in the *American Journal of Medicine* states that cayenne is an effective analgesic for osteoarthritis and is shown to work in cases in which chronic pain doesn't respond to other methods.[16] It's also effective in relieving pain associated with diabetic neuropathy, postmastectomy pain syndrome, skin allergies and tumors, amputation stump pain, and possibly neural dysfunction.[17]

DMSO. Dimethylsulfoxide is the "big brother" of MSM (methyl sulfonyl methane), which is a natural product that suppresses nerve pain impulses and inflammation. DMSO is also a potent pain reliever in its own right. A

While you may have done everything possible to heal an injury, that doesn't mean the hurt will leave once your injury has healed. A good example of this is phantom-limb pain, which is commonly called "stump pain." Amputees often continue to have grief in limbs that are no longer there.[5,6]

A UNIQUE HERBAL BLEND DELIVERS INCREASED PAIN RELIEF ... *continued*

German placebo-controlled double-blind study with 157 patients found that topical use of DMSO resulted in 44 percent of the patients being pain-free after 14 days, while only 9 percent of the placebo group had total relief.[18] Another important property of DMSO is its function as a solvent, allowing the transportation of the other pain-relieving elements of Pain Away to travel through the tissue and reach aching joints. While many products can reach pain just under the skin, DMSO allows Pain Away to penetrate to remote areas usually relegated to oral painkillers.

Limonene oil. This fragrant oil is derived from orange peels. The form used in Pain Away is pH-balanced limonene oil, which buffers the burning effect that may occur following use.

Menthol. Extracted from peppermint, menthol stimulates circulation and cools the injured area. Its traditional uses include pain relief of rheumatism, lumbago, and neuralgia (pain of unknown origin).

Mahanaryan oil. This is a traditional Ayurvedic massage oil used for aches, pains, bruises, muscle fatigue, arthritis, multiple sclerosis pain, gout, and strains. It's a combination of over 30 botanical products known to have tonic properties.

Peppermint. Usually taken internally for digestive problems, peppermint has a reputation as a muscle relaxant and pain reliever.

St. John's Wort. Regarded primarily as an antidepressant, St. John's Wort has also been used for over 100 years for the external treatment of wounds, bruises, sprains, phantom limb pain, and dermatitis.[19]

Wintergreen oil. Methyl salicylate, found in many topical painkillers, is really oil of wintergreen, a common evergreen shrub. The oil has the same analgesic properties as aspirin.

The pain isn't associated with the surgical amputation itself but is a continuance of pain felt from a limb, hand, foot, toe, or finger that's no longer there. (Stump pain appears to be caused by changes in the somatosensory cortex—an area of the brain associated with sensations.)

So, a current injury isn't a prerequisite for pain. This was demonstrated by Swedish researchers, who found that breaking the cycle of discomfort for patients with neuralgia (sudden sharp pain confined to isolated nerve

---

THE HSI BALTIMORE OFFICE TRIED PAIN AWAY— AND IT WORKED LIKE A CHAMP!

We always make an effort to try a product ourselves before we recommend it to you. We did the same with Pain Away and experienced *remarkable* results. One person used it to relieve the pain of a knuckle injury she received last October. The last time she had a similar injury, it took two years for the pain to stop. She applied a few drops of Pain Away to her knuckle, and the pain was gone within a few minutes. That wasn't a big surprise, since she'd expected some relief. But it was the long-lasting effect that particularly impressed her.

Pain Away's pain-relieving properties are renewed or reinvigorated when they come in contact with warmth—such as washing your hands or showering. Even covering the injured spot with your hand to prevent the loss of body heat is enough to renew Pain Away's activity. Over a period of a week, she used Pain Away three or four times. When she left work on a Friday evening, she forgot to take the bottle with her. But it didn't matter. The pain didn't return that weekend—or ever. As we go to print with this issue (over three weeks after the last application), the pain hasn't returned.

Another person, who had a serious wrist injury for six months, was wearing a support bandage and taking over-the-counter painkillers. She rubbed Pain Away on her wrist four times over a period of three days. By the third day, she had such significant relief that she no longer used the support bandage. Again, the pain was relieved immediately; and the effect lasted for hours. She now needs to use Pain Away less and less, as the discomfort in her wrist recedes.

branches) brings extended relief long after prescribed painkillers wear off. While the scientists don't fully understand why this works, they theorized that chronic pain may be partially responsible for its own continuation.[7]

Stop the production of substance P to permanently stop pain

Finding a way to stop the production of substance P led Health Sciences Institute panelist Jon Barron to team with Ron Manwarren of Royal Botanicals in the development of a unique topical pain reliever. While Barron was refining an all-natural transport system that would quickly send herbal extracts through the skin and into deep tissues, Manwarren had just finished formulating a "deep-tissue" healing oil based on traditional herbs—but lacked a botanical-based foundation to transport it. When Manwarren brought his new formula to Barron, their combined efforts resulted in Pain Away.™ While over-the-counter topical products commonly contain one, two, or three pain-relieving substances, such as methyl salicylate, menthol, and camphor, Pain Away has 10 proven painkillers.

Because Pain Away is an easy-spreading and potent liquid, only a few drops are needed. Pain relief can come almost immediately. Even better, it can permanently relieve chronic pain after just a few applications. In fact, we tested it informally here at the Health Sciences Institute Baltimore office. (See the box on this page for our anecdotal results.)

The scented ingredients in Pain Away are mild—contrary to the overpowering smells of most over-the-counter products. Although cayenne can deliver a warming or hot sensation, much of that sensation depends on the type of injury you're treating and your sensitivity to cayenne. Of the five people who tested our sample bottle of Pain Away here in the office, only one commented that he felt an uncomfortable amount of heat.

Because a small amount will go a long way, the pricing is extremely economical. See page 215 for ordering information.

Many of us struggle with ongoing pain, so it's a relief to finally find something that works. While Pain Away may not hold the answer to chronic disease, it may be your solution to chronic pain.

Action:

- Halts the production of substance P the fluid, which causes the nerve fibers surrounding an injury to have a heightened reception to pain.

Benefit:

- Breaks the cyclic "snowball effect" (a cycle of injury, inflammation, distress, and pain). that scientists theorize causes chronic pain to perpetuate itself.

References

[1] Lancet, 355(9199):233-4, 2000

[2] Pain, 90(1-2):191-9, 2001

[3] Reuters Health Information, April 23, 2000

[4] Neurochem Int, 35(6):471-8, 1999

[5] Pain, 87(1):33-41, 2000

[6] Neurosurgery, 48(3):681-7, 2001

[7] Pain, 43(3):287-97, 1990

[8] Biol Chem, 378(9):951-61, 1997

[9] Hautarzt, 31(1):10-17, 1980

[10] Herbal Medicine, p 44

[11] J Pharm Belg, 45(1):12-15, 1990

[12] Pharmazie, 47(12):924-6, 1992

[13] J Am Acad Dermatol, 44(3):471-8, 2000

[14] Neurosci Res, 38(2):147-54, 2000

[15] PDR for Herbal Medicines, pp 715-6

[16] Am J Med, 105(1B):45S-52S, 1998

[17] Clin J Pain, 14(2):97-106, 1998

[18] Fortschr Med, 112(10):142-6, 1994

[19] Br J Dermatol, 142(5):979-84, 2000

26

Butterbur:
Potent Plant Extract Reduces
Migraines by 50 Percent

"I have a terrible migraine."

It's a statement that elicits different reactions from different people—everything from "Isn't it all just in your head" to "You're under too much stress." If you suffer from migraines, you've heard it before.

But let's set the record straight. A migraine headache is a neurological and vascular disease—not a psychologically induced condition—which has recently been proven to have a strong genetic link. In fact, in a few years migraines may actually be diagnosed through a DNA test.

And, contrary to popular belief, a blinding headache is just one symptom of a migraine attack. The disease can also cause nausea and vomiting, sensitivity to light and sound, limb numbness, and speech impairment. Untreated, migraines can even lead to serious physical conditions, including strokes, aneurysms, permanent visual loss, coma, and *even death.*

A migraine attack can last for hours, days...even weeks

Attacks can be caused by environmental factors like bright lights, loud noises, exposure to second-hand smoke, or just by walking outside on a windy day. Physiological causes include lack of sleep, muscle tension, stress, and menstrual cycles. Many foods trigger migraines—anything containing the amino acid tyramine (red wine, aged cheese, smoked fish, some beans), monosodium glutamate (an additive in many foods), or meats containing nitrates (bacon, hot dogs, salami). Specific culprits often include chocolate, citrus fruits, and many dairy products.

Migraine pain is caused by the inflammation of blood vessels in the tissue surrounding the brain. The inflammation in the brain triggers nerve endings to release a flurry of neurotransmitters, sending chemical messages of pain throughout the body.

Butterbur extract proven to reduce migraine incidence by 50 percent

But now there's a solution for those who suffer from crippling migraines. The HSI network has uncovereded a potent plant extract that prevents inflammation of the blood vessels and tissue in the brain. It's been used safely in Europe for 25 years and has recently been proven to reduce the incidence of migraine headaches by 50 percent.[1] Petadolex (derived from the petasites hybridus plant commonly known as butterbur) is a natural supplement that not only prevents occurrences but also helps to manage pain during a migraine attack.

Indigenous to Northern Asia, Europe, and North America, the butterbur plant grows on the banks of rivers and streams. The medicinal use of this large, leafy plant dates back to antiquity, when it was used to treat digestive tract spasms, asthma, and whooping cough. In the Middle Ages, butterbur was used to combat the plague.

Works like prescription drugs...but without the pain!

Virtually ignored during much of the 19th and 20th centuries, butterbur is now garnering the interest of scientists throughout the world who are interested in its pain-relieving properties. Modern studies have shown that the plant extract helps control migraines by reducing muscle and tissue spasms and by easing the inflammation of blood vessels throughout the body. In this respect, Petadolex is similar to prescription migraine medications.

One recent randomized, double-blind clinical study at the University of Munich looked at the effectiveness of Petadolex over a three-month period. Patients were recruited for the study if they experienced at least three migraines per month over a period of at least one year.

Results of the study showed that patients given Petadolex twice a day for three months experienced longer intervals of time between attacks and a reduction in attack intensity.[2]

Petadolex reduced the average number of migraines from 3.4 to 1.3 per month

Patients who took Petadolex experienced a 50 percent reduction in migraine frequency after 12 weeks. By comparison, patients taking the placebo only experienced a 10 percent reduction of migraine occurrences. When asked to assess the overall benefit of their treatment, 74 percent of Petadolex patients said they'd benefited from the study treatment, compared

---

CONVENTIONAL MIGRAINE TREATMENTS FOCUS PRIMARILY ON PAIN MANAGEMENT, NOT PREVENTION

Narcotic analgesics like Demerol, Percodan, and Codeine are used to control severe migraines by acting on the central nervous system to alter the pain perception in the body. But they *don't* prevent the incidence of migraines, and they do require a prescription, and can cause intense physical dependency. Side effects range from depression and disorientation to severe vomiting and constipation.

Nonnarcotic analgesics work by constricting the dilated arteries in your brain. But, again, they do nothing to prevent migraines, the side effects are extreme, and you need a prescription to get them. Over-the-counter drugs, like aspirin and ibuprofen, can be used to relieve mild migraine pain, but routine use can actually cause rebound headaches.

Betablockers are the most commonly prescribed prophylactic, or preventive, drug for migraines. Used typically to treat coronary-circulatory disease and depression, beta blockers dilate the blood vessels and can actually make a migraine worse. They also have side effects like low blood pressure, muscle weakness, digestive disturbances, and depression.[4]

Petadolex is a safe, natural alternative to prescription drugs. It works to prevent migraine attacks without the harmful side effects of beta blockers. And after four to six months it can be discontinued—without losing its healing effects.

to only 26 percent of the placebo group.[3]

> *"Patients given Petadolex twice a day for three months experienced longer intervals of time between attacks and a reduction in attack intensity."*

In addition to lower intensity of pain and shorter duration of migraine attacks, these patients also experienced a significant reduction in the frequency of nausea, lack of appetite, and sensitivity to noise, smell, and light. And there were no side effects associated with taking the supplement.

Find relief with 2 capsules a day

The formulators recommend you take 1 capsule twice a day with food. Continue to take the capsules for four to six months. After that, you can stop, and the benefits will remain with you—even while no longer taking Petadolex.

Made from a completely natural substance, Petadolex is available without a prescription.

If you suffer from the pain of migraines, this could be your ideal, side-effect-free solution.

See page 215 for ordering information.

Actions:

- Prevents inflammation of blood vessels and tissues in the brain that trigger never endings to release neurotransmitters that cause migraine pain.

- Reduces muscle and tissue spasms lessening migraine frequency and aiding in pain relief.

Benefits:

- Decreases the frequency of migraine symptoms including nausea, lack of appetite, and sensitivity to noise, smell, and light

- Diminishes migraine attack intensity and duration.

References

[1] Townsend Letter 202:1-4, 2000

[2] Der Freie Artz 3:44-49, 1996

[3] Townsend Letter 202:1-4, 2000

[4] "A National Understanding for Migraineurs," at http://www.migraines.org/myth/mythreal.htm

27

Relaxin:
Fibromyalgia Patients Find Relief With a Little-Known Hormone

Fibromyalgia is a debilitating disorder that causes chronic, sometimes excruciating, pain throughout the body. Ninety percent of fibromyalgia (FMS) patients are women. The older you get, the greater your chances of developing symptoms. The pain of fibromyalgia usually consists of diffuse aching or burning described as "head to toe," and it is often accompanied by muscle spasms. Its severity varies from day to day and can change location, becoming more severe in the parts of the body that are used the most (i.e., the neck, shoulders, and feet). In some people, the pain can be intense enough to interfere greatly with work and ordinary daily tasks. Treatment aims for FMS have been no more than attempts to manage the disease through a combination of prescription drugs, NSAIDS, exercise, and massage therapy—until now.

Thanks to the work of a pioneer in pain management, patient results show that a little-known hormone called relaxin may be the key to offering safe, long-term relief from FMS pain. But that's not all. The beneficial side effects that patients are reporting may help make relaxin the next big player in fighting the effects of aging—for both women and men.

"Third pregnancy hormone" is similar to insulin

Relaxin is a type of hormone that occurs naturally in humans and other animals. It consists of 56-amino acids in a polypeptide chain, related to insulin. Its presence was first established in the 1930s. In that study, doctors found that it helped relax the pubic ligament during pregnancy.[1] In the ensuing decades, doctors refined their understanding of the hormone, but maintained the focus on its role in pregnancy.

Although relaxin has been known as the "third pregnancy hormone," it's

FMS PAIN DISAPPEARS WITH RELAXIN

Word of Dr. Yue's success is getting out, and doctors around the country are learning of its positive effects for their patients. Dr. M. Marlene Briggs, N.M.D, of Doctors Integrative Medicine in Gold Canyon, Arizona, calls relaxin, "one of the greatest things to happen in medicine in recent history."

As a general practitioner who specializes in treating FMS, as well as all skin and allergy problems, Dr. Briggs has begun using relaxin with many of her FMS patients, and she has seen many positive results. Relaxin has helped to lessen patients' chronic pain and ease their sleep dysfunctions. In addition, her patients have seen some of relaxin's secondary benefits, like stronger nails and hair. Dr. Briggs is very enthusiastic about relaxin's possibilities; she believes the hormone may be found to be the "missing link" in a whole host of other chronic diseases without a cure, such as chronic fatigue syndrome and dysmenorrhea.

Coleen Johnson learned about relaxin from her brother, a medical student. After being diagnosed with FMS in 1996, Coleen was searching for answers that her doctors were unable to provide. The chronic pain and fatigue were making it difficult for her to continue full-time work as a dental hygienist, and the "fibro-fog" was effecting her concentration and alertness. After learning about Dr. Yue and his clinic in her home state of Minnesota, she paid him a visit and began taking relaxin in November of 1999.

Almost immediately, Coleen felt a boost in her energy levels and improvements in her sleep and concentration. In a few weeks, she began feeling relief from the chronic muscle pain. Now she is able to work a full week, just as before, and has energy to spare. Best of all, Coleen experienced no side effects from the treatment. Her 18-year-old daughter is now taking a low dose of relaxin under Dr. Yue's direction for fatigue and insomnia, and she has experienced an amazing boost in energy and mood.

found in men as well. And while its amazing effects on the body during pregnancy have continued to receive the most attention, researchers have begun to examine its effects on other bodily functions—with significant results.

Creates flexible, elastic connective tissues

Relaxin's effects during pregnancy are far-reaching and offer a preview of its powerful possibilities. It causes the cervix to "ripen," promotes the widening of the pelvis, thickens the endometrium, and develops blood vessels in the uterus. It softens the tissues of the birth canal and promotes cell proliferation, which helps the cervix and uterus to grow. It also allows ligaments and other connective tissues to relax and elongate.[2] This is necessary to accommodate a growing baby in the body.

By affecting collagen production and stimulating skin growth, relaxin effectively transforms the female body during pregnancy. Now researchers are beginning to understand the hormone's other responsibilities in the body—in both women and men.

Powers beyond pregnancy

Dr. Samuel Yue at the Minnesota Pain Center in St. Paul was among the first to recognize the significance of relaxin's powers beyond pregnancy. Through his work with fibromyalgia patients, he made an important observation. He noted that his female FMS patients reported relief from their symptoms during pregnancy, as well as fewer symptoms before and during menstruation and during menopause.

During pregnancy, relaxin concentrations increase from normal levels (below 200 picograms per ml of blood) to over 800 picograms. Before and during menstruation, and during menopause, its levels fall below normal levels. Dr. Yue made the connection between the relaxin levels during these time periods and the relief of FMS symptoms.

After further research, Dr. Yue began to treat some of his FMS patients with relaxin derived from pigs, which has a composition very similar to the human hormone. The results were significant. Many of his patients experienced relief from the chronic pain of FMS for the first time. Some felt results immediately, while others took seven to 10 weeks or longer.

Until now, doctors had only been able to mask the symptoms of fibromyalgia and had no clear understanding of the causes of the disease. Now Dr. Yue's research offers a clear indication that FMS may be caused by a relaxin deficiency, or the body's inability to utilize the hormone properly.

Improve the appearance of hair, skin and nails

After finding the link between relaxin and FMS, Dr. Yue hypothesized that its effects during pregnancy may carry over to other conditions as well. He found that the hormone's ability to stimulate skin-cell production and affect collagen synthesis could have an impact on a variety of ailments.

Among the most exciting benefits of relaxin that Dr. Yue has observed are its effects on the regular signs of aging. During the fertile years, most women's ovaries secrete enough relaxin to reap benefits. After menopause, however, the primary source of the hormone is exhausted, and secondary sources like breast tissue and the uterus may not produce enough. If the ovarian function has been prematurely suppressed through the use of birth-control pills, oophorectomy (surgical removal of the ovaries), or tubal ligation, the aging effects of low relaxin levels may be seen before the typical menopausal age.

As relaxin levels decline through menopause, the signs of aging first begin to appear. Dry, dull skin; brittle hair and nails; and general aches and joint pain are all common complaints. Hormone-replacement therapy with relaxin may help address all of these concerns, through its impact on cell production and collagen synthesis. Users report smoother, better-hydrated skin, with less noticeable pores and wrinkles. It may even help repair skin damaged by the sun and help eliminate blotching and age spots.

Relaxin has proven so effective in stimulating the growth of new skin that it is being studied for possible surgical uses. Research has shown that it may effectively aid tissue expansion needed for surgery.[3] It can also help accelerate wound healing, a problem that often develops in elderly patients. Early studies also show that it may be beneficial in the treatment of scleroderma, a severe skin disorder characterized by pathological hardening and thickening of the skin.[4]

Men's bodies depend on relaxin too, though their levels are much lower and more difficult to detect. In males, the hormone is synthesized in the prostate, secreted by the seminal tubules, and can be detected in the seminal fluid.[5] Normal levels are about 200 nanograms per ejaculation. Relaxin has not been as effective in treating FMS in males, possibly due to other hormonal factors. But men still depend on the hormone for healthy connective tissues and may still benefit from relaxin replacement.

Fight osteoporosis and improve cognitive function

Osteoporosis has long been known as a geriatric disease, and one that primarily affects women. Now doctors are beginning to understand the role that relaxin may play in beating the disease. Collagen plays a crucial role in retaining calcium in the bones. By improving the quality of collagen in the body, relaxin may prevent the decalcification that was once thought to be an inevitable effect of aging.

Relaxin has also been shown to improve sleep quality. Although poor sleep quality is a common symptom of FMS, Dr. Yue noted that his FMS patients often reported restoration of healthy sleep patterns during pregnancy. Its interaction with the central nervous system may explain this effect and lead to more understanding of the hormone's effect on cognitive function. Dr. Yue theorizes that relaxin may prevent several cognitive and psychological disorders, such as Alzheimer's disease and postpartum depression.

It has also been found to lower blood pressure by stimulating nitrous oxide production. Nitrous oxide has been shown to help relax blood vessels. Studies have suggested that the presence of relaxin in fertile women may explain the group's low incidence of coronary heart disease.[6]

Relaxin impacts our most important systems

How does relaxin work? Many unanswered questions remain, but research suggests that it works on many of the body's systems either directly, by attaching to a relaxin receptor site, or indirectly, through its impact on collagen production. In one of these ways, the hormone affects many of the most important systems in the body, including the smooth and striated muscles, the central and autonomic nervous systems, the connective tissues, and the cardiac muscles. In animal studies, the smooth muscles, brain tissues, cardiac muscles, and hair and skin follicles have all been shown to have relaxin receptor sites.[7] Further research will help doctors understand more fully how it impacts so many aspects of our health.

No breast-cancer concerns or other serious side effects

Research has shown that relaxin does not have the serious side effects often associated with other forms of hormone-replacement therapy. Research has suggested that the steroid hormones in the estrogen/progesterone family are linked with breast cancer. But this is not a concern with relaxin, because it is not a member of the steroid family but a polypeptide hormone similar to insulin. In fact, preliminary research suggests that it may even inhibit the growth of breast-cancer cells.[8]

There are some minor side effects associated with relaxin, but most of them are temporary. Some female patients experience morning sickness, breast tenderness, and increased menstrual flow while the body adapts to the presence of the hormone. Usually, these side effects dissipate after the first month. Men generally report no side effects.

And there is no fear of becoming dependent on the hormone. If you choose to stop taking it, the symptoms that had disappeared will simply return, but without any additional problems. But once they start, most people choose to continue taking relaxin for the pain relief and other positive benefits it provides.

Relaxin has been shown to be safe in conjunction with most prescription medications. Estrogen and birth-control pills are both compatible, and the two hormones may even work better in concert. However, other medications may need adjustment when one supplements with relaxin. Diabetics and hypoglycemics may find that they need less insulin and other medicines, and many who take antidepressants may be able to reduce their dosages or stop taking them altogether. Check with your doctor or pharmacist about the effects of relaxin on your prescription medications before you start.

What to take

Dr. Yue and Sky BioHealth Solutions, Inc. have developed an oral form of relaxin called Vitalaxin (20- mcg tablets for symptoms of FMS) and Biolaxin (10 mcg tablets for general anti-aging benefits). While other polypeptides with similar compositions require hypodermic injection, Dr. Yue and his associates claim to have seen results with oral administration. With insulin and other long-chain polypeptides, the substance is broken down in the stomach before it can be absorbed, negating its effectiveness. Relaxin capsules are enteric-coated, so they bypass the stomach and pass on to the gastrointestinal tract. Since receptor sites for relaxin have been identified in the GI tract, it is possible that they facilitate its absorption.

More research needs to be done to clarify how oral relaxin is processed in the body, but for now Dr.Yue's patients are seeing results with the oral administration. According to Dr. Yue, patients have seen changes, and experienced the transient side effects of morning sickness and breast tenderness, indicating that the hormone has been absorbed and is exerting its effects on the body.

Dr. Yue recommends that patients start with 1 tablet in the evening for 2-3 days. If no side effects are experienced, they should increase the dosage to 1 tablet in the morning and 1 at night. For women, after about a month, depending on side effects (and financial considerations, since, unfortunately, the product is expensive), the dosage can increase to 1 tablet in the morning and 2 in the evening for 2-3 days and then 2 tablets in the morning and 2 in the evening.

Be careful when shopping for relaxin. There are some herbal remedies available with the same name, that are designed to promote relaxation, sleep, and general feelings of well-being. These products **do not** contain the hormone relaxin and will not produce the desired results. Check the active ingredients to be sure of what you are buying. See the "Guide to Sources and Availability" on page 215 for recommended sources.

Actions:

- Stimulates skin cell production and affects collagen synthesis

- By improving collagen production prevents the decalcification of bones that can lead to osteoporosis.

- Relaxes blood vessels lowering the risks of coronary heart disease.

- Interacts with the central nervous system and has an effect on cognitive functioning lessening the symptoms of, or possibly preventing, psychological disorders such as Alzheimer's disease and postpartum depression.

Benefits:

- Accelarates wound healing.

- Improves sleep quality.

- Slows the aging effects of low relaxin levels such as dry or dull skin, brittle hair and nails, and general aches and joint pains.

- Successfully lessens the pain and fatigue caused by Fibromyalgia and other chronic pain conditions.

References

[1] Arch Otolaryngol Head Neck Surgery, 118:153-156, 1992

[2] Journal of Neuroendocrinology, 7:411-417, 1995

[3] Arch Otolaryngol Head Neck Surgery, 118:153-156, 1992

[4] J Rheumatol, 25(2): 302-7, 1998

[5] Gen Pharmac, 28: 13-122, 1997

[6] British Journal of Pharmacology, 116: 1589-1594, 1995

[7] Townsend Letter for Doctors and Patients, pp. 76-82, January 2000

[8] Cancer, 70: 639-643, 1992

Anti-Aging Secrets

It's a fact. Aging is inevitable. But are the detrimental changes and disabling conditions that all to often accompany the aging process inevitable as well? Scientists on the cutting edge of anti-aging technologies are saying, "No, they don't have to be." The cumulative effects of free-radical damage and a weakening immune system as we age can lead to the deterioration of our joints, bones, muscles and even our hair, skin, and nails. But exciting new therapies are slowing, or even reversing, the effects of aging.

In this section you will find chapters on trienelle a skin cream that features an advanced liposomal delivery system, jiaogulan China's "immortality herb, and the anti-aging "miracle" pill H-3.

C H A P T E R **28**

Trienelle®:
An Anti-Aging Cream that Might Save Your Life
Trienelle® Takes On Skin Cancer and Aging

Half of all new cancers are skin cancers. In fact, they're more common than cancers of any other organ. Over 1.3 millions cases of basal cell and squamous cell skin cancer are expected to be diagnosed this year.[1]

Sobering isn't it? But now a powerful form of an old standby offers new hope.

The antioxidant advantage

Antioxidants like vitamin C and E have become very popular in skin products—and for good reason. There's a wealth of research documenting their value in protecting the skin from sun damage.

Most skin cancer is caused by overexposure to the sun. The ultraviolet (UV) radiation generates an excessive number of superoxide radicals in exposed skin cells. These highly reactive molecules can, among other things, cause serious damage to your DNA. As a result of this, skin cells may begin to reproduce uncontrollably, leading to benign, precancerous, or malignant lesions on the skin.[2] In short, sun exposure can lead to skin weathering,[3] abnormal growths, and in serious cases, skin cancer.[4]

Antioxidants counteract this effect by coupling with the free radicals before they can harm the DNA. The effectiveness of antioxidants in protecting the skin against sun damage has been well documented. A double-blind placebo study held at the University of Munich found that combined antioxidants (vitamins C and E in the study) reduce the sunburn reaction—stopping the skin damage before it degenerates to something more serious.[5]

The following year, University of Leiden researchers demonstrated that topically applied antioxidants can be used to prevent UV rays from damaging epidermal layers. (In this study, the experiments were conducted on mice.)[6]

In a study carried out specifically on the antioxidant qualities of vitamin E, researchers concluded that it's an effective sunscreen, and prevents the formation of DNA lesions that lead to skin cancer.[7]

Natural compound combats aging and cancer

One of our panelists, Dr. Randall Wilkinson, has developed a skin cream to help you win the war against skin cancer and aging. It's a combination of several elements—all of which add up to one of the most powerful skin-care products on the market, both for its disease-fighting capabilities and for its ability to restore a youthful appearance to the skin.

Trienelle Daily Renewal Creme is designed to address both the issue of cellular damage that can lead to skin malignancies as well as the more cosmetic issue of premature aging and skin weathering. In doing so, it uses a very unique and scientifically supported combination of natural ingredients.

Trienelle harnesses the proven power of tocotrienols

While vitamin E is helpful in protecting the skin from UV damage, not all vitamin E is created equal. The key is to find the most effective form to carry out this all-important task. That's where tocotrienols come in. There are two primary forms of vitamin E: tocotrienol and the more common alpha-tocopherol. While alpha-tocopherols are used in face creams and the majority of nutritional supplements on the market, tocotrienols are actually far more potent—up to 60 times more effective.[8]

Trienelle includes both tocotrienols and mixed tocopherols, to take advantage of the full range of both forms of vitamin E.

Recent studies have verified this, concluding that the physiological activities of tocotrienols make them superior to alpha-tocopherols and that its role in cancer prevention may have "significant clinical implications."[9]

Tocotrienols offers other distinct advantages over alpha-tocopherols and other antioxidant nutrients used in skin-care products. They're better absorbed and distributed in the superficial and deep skin layers.[10] Unlike alpha-tocopherol, which is quickly depleted by UV exposure, tocotrienols remain in the skin at greater concentrations and even help to preserve the levels of tocopherols in the skin. Tocotri-enols, when applied to the skin, also help to retain vitamin E, even after UV exposure.[11]

And, in addition to its antioxidant capacity, tocotrienols have another important role in derailing the cancer process at the cellular level. Tocotrienols also regulate a key biochemical supply necessary for cell prolif- eration. To put it simply, tocotrienols help short-circuit the excess spreading of cells, *even when DNA damage has occurred.*

> *Recent studies have verified that the physiological activities of tocotrienols make them superior to alpha-tocopherols and that its role in cancer prevention may have "significant clinical applications."*

Trienelle includes both tocotrienols *and* mixed tocopherols, to take advantage of the full range of both forms of vitamin E, incorporating a particularly potent concentration of tocotrienols (extracted from rice bran and palm oil) for maximum benefit. Trienelle is the *only* skin-care product that uses tocotrienols, while alpha-tocopherol cremes are readily available.

A new technology for skin care

Trienelle uses a newly developed technology to deliver the maximum benefit to your skin. It's called the Tocolur™ Skin Nutrition Complex, and it features an advanced liposomal delivery system. Liposomes are tiny drop like particles 300 times smaller than cells. Encased by fat-soluble membranes made from the same material as actual cells, liposomes penetrate quickly and deeply through the waterproof outer layer of the skin. When the liposomes come into contact with the cells of the dermis, the nutrients contained inside are transferred via osmosis into the living cells.

Each Tocolur liposome contains both tocotrienols and tocopherols. In addition, the formulators have included applephenone—a recently discovered super-potent antioxidant. Extracted from green apples, applephenone also protects cells against carcinogens and is a natural antihistamine (helping to block allergic reactions like hives).

Trienelle offers complete skin protection

Dr. Wilkinson's goal in creating Trienelle was to have a skin care product that provided "the very best protection against skin cancer, sun, and aging-related damage available anywhere. Period."

Although Trienelle is priced the same as other premium skin care products, no expense was spared in using the best materials. Dr. Ron DiSalvo, the cream's chief formulator, noted, "The quality of ingredients and the high potencies of cutting-edge and active ingredients make Trienelle probably the most expensive formula [to manufacture] that I've ever put together."

TRIENELLE'S OTHER INGREDIENTS BUILD A WALL OF PROTECTION

MELATONIN HEALS DAMAGED SKIN

Melatonin increases Trienelle's antioxidant and antiaging properties. In fact, topically applied melatonin has been shown to protect against sunburn and to heal skin already burned.[12]

IMMUNOPROTECTIVE COMPLEX

Radiation from the sun can seriously suppress the cellular immune system of the skin, which is the body's largest immuno-protective organ. Skin care ingredients are now being developed and evaluated for their IPF value (immuno-protective factor). Similar to the widely used SPF, the IPF describes the ability of a substance to protect against immune suppression caused by UV radiation.

Trienelle uses reishi and versicolor mushroom extracts and Hi-IG colostrum to shield against the immuno-suppression caused by UV radiation.

ALPHA-HYDROXY ACID (AHA) IS A POWERFUL SKIN EXFOLIANT

AHA has become one of the most popular and widely used skin-care ingredient, mostly for its ability to improve the look of mature and prematurely aging skin through its natural exfoliating qualities.[13]

By speeding the rate of turnover of dead skin cells on the surface of the skin, AHA reduces the appearance of fine lines and wrinkles by revealing the fresher layers beneath the surface. Trienelle includes multi-fruit hydroxy acids (from bilberry, maple, orange, and lemon) at a level that maximizes the therapeutic benefit and minimizes any possible sensitivity or irritation.

Trienelle should be massaged into clean skin once in the morning and once before bedtime. Care should be taken to cover those areas most susceptible to sun damage—the face, the back of the neck, and the ears. There's no need to wear an additional moisturizer, as the cream has a highly emollient lotion base (featuring chlorella) that attracts and holds moisture in the skin.

See page 215 for ordering details.

WALL OF PROTECTION ... *continued*

MATRIXYL REPLENISHES COLLAGEN AND DISSOLVES WRINKLES

One of the chief factors in the aging of skin is the decline of collagen, the supportive infrastructure that gives the skin its elasticity and plumpness. Collagen naturally breaks down and degrades with age, causing sagging, wrinkling, and a crepe-like appearance. Sun exposure, as we've mentioned, greatly accelerates this process. For years, collagen itself has been used in skin-care products to attempt to bolster a dwindling collagen matrix.

Trienelle uses Matrixyl, the state-of-the-art in collagen maintenance. This ingredient supports and refurbishes deteriorating collagen, and is backed up by dramatic human trials. In one double-blind placebo study, Matrixyl was found to reduce deep wrinkles by 68 percent over six months; moderate wrinkles were reduced by 51 percent in the same period.[14]

BROAD-SPECTRUM UVA/UVB SUNSCREEN SHIELDS THE SKIN FROM SUN DAMAGE

Despite the dramatic new findings on antioxidant skin nutrition, many dermatologists still hold that the most important factor in preventing skin cancer is the consistent use of a high-quality sunscreen. Trienelle provides everything the consumer needs in a daily skin-care regimen, including the all-important skin-care protection (with an SPF of 15). The sunscreen agents in Trienelle have been selected to protect against the broadest possible range of UV radiation.

Action:

- Uses the more powerful form of vitamin E, tocotrienols, to counteract the superoxide radicals generated in skin cells exposed to ultraviolet light that can damage DNA causing it to reproduce uncontrollably leading to abnormal growths and skin lesions

Benefits:

- Restores a youthful appearance to skin damaged on the cellular level causing premature againg and skin weathering.

- Protects against skin cancer, sun exposure, and age-related damage to the skin.

References

[1] Skin Cancer Fact Sheet, American Academy of Dermatology, 1999

[2] Free Radic Biol Med 24(1):55-65, 1998

[3] J Biol Chem 274(22):15345-9, 1999

[4] J Eur Acad Dermatol Venereol 113(2):96-101, 1999

[5] J Am Acad Dermatol, 38(1): 45-48, 1998

[6] Int J Radiat Biol 75(6):747-755, 1999

[7] Nutr Cancer 29(3): 205-211, 1997

[8] Free Radical Biology & Medicine, 10: 263-275, 1991

[9] Clin Biochem 32(5):309-319, 1999

[10] Lipids 33(1):87-91, 1998

[11] Free Radic Biol Med 22(5):761-769, 1997

[12] Archives of Dermatological Research 288(9): 552-526, 1996

[13] Percept Mot Skills 86(1):137-138, 1998

[14] "Matrixyl Tested In Vivo on a Panel of 35 Subjects During 2-4-6 Months," Sederma, 1999

29

Jiaogulan:

China's "Immortality Herb" Super-Charges Your Health; Live Longer and Better

We've all heard about the effectiveness of ginseng for boosting the immune system and energizing the body. However, there's a lesser-known Asian herb—one that many Chinese use to extend their lives to 100 years or more.[1] In fact, among those in China who take advantage of its healing powers, it's regarded as "like ginseng...but better."

The herb is called jiaogulan (JOW-goo-lawn), and it's poised to be the next big thing in herbal supplements. Its catalog of benefits is dizzying—as is the amount of scientific research behind it. Treating everything from high blood pressure to bronchitis, this potent antioxidant has also shown anticancer effects in lab studies.

If the body needs rest, jiaogulan promotes rest. If it needs to be energized, the herb does that as well.

An herb that adapts to your body's needs

From the mountains of southern China, jiaogulan was first recognized as a medicinal herb in the 16th century. Since then, the evidence has mounted for its ability to heal and regulate the body's functions. Jiaogulan is a powerful adaptogen—an herb that helps the body adapt and deal efficiently with the various stresses put upon it. In other words, it harmonizes the functions of the body.

When stress arises, the adaptogen equips your body to meet the challenge on equal terms. It strengthens the immune system and prevents the stress (be it the pressures of work, toxins in the air, an excessively poor diet, or whatever) from harming the body.

Animal studies conducted in 1990 demonstrated that the herb enhanced resistance in mice against the effects of excessive exercise, oxygen deprivation, electric stimulus, and high temperature.[2]

Similarly, in human studies, jiaogulan is shown to be a potent adaptogenic. 300 athletes were tested with jiaogulan prior to a competition (with a control group given a placebo). *Every member* of the test group reported increased vigor and alertness, quicker reflexes, and less nervousness.[3]

This effect is coupled with the herb's ability to promote and improve sleep—with a tested effectiveness of 89-95 percent.[4] So, if the body needs rest, jiaogulan promotes rest. If it needs to be energized, the herb does that as well.

High-powered antioxidant protection

The active elements of jiaogulan are high-powered antioxidants, scavenging the body for free radicals. In doing so, they protect the body from DNA damage (caused by oxidation) and stave off the inevitable physical decline of aging—accounting for the 100-year life span of many Chinese jiaogulan users.

A 1992 study at Loma Linda University demonstrated the antioxidant qualities of jiaogulan. The different elements of the herb prevented a range of oxidation damage. The researchers concluded that "the extensive antioxidant effect of gypenosides [the active molecular component of jiaogulan] may be valuable in the prevention and treatment of various diseases such as atherosclerosis, liver disease, and inflammation."[5]

A proven cancer inhibitor

Partially as a result of its high-powered antioxidant effect, jiaogulan has been shown to obstruct the growth of cancer. In an animal study, a test group of rats was given jiaogulan two weeks prior to the introduction of a carcinogen. After 18 weeks of receiving the carcinogen, the rats were killed and studied.

Not only was the number of tumors in the test group lower than those in the control group (who received only the carcinogen), but jiaogulan actually delayed the onset of the cancer for six weeks (even while the rats received regular injections of carcinogens).[6]

Similarly, in clinical studies, researchers discovered that jiaogulan increased the Natural Killer cell activity in patients with urogenital cancers, empowering their bodies to fight back against the invading tumors.[7]

Jiaogulan regulates blood pressure and cholesterol

Both high *and* low blood pressures are dangerous to your health. Causing everything from heart attack in the case of high blood pressure to cerebral collapse in the case of low, they're serious conditions that must be addressed immediately. Jiaogulan does this, by bringing the blood pressure into the normal level (whether it's high *or* low).

In the area of hypertension (a result of dangerously high blood pressure), jiaogulan was tested in a clinical study against ginseng. The results were surprising: 82 percent of those taking jiaogulan noted improvement in their condition, vs. only 46 percent taking ginseng.[8]

The herb has an equally powerful effect in lowering dangerous cholesterol levels. Numerous clinical studies have been published showing that jiaogulan is effective in lowering LDL (bad cholesterol) levels, and raising the HDL (good cholesterol) levels.[9]

In lowering the dangerous LDL cholesterol, jiaogulan helps prevent atherosclerosis, stroke, and heart attack.

Jiaogulan makes your heart more efficient

Gypenosides have been found to enhance the contractility of the heart. In doing so, they increase the efficiency of the heart's pumping mechanism. Simply put, jiaogulan reduces the burden on your heart, by helping it pump the same amount of blood with less stress and effort.[10]

For this reason, the "immortality herb" would be perfect for an athlete, or active person, concerned with his physical output. Endurance is increased and recovery time shortened. This was born out in a study on 220 athletes and 30 healthy non-athletes. Using a color DOPLER examination, researchers found that the active components of jiaogulan, in concert with other medicinal herbs, increased heart output measurably, *without raising the heart rate or blood pressure.*[11]

Liver damage and bronchitis

But the heart isn't the only organ aided and protected by jiaogulan. Its healing power also extends to the liver, which the herb shields against toxic chemicals.[12]

The lungs, too, benefit from the herb. Jiaogulan is remarkably effective in treating bronchitis—the disease it was originally used to cure in traditional China. In one study of 86 cases of bronchitis, *jiaogulan improved 93 percent of those suffering.*[13] A study of 96 cases showed an effectiveness of 92 percent.[14]

Where to find jiaogulan

At this time, there aren't many sources for jiaogulan in the United States; most health-food stores don't sell it (and haven't heard of it). This will undoubtedly change as more consumers learn of its proven benefits and wide range of uses.

However, Jiaogulan Herbal Products Inc., a company that sells exclusively jiaogulan-related medicines, carries a range of items featuring the herb. Michael Blumert, researcher and author of the comprehensive *Jiaogulan: China's Immortality Herb*, recommends 1 pill three times a day for prevention of illness. A therapeutic dose would increase the intake to 3 pills three times a day.

For additional supplementation, you can obtain jiaogulan tea bags. See page 215 for ordering information.

Actions:

- Obstructs the growth of cancer, delaying onset and increasing the Natural Killer cell activity to fight existing tumors.
- Lowers bad cholesterol (LDL) levels and raises good cholesterol (HDL) levels leading to increased protection against, atherosclerosis, stroke, and heart attack.
- Increases the heart's ability to contract allowing the heart to pump blood with less stress and effort.

Benefits:

- Protects the body from free radical damage to DNA effectively slowing the physical decline of aging and increasing the life span.

- Brings high or low blood pressures into a normal range.

- Aids other organs in the body including shielding the liver against toxic chemicals and treating bronchitis in the lungs.

- Promotes and improves an effective sleep cycle.

- Enhances the body's resistance to a variety of stress allowing for alertness, quicker reflexes, and less nervousness.

References

[1] Michael Blumbert, Dr. Jialiu Liu, Jiaogulan: China's "Immortality" Herb, Torchlight Publishing Inc., 1999, p. 27

[2] Asia Pacific Journal of Pharmacology, 5(4):321-322, 1990

[3] Journal of Guiyang Medical College, 18(4):261, 1993

[4] Journal of Guiyang Medical College, 18(3):146, 1993

[5] Cancer Biotherapy, 8(3):263, 1993

[6] Journal of West China University of Medical Sciences, 26(4):430-432, 1995

[7] Zhong Yao Li Yu Lin Chuang, 7(2):39, 1991

[8] Guizhou Medical Journal, 20(1), 1996

[9] Blumert, op. cit., p. 43

[10] Zhongguo Yaolixue Zazhi, 4(1):17-20, 1990

[11] Journal of Pharmacology, 5(4):321-322, 1990

[12] Industiral Hygiene and Professional Disease, 24(2):74, 1998

[13] Hunan Journal of Traditional Chinese Medicine, 9(4):11, 1993

[14] Research on Chinese Herbs, 4:136, 1996

30

H-3 Plus:
Turn Back the Clock With
Nature's New Fountain of Youth

Imagine if the fountain of youth really existed. Imagine if you could wash yourself in its healing waters and walk away feeling and looking like you were in your prime again. What if you didn't have to worry about cancer, hypertension, or other age-related diseases?

Just think about it…would you live your life differently? Would you spend more time visiting friends, outdoors, or at the beach? Would you get started on all those projects around the house that you never have the energy for? Would you lead a more active love life, take up a new hobby, change careers, or just play with your grandchildren on the floor once in a while?

This doesn't have to be just a fantasy. You can now slow, halt, and even *reverse* the effects of aging on your body. Health Sciences Institute has recently uncovered what could be the most powerful anti-aging supplement ever developed. This breakthrough has been proven to literally reverse the body's aging process by rebuilding old, damaged cells. With this powerful, life-changing panacea you can:

- Protect your cells from degenerative ailments like heart disease, MS, and Parkinson's disease
- Improve chronic age-related conditions like arthritis and osteoporosis
- Wipe away wrinkles and liver spots
- Feel an overwhelming sense of well-being throughout the day
- Regain muscle mass and mobility in your limbs
- Improve the luster and vitality of your hair, nails, and skin
- Sleep through the night and wake up feeling alert and energized

• Boost your immune system

H-3 Plus promises all this and more. It's the next generation of an anti-aging formula developed in Romania almost 50 years ago and heralded by the TV show 60 Minutes back in 1972. The difference is, H-3 Plus is *six times stronger and lasts 15 times longer* than the original Romanian formula.

This cutting-edge compound has been developed by a distinguished think-tank of scientists and researchers—including HSI panelist, acclaimed author, and nutritional expert, Ann Louise Gittleman, N.D., C.N.S, M.S. It's just been patented in the United States, so there aren't many clinical studies yet. However, the initial results collected by Gittleman and her associates are *so astonishing*, we wanted to tell you about it immediately...so you don't have to wait years for Mike Wallace to get wind of it.

The Romanian anti-aging miracle similar to an ingredient every dentist uses

The story of H-3 Plus actually begins almost 100 years ago in Austria.

DOUBLE-BLIND STUDIES SHOW H-3 PLUS IS A SAFE AND EFFECTIVE REMEDY AGAINST DEPRESSION

Nineteen million Americans suffer from depression—particularly a large number of seniors. Now with H-3 Plus, we can finally control depression naturally.

The monoamine oxidase (MAO) is an enzyme in the body vital to maintaining good health. But after age 45, research shows that your body begins to produce higher levels of this enzyme. As MAO builds up in the brain, it replaces other vital substances such as norepinephrine (a hormone essential to our well-being and vitality), and can cause depression and premature aging.

Twenty years ago, David MacFarlane, Ph.D., of the University of Southern California tested GH-3 (H-3 Plus's predecessor) for its ability to inhibit the build up of MAO in the body. MacFarlane's research

---

Procaine—the primary active ingredient in H-3 Plus—was first discovered in 1905 by biochemist Dr. Alfred Einhorn while he was looking for a non-toxic, non-addictive anesthetic. At the time, cocaine was primarily used, but its negative characteristics were becoming apparent and its use was going to be outlawed. Procaine (very similar to Novocain) became a safe alternative anesthetic.

Nearly 50 years later in 1949, Dr. Ana Aslan of the National Geriatric Institute in Bucharest, Romania, discovered Procaine's anti-aging properties virtually by accident. Familiar with its anesthetic properties, Dr. Aslan began to inject her elderly arthritis patients with Procaine. To her surprise, not only did her patients experience decreased pain and increased mobility, they also began to experience overwhelming physical and mental improvements.

Dr. Aslan called her new discovery GH-3 and began a massive series of clinical trials that studied the effects of Procaine on 15,000 patients between ages 38 and 62. The study included over 400 doctors and 154 clinics, and at that point may have been the largest double-blind trial ever undertaken.

A SAFE AND EFFECTIVE REMEDY AGAINST DEPRESSION ... *continued*

unquestionably proved that GH-3 does inhibit MAO. He published these remarkable results in the Journal of the American Geriatric Society in 1973.

Panelist Ann Louise Gittleman has witnessed the anti-depressant effect of H-3 Plus on many of her patients. Gittleman commented, "Many people report they are able to cope with stress better after the first two weeks and maintain a constant feeling of well-being. Some patients have even been able to wean themselves off prescription drugs like Prozac."

What GH-3 could do in 1972, H-3 Plus can do today...and 6 times more effectively. If you suffer from depression—especially if you're on unsafe prescription antidepressants—this important treatment may provide the relief you need naturally.

Be sure to work with your doctor in making any changes in your medical program.

Procaine repairs the damage of old age, toxins, and disease from the inside out

By the time most of us reach 30, our bodies stop reproducing cells at the rate they once did. We literally lose more cells than we gain. And the cell membranes begin to erode and don't absorb nutrients as efficiently. New scientific evidence even suggests that many degenerative diseases—such as cancer, MS, and Parkinson's—are manifestations of damage to these cell membranes.[1]

Dr. Aslan and her research team found that Procaine works by penetrating

---

AVOID DANGEROUS IMITATIONS
KNOCK-OFF SUPPLEMENTS CAN WASTE YOUR MONEY... AND YOUR HEALTH

H-3 Plus is an amazing anti-aging supplement that's sure to change the way we approach age-related disease. One of our own panelists, Ann Louise Gittleman, helped research and design this medical breakthrough, and gave us the alert when the final formulation was complete.

But there's a much bigger story behind this particular product. You see, H-3 Plus is based on a much older formula, GH-3. You may remember GH-3 from the media splash it caused about 30 years ago (it even made it onto the TV show 60 Minutes), when several major studies showed promising results for reversing the effects of aging. The market was soon flooded with additional studies, disease-cure claims, and GH-3 products. There was just one problem:

Most of it was bogus.

That's not to say that GH-3 itself was a fraud; it wasn't. The initial studies were then and continue to be impressive. However, fast-acting swindlers, eager to make a buck, jumped onto the GH-3 train with knock-off products and unfounded medical claims. The real GH-3 continued along, still impressing researchers in clinical tests, but its reputation among the general public was tarnished. Too many people had tried the ineffective (sometimes harmful) GH-3 imitators, and they never tired of retelling their poor experiences.

---

old or damaged cell membranes and repairing the erosion caused by old age, disease, toxins, food additives, and stress. Bathed in this powerful elixir, cells in the body are then able to receive nutrients and vitamins and expel toxins effectively. This makes for a healthier—and younger—body, from the inside out.

In 1956, Dr. Aslan presented her findings to the European Congress for Gerontology meeting in Karlsruhe, West Germany. While her claims were initially met with skepticism, Aslan's astonishing conclusions could not be ignored for long:

- Close to 70 percent of GH-3 patients never contracted a disease
- Overall, the death rate in the GH-3 group was more than 5 times lower than the placebo group over 3 years
- Patients were less prone to infectious diseases and seasonal influenza
- Reduction of sick days off work by almost 40 percent

AVOID DANGEROUS IMITATIONS ... *continued*

And so a powerful, helpful supplement fell into disrepute.

Sadly, this pattern is repeated time and time again. A strong alternative treatment will be released and lauded....only to be followed by a storm of cheap imitations. HSI has made it a priority to find suppliers with integrity—people who don't stoop to sell knock-offs. It's essential to our network that you be able to trust the vendors and items we recommend.

That's why we only go with the best...and when we choose a product or treatment to feature, we make sure it's the real thing. You should expect nothing less. You may see rival products featured on the internet, or maybe even in health food stores, but be wary of them. While vitamins and herbs come in several equally effective brands, other treatments do not. Imitation formulas are just that... imitations—unworthy of your money and your time.

- Joint mobility improved in 56 percent of cases[2]

While not a cure to any single disease, GH-3 was proven to target and improve many common chronic diseases and conditions including:

Arthritis	Poor circulation	Liver spots
Chronic fatigue disorder	Excessive cholesterol	Failing memory
Depression	Parkinson's disease	Varicose veins
Sleep disorder	Peptic ulcers	Hypertension
Migraine headaches	Heart disease	Emphysema
Lethargy	Acne	Rheumatism
Multiple sclerosis	Osteoporosis	Dementia
Decreased sex drive	Hodgkin's disease	Sickle cell anemia

60 Minutes uncovers Dick Clark's anti-aging secret

During most of the 1960s, GH-3 fought its way through U.S. federal regulations. Then in 1972, Mike Wallace of *60 Minutes* did an investigative piece on this underground anti-aging formula and much of the western world finally took notice.

Since it was first developed, over 100 million people in more than 70 countries have used Dr. Aslan's formula. Hundreds of thousands of people were treated with GH-3 at her Romanian clinic, including many leaders from around the world, such as Mao Tse-Tung, Charles de Gaulle, Ho Chi Minh, Winston Churchill, and John F. Kennedy. Even many Hollywood stars— including Dick Clark, the Gabor sisters, Marlene Dietrich, Charlie Chaplin, Lillian Gish, Lena Horne, Charles Bronson, Kirk Douglas and Greta Garbo. All traveled to Romania for Dr. Aslan's GH-3 treatments.

Next generation formula is six times stronger than the GH-3—and without the downside

While Dr. Aslan's results were extraordinary, her Procaine formula has its limitations—its beneficial effects wore off too quickly and the market was (and is) flooded by cheap and ineffective imitations. But now, through the HSI network, you are among the very first in the United States to hear about H-3 Plus, the new and improved Procaine compound.

> *"H-3 Plus actually lasts 15 times longer and is 6 times stronger than Dr. Aslan's formula, which only delivered 15 percent of the nutrients and cost thousands of dollars to administer"*

According to Gittleman, "H-3 Plus is the most advanced and only patented Procaine formula ever developed. It's so powerful, many people respond to it within the first three days. I have actually had to reduce my dosage to half a pill because it's so powerful."

The secret to the new formula lies in the purification process. H-3 Plus is run through a highly complex filtering process—making it 100 percent bioavailable. That means *all* the Procaine nutrients can be absorbed into the blood stream. Otherwise, Procaine leaves the body too quickly, providing only temporary relief.

H-3 Plus actually lasts 15 times longer and is 6 times stronger than Dr. Aslan's formula, which only delivered 15 percent of the nutrients and costs thousands of dollars to administer.

According to Gittleman, "H-3 Plus is a potent anti-aging supplement that keeps you feeling energized all day long. We have an enormous number of success stories from people who've felt relief from arthritis, depression, and lowered libido, and other chronic ailments associated with aging. We have even seen a return of some patients' original hair color. But most of all, you feel this overwhelming sense of well-being." Gittleman added, "It's almost like an adaptogenic herb—it seems to provide whatever your body needs."

H-3 Plus is all-natural, and you don't have to go to Romania to get it

Like the original formula, H-3 Plus is a completely natural substance, and you don't need a prescription. It comes in pill form and should be taken once or twice daily (six to eight hours apart) with a glass of water, one hour before or two hours after eating. For most people, taking H-3 Plus twice a day on an empty stomach for three months gets the best results.

H-3 Plus can be taken with other vitamins and supplements. In fact, your regular supplements may be absorbed more efficiently while taking it. For more information see the "Guide to Sources and Availability" on page 215.

Actions:

- Produces significant mental and physical improvements resulting in a sense of well-being.

- Rebuilds old and damaged cells to improve age related damage to hair, nails, and skin.

Benefits:

- Improves chronic age-related conditions like arthritis and osteoporosis.

- Provides protection against degenerative ailments such as heart disease, Multiple sclerosis, and Parkinson's disease.

References

[1] Science 287:2486-2492, 2000

[2] "Gerovital-H3; Its prophylactic and regenerative effects," www.smart-drugs.com/ias-info/gh3-prevention.htm

Guide to Sources and Availability

Due to their breakthrough, underground nature, many of the remedies presented in Underground Cures may not be readily available in health-food stores or other retail outlets. As a service to our readers, we have identified several high-quality, reliable sources for the products discussed in this book.

If you are interested in continuing to have access to the latest, most powerful discoveries and modern, underground treatments like the ones in this book, please turn to page 227 to find out how you can receive monthly Members Alerts from the Health Sciences Institute.

The foregoing chapters have not been evaluated by the U.S. Food and Drug Administration. This information is not intended to diagnose, treat, cure, or prevent any disease.

Arjuna (T. arjuna) *(Chapter 10)*
Himalaya USA
6950 Port West Drive, Suite
170 Houston, TX 77024
Tel: (800) 869-4640 or (713) 863-1622
www.himalayausa.com

Body Oxygen *(Chapter 9)*
Bio-Nutritional Products
41 Bergenline Avenue
Westwood, NJ 07675
Tel: (800) 431-2582 or (201) 666-2300

Burgstiner's Thymic Formula
(Chapter 13)
Preventive Therapeutics Inc.
2020 Westside Court, Suite A
Snellville, GA 30078
Tel: (800) 556-5530 or (770) 972-2129
Fax: (770) 972-3646
www.thymic.com

Butterbur (Petadolex) *(Chapter 26)*
Natural Health Consultants
P.O. Box 1091
Vallejo, CA 94590
Tel: (888) 852-4993 or (707) 554-1820
Fax: (707) 647-3055

Calcium elenolate (olive-leaf extract) *(Chapter 1)*
Advanced Nutritional Products
1300 Piccard Drive, Suite 204
Rockville, MD 20850
Tel: (888) 436-7200 or (301) 987-9000
Fax: (301) 963-3886

Vitacost
2049 High Ridge Road
Boynton Bech, FL 32426
Tel: (800) 793-2601
Fax: (561) 752-8900
www.vitacost.com

CellAid *(Chapter 4)*
CellAid, Herbaceuticals, Inc.
630 Airpark Road
Napa, CA 94558
Tel: (800) 784-8212 or (707) 259-6266

Citrudex *(Chapter 21)*
Center for Natural Medicine
Dispensary
1330 SE 39th Avenue
Portland, OR 97214
Tel: (888) 305-4288 or (503) 232-0475
Fax: (503) 232-7751
www.cnm-inc.com

Galantamine (GalantaMind)
(Chapter 19)
Life Enhancement Products, Inc.
P.O. Box 751390
Petaluma, CA 94975-1390
Tel: (800) 543-3873 or (707) 762-6144
Fax: (707) 769-8016

Glycalkaloid Cream (SkinAnswer)
(Chapter 6)
CompassioNet
P.O. Box 710
Saddle River, NJ 07458
Tel: (800) 510-2010 or (201) 236-3900
Fax: (201) 236-0090

Grapefruit Pectin (ProFibe)
(Chapter 11)
Optimal Health Resource
550 Kane Court, Suite 100
Oviedo, FL 32765
Tel: (888) 727-6388

Graviola *(Chapter 8)*
Raintree Nutrition Inc.
10609 Metric Boulevard, Suite 101
Austin, TX 78758
Tel: (800) 780-5902 or (512) 833-5006
Fax: (512) 833-5414

H-3 Plus *(Chapter 30)*
Uni Key Health Systems, Inc.
P.O. Box 7168
Bozeman, MT 59771
Tel: (800) 888-4353 or (406) 586-9424
Fax: (406) 585-9892
www.unikeyhealth.com

**Hybridized mushroom extract
(AHCC)** *(Chapter 5)*
American BioSciences
Tel: (888)-884-7770
(call for a location near you)
www.americanbiosciences.com/abs_i
mmpower.htm

Infopeptides *(Chapter 3)*
Vitacost
2049 High Ridge Road
Boynton Bech, FL 32426
Tel: (800) 793-2601
Fax: (561) 752-8900
www.vitacost.com

Inositol *(Chapter 20)*
Advanced Nutritional Products
1300 Piccard Drive, Suite 204
Rockville, MD 20850
Tel: (888) 436-7200 or (301) 987-9000
Fax: (301) 963-3886

Jiaogulan *(Chapter 29)*
Jagulana Herbal Products
P.O. Box 45
Badger, CA 93603
Tel: (888) 465-3686 or (559) 337-2188
Fax: (559) 337-2354

Juzen-taiho-to (Energy Kampo)
(Chapter 7)
Willner Chemists
100 Park Avenue
New York, NY 10017
Tel: (800) 633-1106 or (212) 682-6192
Fax: (212) 682-6192
www.willner.com/honso.htm

Lactoferrin *(Chapter 2)*
Advanced Nutritional Products
1300 Piccard Drive, Suite 204
Rockville, MD 20850
Tel: (888) 436-7200 or (301) 987-9000
Fax: (301) 963-3886

Vitacost
2049 High Ridge Road
Boynton Bech, FL 32426
Tel: (800) 793-2601
Fax: (561) 752-8900
www.vitacost.com

Larreastat *(Chapter 17)*
Herbal Technologies
2588 Progress Street, Suite 1
Vista, CA 92083
Tel: (800) 211-9619 or (760) 734-1899
Fax: (760) 734-1876

Maca (MacaPure) *(Chapter 23)*
PureWorld Botanicals
375 Huyler Street
South Hackensack, NJ 07606
Tel: (201) 440-5000
Fax: (201) 342-8000
www.pureworld.com/news/maca-
pure_spec.html

Myco+ *(Chapter 16)*
Raintree Nutrition, Inc.
10609 Metric Boulevard, Suite 101
Austin, TX 78758
Tel: (800) 780-5902 or (512) 833-5006
Fax: (512) 833-5414

Natural Killer Cell Function Test
(Chapter 5)
Immunosciences Lab, Inc.
8693 Wilshire Boulevard
Beverly Hills, CA 90210
Tel: (800) 950-4686 or (310) 657-1077
Fax: (310) 657-1053

N-Tense *(Chapter 8)*
Raintree Nutrition, Inc.
10609 Metric Boulevard, Suite 101
Austin, TX 78758
Tel: (800) 780-5902 or (512) 833-5006
Fax: (512) 833-5414

Pain Away *(Chapter 25)*
Healing America, Department #17575
426 Salem Drive
Owensboro, KY 42303
Tel: (850) 302-0170
Fax: (512) 833-5414
www.love.healingamerica.com

Perilla Oil *(Chapter 12)*
Health-n-Energy
P.O. Box 637
Jacksonville, FL 32234
Tel: (800) 571-2999
Fax: (904) 289-9905

**Phosphatidylserine (Brain Power
Plus)** *(Chapter 18)*
Advanced Nutritional Products
1300 Piccard Drive, Suite 204
Rockville, MD 20850
Tel: (888) 436-7200 or (301) 987-9000
Fax: (301) 963-3886

Red Deer Antler Velvet *(Chapter 24)*
Lifestar Millennium
2175 East Francisco Blvd. #A-2
San Rafael, CA 94901
Tel: (800) 858-7477 or (415) 457-1400
Fax: (415) 457-8887

Relaxin (Vitalaxin) *(Chapter 27)*
Vitacost
2049 High Ridge Road
Boynton Bech, FL 32426
Tel: (800) 793-2601
Fax: (561) 752-8900
www.vitacost.com

Shark Cartilage (BeneJoint)
(Chapter 14) CompassioNet
P.O. Box 710
Saddle River, NJ 07458
Tel: (800) 510-2010 or (201) 236-3900
Fax: (201) 236-0090

Trienelle *(Chapter 28)*
Aspen Benefits Group
7950 Meadowlark Way, Suite B
Coeur d'Alene, ID 83815
Tel: (800) 539-5195 or (208) 762-9883
Fax: (208) 762-8773

Virility Formula (V-Power) *(Chapter 22)* Advanced Nutritional Products
1300 Piccard Drive, Suite 204
Rockville, MD 20850
Tel: (888) 436-7200 or (301) 987-9000
Fax: (301) 963-3886

Wobenzyme *(Chapter 15)*
Optimal Health Resources
12472 Lake Underhill Road #275
Orlando, FL 32828
Tel: (888) 727-6388
Fax: (407) 366-3343

Index

Get the underground cures of tomorrow—today!
And be among the first to know!

This book is based on the research and discoveries of the Health Sciences Institute (HSI). HSI is a unique members-only organization, built upon a vast network of doctors and researchers from around the world, that's dedicated to doing one thing: breaking the barriers that big-money medicine has placed before revolutionary natural cures—and bringing those cures to you *right now*!

Unlike anything before it, HSI doesn't represent the opinion of a single, self-appointed "guru," but contains the unmatched combined wisdom of the world's most formidable medical minds.

Through the monthly HSI *Members Alert* newsletter, regular e-mail updates, Members Forum discussions, and symposia, we alert our members to exciting new breakthroughs in natural healing, show them how to use them, what results to expect, and where to get them.

The clear and easy-to-read HSI *Members Alert* has become a legend in the alternative medical industry as a quintessential source for cutting-edge medical discoveries. Many physicians all over the world use the *Members Alert* to bring their own patients medical solutions and treatments available nowhere else—including the underground cures you've read about here.

Hundreds of members have thanked us for bringing them the newest solutions that work where other therapies—mainstream and alternative—have failed.

- *"I cannot thank HSI enough for helping my daughter eliminate her unrelenting bought with psoriasis. Because of you, the Lovelands have a lot to be thankful for this Thanksgiving. Best Wishes." G. Loveland.*

- *"My health has really improved over the last several months. I get a lot of brand-new, cutting-edge information from you that cannot be found easily anywhere else." Bob A.*

• *"Every day we fervently thank God for guiding me to choose [the therapy HSI featured] to treat my husband's liver cancer. From the day of his first dose, he began improving almost overnight. Now, he's completely tumor free!" J. Webb*

Now, you can continue to get the latest breakthrough cures for everything from arthritis, to cancer, to heart disease, and more by joining the Health Sciences Institute today. As a member of HSI, you'll have the opportunity to take advantage of exclusive special reports, first access to hard-to-get products and services, access to a worldwide network of doctors and researchers, and much more.

Simply return the New Member Certificate below, along with your first annual membership payment of $49 to activate your membership, which includes 12 monthly issues of the HSI Members Alert and all the benefits described above. Reply today!

(Cut along dotted line and return to HSI, P.O. Box 925, Frederick, MD 21705-9913)

New Membership Certificate

❏ **YES!** I would like to join the Health Sciences Institute for the low price of $49 today. That includes 12 issues of the HSI Members Alert, which I can cancel at any time for a full refund of all unmailed issues.

Name:_____

Address:_____

City:_____ State:_____ Zip:_____

Phone: (_____)_____

E-mail: _____
        (required to receive FREE health updates)

❏ My check is enclosed for $ _____ made payable to Health Sciences Institute (MD residents add 5% sales tax). *(Maryland residents add 5% sales tax)*

❏ Please charge my: ❏ Visa   ❏ MasterCard   ❏ American Express

Card #:_____ Expires:_____

Signature:_____

PHSIBC01

Return this reply to: Health Sciences Institute
PO Box 925 • Frederick, MD 21705-9913
www.HSIBaltimore.com

New breakthroughs and urgent health news sent directly to you... ABSOLUTELY FREE!

Be among the first to benefit from all-natural cures and life-extending discoveries that the rest of the world won't know about for another generation—or longer. Best of all…it's absolutely FREE—no strings attached.

Now you can receive the Health Sciences Institute's exclusive e-Alerts, normally sent only to its members. Using the power of the internet, HSI is able to share their breaking discoveries and insights as they happen. And now you can receive them—FREE.

Each day, they receive hundreds of e-mails from members. Here are just a few examples:

- *Boris S. wrote, "Thank you again for your updates and alerts. You have been consistent and perfect," following our story on the food industry's attempt to introduce natural bacteria killers.*

- *Ruth W. wrote to say, "What a wonderful report on NIH ignoring the true cause(s) of disease," after reading our alert about NIH's decision to lower standards for high cholesterol, in turn recommending drugs for millions more Americans.*

- *And Dr. Fritz writes: "Your e-mails, just as your newsletter, are most important for me. Thank you for what you are doing for your members."*

Signing up is simple. If you are already a member of HSI, just send a blank e-mail to hsi_sub@agoramail.net. If you are not a member, send a blank e-mail to nonhsi_sub@agoramail.net.

(We share your concerns over privacy. HSI will never sell your e-mail address. And, of course, you can unsubscribe at any time.)

Sign up for FREE today!

Black Listed Cancer Treatment Could Save Your Life

Baltimore, MD— As unbelievable as it seems the key to stopping many cancers has been around for over 30 years. Yet it has been banned. Blocked. And kept out of your medicine cabinet by the very agency designed to protect your health—the FDA.

In 1966, the senior oncologist at St. Vincent's Hospital in New York rocked the medical world when he developed a serum that **"shrank cancer tumors in 45 minutes!"** 90 minutes later they were gone... Headlines hit every major paper around the world. Scientists and researchers applauded. Time and again this life saving treatment worked miracles, but the FDA ignored the research and hope he brought and shut him down.

You read that right. He was not only shut down—but also forced out of the country where others benefited from his discovery. That was over 35 years ago. How many other treatments have they been allowed to hide? Just as in the case of Dr. Burton's miracle serum these too go unmentioned.

Two-Nutrient Cancer Breakthrough...

Decades ago, European research scientist Dr. Johanna Budwig, a six-time Nobel Award nominee, discovered a totally natural formula that not only protects against the development of cancer, but people all over the world who have been diagnosed with incurable cancer and sent home to die have actually benefited from her research—and now lead normal lives.

After 30 years of study, Dr. Budwig discovered that the blood of seriously ill cancer patients was deficient in certain substances and nutrients. Yet, healthy blood always contained these ingredients. It was the lack of these nutrients that allowed cancer cells to grow wild and out of control.

By simply eating a combination of two natural and delicious foods (found on page 127) not only can cancer be prevented—but in case after case it was actually healed! "Symptoms of cancer, liver dysfunction, and diabetes were completely alleviated." Remarkably, what Dr. Budwig discovered was a totally natural way for eradicating cancer.

However, when she went to publish these results so that everyone could benefit—**she was blocked by manufacturers with heavy financial stakes!** For over 10 years now her methods have proved effective—yet she is denied publication—blocked by the giants who don't want you to read her words.

What's more, the world is full of expert minds like Dr. Budwig who have pursued cancer remedies and come up with remarkable natural formulas and diets that work for hundreds and thousands of patients. *How to Fight Cancer and Win* author William Fischer has studied these methods and revealed their secrets for you—so that you or someone you love may be spared the horrors of conventional cancer treatments.

As early as 1947, Virginia Livingston, M.D., isolated a cancer-causing microbe. She noted that every cancer sample analyzed (whether human or other animal) contained it.

This microbe—a bacteria that is actually in each of us from birth to death—multiplies and promotes cancer when the immune system is weakened by disease, stress, or poor nutrition. Worst of all, the microbes secrete a special hormone protector that short-circuits our body's immune system—allowing the microbes to grow undetected for years. No wonder so many patients are riddled with cancer by the time it is detected. But there is hope even for them...

Turn to page 76 of *How to Fight Cancer and Win* for the delicious diet that can help stop the formation of cancer cells and shrink tumors.

They walked away from traditional cancer treatments...and were healed! Throughout the pages of *How to Fight Cancer and Win* you'll meet real people who were diagnosed with cancer—suffered through harsh conventional treatments—turned their backs on so called modern medicine—only to be miraculously healed by natural means! Here is just a sampling of what others have to say about the book.

"We purchased *How to Fight Cancer and Win*, and immediately my husband started following the recommended diet for his just diagnosed colon cancer. He refused the surgery that our doctors advised. Since following the regime recommended in the book he has had no problems at all, cancer-wise. If not cured, we believe the cancer has to be in remission."

—*Thelma B.*

"I bought *How to Fight Cancer and Win* and this has to be the greatest book I've ever read. I have had astounding results from the easy to understand knowledge found in this book. My whole life has improved drastically and I have done so much for many others. The information goes far beyond the health thinking of today."

—*Hugh M.*

"I can't find adequate words to describe my appreciation of your work in providing *How to Fight Cancer and Win*. You had to do an enormous amount of research to bring this vast and most important knowledge to your readers.

My doctor found two tumors on my prostate with a high P.S.A. He scheduled a time to surgically remove the prostate, but I canceled the appointment. Instead I went on the diet discussed in the book combined with another supplement. Over the months my P.S.A. has lowered until the last reading was one point two."

—*Duncan M.*

"In my 55 years as a Country Family Physician, I have never read a more 'down to earth,' practical resume of cancer prevention and treatments, than in this book. It needs to be studied worldwide for the prevention of cancer by all researchers who are looking for a cure."

—*Edward S.,MD*

"As a cancer patient who has been battling lymphatic cancer on and off for almost three years now, I was very pleased to stumble across *How to fight Cancer and Win*. The book was inspiring, well-written and packed with useful information for any cancer patient looking to maximize his or her chances for recovery."

—*Romany S.*

"I've been incorporating Dr. Budgwig's natural remedy into my diet and have told others about it. Your book is very informative and has information I've never heard about before (and I've read many books on the cancer and nutrition link). Thanks for the wonderful information."

—*Molly G.*

Don't waste another minute. There are only a limited number of books in stock—and unless order volume is extraordinarily high we may not be able to print more life-saving copies. Claim your book today and you will be one of the lucky few who no longer have to wait for cures that get pushed "underground" by big business and money hungry giants.

Your satisfaction is fully guaranteed. This will probably be the most important information you and your loved ones receive—so order today!

China's great healing Master reveals his astonishing
"SECRET" CHINESE FOOD CURES

Baltimore, MD—For thousands of years, China's great healing Masters have known a secret that Western doctors are just starting to discover. The cures to the world's great plagues aren't in your medicine chest...They're hiding in your pantry! Beyond drugs, vitamin supplements or any other pill...Nothing else even comes close to the life-giving power of food.

Now, for the first time ever, China's great living Healing Master has agreed to reveal all his most celebrated food cures, in the most important book of its kind ever published. **Unleashing the Power of Food: Recipes to Heal By** is the most life-saving cookbook you'll ever own!

Here, in one incredible volume, are more than 200 life-giving, healing meals from China's legendary *Master FaXiang Hou*. Revered in Asia, Master Hou is winning fame in the West as well...

With uncanny speed, he is able to clear up heart disease, cancer, diabetes, high blood pressure, asthma, allergies, migraine headaches, emphysema, chronic fatigue syndrome and many other health nightmares...

Precisely targeting each disease with the exact foods shown to heal it!

Already, many medical doctors, film stars, sports heroes, and other Westerners in the know have traveled thousands of miles to be healed by Master Hou. **But now you can experience his healing miracles without even leaving your home.**

Because now you'll have all the very same recipes that Master Hou prescribes for his famous patients and prepares for himself. With more than 310 pages, **Unleashing the Power of Food** is your ultimate guide to cooking the world's healthiest meals.

Master Hou's food cures work better than Western "diets"

First of all, *they're not diets.* They *don't* deprive you of "forbidden" foods you can't help loving.

You see, when a Western doctor puts you on a diet, it's all about *cutting stuff out.* Cut out the fat. Cut out the calories. Cut out the meat. Cut out the carbs. *Cut out the fun.* No wonder nobody sticks to those diets!

But Chinese food healing isn't about *eliminating foods....*

It's about combining the foods you love to UNLOCK THEIR HEALING POWER

For example, instead of forbidding red meat, Master Hou shows you how to combine it with other foods—in recipes that actually *make meat healthier.*

So instead of denying your desires, these recipes totally satisfy you. Balancing one food with another, they bring *your whole body* into healthy balance. As a result, these food cures can do much more than any conventional diet. They're not just a few years ahead of Western medicine... When it comes to healing with food, China is 2500 years ahead of the west.

Master Hou is the living inheritor of 2,500 years of careful observation and continuous discovery by healing Masters before him. And he'll put this *entire* awesome legacy in your hands including:

Hundreds of Mouth-Watering Meals That Heal

They're so delicious, you may *not* want to tell your family these are actually *curative recipes.* Just serve up the best Chinese cooking they've ever tasted — and smile at the compliments!

Let Master Hou show you how to unlock the *curative power* in these foods, by serving up:

• BEEF WITH BAMBOO SHOOTS. Rebuild bones and build stronger muscles with this quick dish! The bamboo shoots "balance out" the beef and unleash its strengthening powers.

• MINCED PORK WITH MELON. In minutes, you've got a spouse-thrilling dinner that *actually lowers blood sugar.* Master Hou calls it the "*ideal food for diabetes!*"

• Want to peel off pounds? Dig into spicy CHICKEN WITH HOT GREEN PEPPERS!

• *Fight cancer* as you strengthen your immune system with HERBED LAMB SOUP!

Then, whenever your loved ones are threatened by major illness, your new book will provide you with...

Complete 7-Day menu planners for beating the world's deadliest ailments

Five entire chapters! Each targets a different condition. And each contains its own special 7-day menu, with delicious selections for breakfast, lunch and dinner, plus detailed instructions from Master Hou. So now you'll have the *ultimate food cures* to help you...

• CONQUER CANCER. You'll banish carcinogens from your body and help repair damage they may have already done...while savoring these delicious recipes.

• HEAL HEART DISEASE. Before the doctor says "bypass surgery," try this high-powered food cure first!

• DIAL DOWN DIABETES. Controlling blood sugar is so much easier when the foods you eat actually *lower* it. Let Master Hou show you how to drop your need for insulin or diabetes drugs...while dining on these satisfying selections.

Cook with it for 60 days, risk-free!

There's no space to describe *all* the healing tools you'll find in this book. So let me invite you now to evaluate it for yourself, risk-free!

Just start using this miraculous book and I promise you'll *taste* the difference immediately,*feel* incredibly better, and *hear* a lot of compliments from your family. In fact, your satisfaction is fully guaranteed. So what have you got to lose?

Act now and get a FREE BONUS REPORT—*Speed-Cooking The Healthy Chinese Way*.

This FREE BONUS REPORT is yours to keep forever, even if you return your new cookbook. So don't wait another day to start *eating your hurts away!*

Manuscript Of Ancient Chinese Healing Techniques Reveals...

How to Breathe Disease Out of Your Body

Secret Methods Date Back Over Four Thousand Years— Harness the Most Fundamental Life Force Known to Eastern Disciplines

We recently discovered an obscure, paper-bound manuscript that turned out to be the only known record of a secret system of Chinese healing. It's a system of breathing techniques combined with simple body postures, handed down for centuries by traditional Chinese doctors. These powerful techniques use the principle of chi, considered by Eastern disciplines to be the energy source that carries life through your body.

• Imagine successfully **treating cancer, colds, viruses, ulcers, heart disease, arthritis, impotence,** and discomforts from **menopause**—simply by breathing...

• Imagine banishing **headaches, fatigue, nervousness, stiffness** and **pain**, simply by breathing...

• And imagine harnessing the most powerful force in your body, channeling it, and using it to heal yourself...

• Imagine all this, and you will understand how important a discovery we've made.

The techniques are based on a force called *chi*. (Also known as "ki," or "qi" by Eastern philosophies.) It's the same force the ancient Vedics of India called "prana," and was identified as "pneuma" by the classical Greeks.

Chi is the vital, essential force behind all life. One ancient saying states that "Chi is the mother of blood." Acupuncture, traditional Chinese medicine, shiatsu and reiki are all based on the principles of chi, and work on the paths through the body that this energy flows through.

In fact, anyone familiar with Eastern forms of exercise and meditation has probably heard of chi. Tai chi, yoga, qi gong, karate, and Zen meditation all teach correct breathing as the basic necessity for practice. That's because correct breathing focuses the power of chi, and radiates it through your body.

Here are just a few of the techniques you can use to heal and prevent disease:

• Treat **cancer** with "ton-ren-mai-zan." (In this technique, you'll also learn to use two secret pressure points, known as dan-chun and hya-kkai, along with the breathing. These are critical areas where chi can be stalled in the body, causing illness and disease.)

• Relieve **angina** with "fei-je-jan-yo"—simple movements that Western doctors may not discover for another hundred years...

• End **fatigue** with "pei-ta-chuen-shen." (This technique uses a secret system of tapping and patting the body—more concentrated than massage, but more gentle than acupressure—to free energy throughout the body. It's fast, it's easy, and the results are amazing.)

• Banish **arthritis** pain with "woo-rong-tan-jao:" Forget drugs! They simply mask pain and suppress inflammation.

Healing techniques such as woo-rong-tan-jao combine gentle movements, breathing, and the body's own energy to relieve and heal afflicted areas.

• Successfully treat **asthma** with "chu-chi-jun-pi." This technique will remind you of the most classic yoga postures. Simple and easy—but combined with a certain stretch and proper breathing, the lower lungs are expanded and used. At the same TIME, healing energy is freed throughout your chest, lungs, and entire body.

• Boost your **sex** drive with "jo-tie-nho-hao." Western medicine keeps looking for a magic pill to boost your sex drive and cure impotence. Unfortunately, it's usually just another drug—with side effects and long-term damage that's only discovered way down the line. But this technique uses a simple princi-ple and gentle internal movements to stimulate your body's natural functions. It's absolutely the simplest and safest way in the world to rejuvenate yourself.

• Find deep, restful **sleep** with "an-chi-wan-jo" (once again, using secret pressure points can produce miraculous results in the body...)

Each one of these techniques is beautifully diagrammed and carefully explained. They're easy to follow, and easy to do. No confusion, no mis-understanding. The author has brought these ancient secrets alive, and delivered them right into your hands. And, in *Healing with Ki-Kou: The Secrets of Ancient Chinese Breathing Techniques*, you'll find over 125 pages of these ancient secrets, covering almost every imagi-nable pain and illness.

Notes

NIAGARA
FOOD

A FLAVOURFUL HISTORY OF THE
PENINSULA'S BOUNTY

TIFFANY MAYER

Charleston · London

THE
History
PRESS

Published by The History Press
Charleston, SC 29403
www.historypress.net

First published 2014

Manufactured in the United States

ISBN 978.1.62619.535.6

Library of Congress CIP data applied for.

For Olivia, who was with me every step of the way, and for Steven, who wasn't far behind.

Contents

Acknowledgements

Though only one name appears on the cover of this book, the words and photos on these pages wouldn't be possible without the contributions of so many people.

First and foremost, I'm grateful to everyone who took the time to share their stories with me so I could include them in *Niagara Food*. You help make this region the rich, fascinating and tasty place that it is and inspire me every day.

Much gratitude goes to Rowan Shirkie for overwhelming me with wine history books and being a fact checker extraordinaire. Your help and eagle eye have been invaluable. Likewise to Jared Dyck of the Vineland Growers Co-operative, curator of historical photos and ever-patient person for putting up with my pestering. I'm also immensely grateful to Karen Moncur, Sarah Marshall and Alison Oppenlaender for sharing research materials.

Thanks to Dave Johnson, Scott Rosts and Melinda Cheevers for your help with the photos and telling Niagara's story visually.

I owe so much, though, to four people, who have taught this city slicker tons over the years and instilled in me a passion for telling stories about the travails and the joys of farm life. Len Troup, Linda Crago and Albert Witteveen, you have been mentors to me during my years here in Niagara and are a big reason why I found myself in any position at all to write a book about food and farming here. And Karen Briere, my agriculture journalism professor at the University of Regina, this really all starts with you in a classroom so many years ago. You ignited my curiosity and gave me a direction in my career that I never would have imagined and now can't imagine working without.

Thank you to my family and friends for cheering me on through this project and especially to my biggest cheerleader, my husband, Steven. Without your support, I wouldn't be able to accomplish what I do. It's as simple as that.

Finally, thank you to Katie Orlando from The History Press. It just shows that you never know who's reading your blog. You took a chance on me and had confidence in my abilities to pull off this project, and for that, I am eternally grateful. And to think we've never even met. I hope to share a meal with you one day.

Introduction

As I packed up my notebook and pulled on my jacket, Mark Picone slid me an apple across the heavy wooden table in his culinary studio.

I had just spent the last hour talking about Niagara wine country cuisine with the storied chef when he offered me the fruit with pale green skin for the road. Earlier in our discussion, Picone had used the apple—a rare hybrid called Pink Pearl—as a prop in our conversation to highlight some of the unique, locally grown produce he makes a point of using in the meals he creates.

"And this, as you'd know, is a pink-fleshed apple," Picone said gesturing to it before moving on to say something about a pile of heart-shaped—and aptly named—heart nuts he had handy to further his point about the uniqueness of his muse, Niagara's bounty.

Did I know that? I suppose it made sense, given the blush cheek peeking through the Pink Pearl's sallow complexion. Still, I hesitated before saying yes, which I sputtered more as a question than a statement.

I thanked Picone for his time and the apple as I headed back out into a grey November afternoon. I wasn't expecting much from my edible gift as I sank my teeth into it on the ride home. I was sure the flesh of the Pink Pearl would still be white, like most of its apple cousins that I was used to eating. At most, it would have a slightly pink tinge, but the name would be largely hyperbole.

When I pulled away from the apple after that first bite, chewing flavourful flesh that flitted between sweet and tart, my eyes widened in amazement and I hit the brakes to take a moment to marvel at the sight before me.

"Holy cow," I exclaimed out loud to myself, in awe of the vibrant bubble gum pink flesh revealed to me. And then I did what any excited foodie would do. I took a photo and put it on Instagram to share it with the world—this eye-opening, mind-blowing apple grown on a farm in quiet west Niagara.

In my nearly nine years living in this region, covering agriculture as a news reporter, shopping at farmers' markets and farm stands and being a regular member of a CSA or local harvest share program, I had never crossed paths with the Pink Pearl. I had never even heard its name uttered.

In that moment, at the side of a rural Vineland road, a vineyard to one side of me and a stand of Carolinian forest to the other, that apple became more than a midafternoon snack for a hungry scribe. It became the raison d'être for this book, a metaphor for my task at hand. It made me realize how much I had to learn about a place I was so sure I knew intimately. And I wanted not just the world but also Niagarans themselves to learn about this magical, surprising place, too.

My mission as the writer of this book became clear as a diamond as I took another bite of the Pink Pearl. Yes, I would tell some of the familiar Niagara stories, those of peach crops, grapes turned into world-class wines, the food artisans who became household names, the restaurateurs who built landmarks in their communities and the tireless food security activists who ensured there was room enough at the table for everyone. As the person given the honour of penning those quintessential stories, I also wanted there to be a Pink Pearl or two among them for readers—something to take them by surprise.

Whatever your familiarity with Niagara, I hope as you read these pages that you'll feel the same wonder and awe, much as I did that grey November afternoon when I met the Pink Pearl.

Chapter 1
Roots and Shoots

Farming in Niagara

My grandfather used to say that once in your life you need a doctor, a lawyer, a policeman and a preacher, but every day, three times a day, you need a farmer.
—Brenda Schoepp

Len Troup puts his head in his hands and shakes it at the question. Would he ever consider selling his family's two hundred acres of peach, pear and cherry orchards? "I bet if you asked Ron tonight, he'd say yes," Troup says, a rueful smile spreading across his lips.[1]

Ron is Troup's eldest son and to whom he is relinquishing the reins of the family farm as Troup, himself a lifelong farmer, eases into retirement. It's an early September evening at the family's Lakelee Orchards in Jordan Station, and the weakening summer sun has sunk below the horizon. Though it's dark outside, the family's packing shed is alight as Ron and his crew of workers continue toiling, nowhere near calling it a day. They're drowning in a flood of peaches that need to be graded, packed and prepared to go to market—if they can find a market. It has been five years since the last fruit cannery in Niagara—in Canada, in fact—closed in 2008.[2] The peach trees the Troups planted in 2009 to replace those bearing fruit for canning with varieties suited for fresh market sales are just starting to produce crops. The young trees aren't even in full production, yet the Troups, like many local farmers this particular fall, are "jammed" with huge volumes of fruit, keeping consumers in more peaches later in the year than ever before.

Jordan Station fruit grower Len Troup in his orchard. *Photo by Nathaniel David Johnson.*

Troup rarely concedes to uncertainty and worries about sounding depressing. Still, it's clear circumstances have unnerved the usually stoic farmer. It has been ten years since the Troups have expanded the capacity of their packing shed, and it's clear the yellow-sided building overlooking that ultimate symbol of urbanism—a multilane highway called the Queen Elizabeth Way—is inadequate when the season yields a good crop. The family is going to have to consider doing something, Troup says. Perhaps a new grading line is in order. But that's a big expense, and who knows what the future holds for the farm?

"It's such a struggle. The family wants to keep it going, but it's a financial struggle, and at some point, people have to say, 'Is it worth it?' It's a lot of stress," Troup admits as he sits at his kitchen table, removed physically, if not emotionally, from the scene in the packing shed.

"You're rolling the dice with a lot of cash. This isn't nickel-and-dime stuff," he adds about the business of fruit farming. "You shouldn't be this close to the edge."

Fertile Ground

The Niagara Peninsula comes by its moniker as the buckle of Ontario's fruit belt honestly. The northern tier of the region is the largest and most important fruit-producing area in Ontario, with nearly twenty-six thousand acres of orchards and vineyards.[3] Farmers grow more than 90 percent of Ontario's peaches, nectarines and apricots; 80 percent of its plums; more than 70 percent of its sweet cherries and pears; and 60 percent of its sour cherries. That's thanks largely to a body of water and rocky ridge joining forces to foster the perfect microclimate for these tender fruits to flourish.[4]

Lake Ontario and the Niagara Escarpment border the peninsula's fruit lands, which stretch roughly sixty-five kilometres from Stoney Creek, just outside Niagara, to the Niagara River. Together, they create an air circulation system that sees southwesterly breezes spill down from the escarpment and sweep air toward the lake. In the spring, cool lake air is then drawn back over orchards and vineyards as the land warms up. This delays bud burst and lessens the chance of damage from spring frosts. In the fall, the reverse happens. Air is warmed over the lake and then moves inland, staving off season-ending frosts. As that warm air hits the escarpment, it's deflected upward, drawing in more of the mild air behind it and extending the growing season.

Peach, nectarine, cherry and apricot trees also thrive because of the northern tier's well-drained sandy soils near Lake Ontario, along the Niagara River and in Pelham, while the silt and clay loam elsewhere suit pear, plum, apple and grape production.

The potential of both the climate and those soils was capitalized on in the 1700s when the Loyalists began cultivating the region. Peter Secord, the uncle of War of 1812 hero Laura Secord, is believed to be the first Loyalist farmer to plant fruit trees, settling here after taking a land grant in the mid-1780s. Less than one hundred years later, there were 375,000 peach trees growing in Ontario, though none of those varieties exists today. By this point, fruit farming had blossomed into Niagara's main industry.[5] It wouldn't be long, though, before it would start to come under threat with the construction of the Queen Elizabeth Way highway in the 1930s, followed by decades of urban encroachment.

The Niagara Escarpment forms a dividing line in the region. While the farmland above the escarpment in south Niagara covers an area larger than the region's tender fruit land, it's filled with more generic crops—corn, soy, wheat and livestock—that make it indistinguishable from other farming

Reginald Francis Thwaites packing peaches in his Jordan Station orchard in 1952. *Photo courtesy of Vineland Growers Co-operative.*

James Troup (right) and help with an apple harvest from Troup's Jordan Station farm destined for Dominion Canners, circa 1900. *Photo courtesy of Vineland Growers Co-operative.*

regions in Ontario. However, it's the fruit, grown on 637 farms that's synonymous with Niagara and is the region's claim to farming fame.[6]

Environmentalists cheered in 2005 when the Ontario government legislated to protect that fruit land. It's now part of a two-million-acre swath called the Greenbelt that stretches from the Niagara River to east of Toronto. It meant the end of urban sprawl that had been threatening Niagara's orchards and vineyards for decades. Statistics from the 1950s and

Aron Wall sits on his horse-drawn water sprayer on his St. Catharines farm while Gerry Wall looks on, circa 1946. *Photo courtesy of Vineland Growers Co-operative.*

1960s showed that Niagara was developing its agricultural land faster than any other metropolitan area in Canada, and now, with the advent of the Greenbelt, cities within the protected area were forced to grow up rather than out.[7]

But for the farmers who owned farmland in the Greenbelt, it was an imposition that meant the end of a say in how they could use their property, at least for the next ten years until a policy review in 2015. They were bound to farm, rent or sell their land to someone who would cultivate it or, barring any takers, let it go to weeds. Depending on whom you ask, the Greenbelt is either a two-million-acre agriculture preserve or a two-million-pound millstone weighing landowners' down because of the limits it puts on land use.

"The easy part of the Greenbelt was just establishing it," Jordan Station fruit grower Len Troup says. "The hard part is now, and that is to make it work. Financially, it has to function. The business environment in which we operate has to allow farming to be profitable and this hasn't been addressed by those who created the Greenbelt."

Today, agriculture remains one of the main industries in Niagara, but the tender fruit so emblematic of the region has lost ground despite the Greenbelt. Some of the biggest blows to Niagara's quintessential crops have come in the past few decades with the loss of processing plants, the most recent being CanGro Foods Inc. in St. Davids. The factory, which shuttered in 2008, was the last major fruit cannery in Canada, taking with it a buyer for Niagara's canning peaches and imperfect pears that couldn't find a home on the fresh market.[8]

With nowhere to sell their fruit, farmers razed their orchards, replacing them with more profitable crops, including wine grapes and freestone peaches suited to be eaten out of hand rather than a can. It's also around this time that something else started to encroach on this precious farmland, raising the question of whether protecting that tender fruit land in the Greenbelt was for naught. Corn—a crop that can be farmed virtually anywhere and doesn't need Class 1 farmland in a microclimate to grow—started popping up where orchards once blossomed. Troup calls it the proverbial canary in the coal mine for the tender fruit industry.

"In the old days, the grape or fruit guys would have run around buying that land, but they're saying now, 'I don't want it,'" Troup says. "The one that's profitable is filling the void."

Stalking the Money

The sight of those cornfields growing below the escarpment has caused some to wonder—and worry—what it means for the future of Niagara's signature crops. Jerry Winnicki isn't one of them. If anything, corn is sparing Niagara a fate far worse.

"We have the most unique land in Canada. I don't mind it going into corn because it can go back into cherries and grapes," Winnicki says. "It's better than going into housing."[9]

Winnicki is an agronomy manager at Clark Agri Service in Wellandport, which sells seed and fertilizer for corn, soybean and wheat farming. He joined Clark at "one of the most fascinating times of change" in agriculture: the rise of technology in farming.

As he sits in the office of a Wainfleet grain elevator belonging to Lennie and Peter Aarts, a combine works its way up and down the field behind him, guided by a satellite that sends a pixelated image to a computer. It tells the driver what sections of the field he has left to harvest and how many bushels he's netting per acre. At the moment, he's pushing two hundred.

That's almost twice as much as a decade earlier, thanks to another kind of technology. Approximately 98 percent of the corn seed Winnicki sells is genetically modified. The data he collects from the computer in the combine will help him decide what seeds to recommend next year to his clients, who are partaking in a type of farming called cash cropping that has been living up to its name in the past few years.

The profits to be made growing such crops are luring young people to farming, Winnicki notes. He's recognizing fewer people at his growers meetings attended by clients farming upward of four thousand acres of corn and soybeans. It turns out those unfamiliar faces are the sons of some of his longtime customers, beckoned back to the land by the prospect of high yields and higher returns. These crops created by scientists are necessary, Winnicki maintains, because it's the only way farmers will be able to feed the world's exploding and increasingly hungry population, projected to hit nearly nine billion by 2050.[10] In the past ten years, the production of corn and soybeans has nearly doubled in Niagara.[11]

"It made farming easier for farmers and it also improved yields," Winnicki says. "Biotech crops help farmers get higher yields from the same land, or extend crops into marginal areas, under harsher growing conditions."

But what about the risk to genetic diversity such crops pose? Or the controversy over neonicotinoid insecticides used as seed and crop treatments wreaking havoc with bee populations? Winnicki asserts there's still plenty of genetic diversity. As for the bees, he says the industry is waiting for definitive science that says "neonics" are responsible for killing colonies of the life-sustaining insects. "If it's not good for the bees, it's not good for me, it's not good for Lennie and we want to know," he maintains.

Picking fruit near Vineland in 1911. *Photo courtesy of Vineland Growers Co-operative.*

Corn has always been a major crop in Wainfleet, where the earliest account of any sort of farming dates back to 1822. Soybeans started to appear as recently as the 1980s, and at the time, Wainfleet grew more than any other municipality in Niagara. Today, Winnicki wagers 90 percent of soy grown in Niagara is genetically modified.

The largely rural Wainfleet was more diversified in its early days as a farming community, however. There were nearly four hundred acres of orchards in 1861. By 1986, they had all but disappeared, with only fifty-six acres of apples and twenty-one acres of tender fruits remaining, the latter better suited to the climate below the Niagara Escarpment.[12] Tomatoes were also a major crop through much of the 1900s, with growers selling on contract to Campbell's in Toronto, a handful of regional canneries and to E.D. Smith in nearby Winona.

Lennie Aarts was one of many growers who lost his market for tomatoes when E.D. Smith closed one of its lines. He ramped up his corn and pork production to make up for the loss. When pork prices bottomed out in the 1990s and early 2000s, he went whole hog into growing corn with his brother Peter. They participate in seed trials, like the one Winnicki is doing, in their quest for profitable crops. Genetically modified corn and soybeans have been proving to have the winning combination of good market demand and sustainable production costs.

The corn the Aarts brothers grow is destined for the Ingredion plant in Port Colborne's Carbohydrate Valley, where it will be turned into fructose and corn syrup to feed the food and beverage industries. Ingredion also converts corn into dextrose and sells it to the neighbouring Jungbunzlauer plant, where it becomes citric acid for food, beverage and cosmetics production.

Winnicki makes the case earnestly for genetically modified crops. He points out that scientists are only trying to reduce crop losses to insects and disease. "We need to include biotech in modern agriculture practices. Otherwise, we will never be able to feed the world," he asserts. "We cannot do it with organic farming."

Canned Industry

While the economics bode well for those growing corn and soy, they haven't done much to benefit Niagara's food processing industry. At one time, there were twenty-two fruit and vegetable canneries operated by Canadian

Canners in the region that provided a market for local farmers to sell their harvests.[13] Some crops were grown specifically to end up in a can. Others were too imperfect for consumers' tastes to sell fresh but whose flaws could be covered with a little dicing and dousing with simple syrup.

Consolidation and, more recently, corporations giving in to the temptation of cheaper labour and raw materials overseas have dealt huge blows to Niagara farmers who once relied on canning factory contracts to help sustain them. Today, there are no canneries left in Niagara. The last one closed in 2008, when CanGro Foods Inc. in St. Davids shuttered. It took with it a market for 150 farmers to sell $2.5 million of clingstone peaches and $1.8 million of pears each year.[14] As it turns out, CanGro, which owns the Del Monte and Aylmer brands, was the last fruit cannery in Canada at the time.[15]

No one will deny how emotional it was to see bulldozers level hundreds of acres of clingstone peach trees, some of them newly planted, as farmers erased from the landscape unfulfilled promises of their fruit going into Del Monte tins for years to come. Those trees were replaced with peaches better suited to eating fresh, grapes for wine or corn. Some land was left vacant as farmers took time to determine replacement crops with the greatest job security. Meanwhile, the pears once destined to be canned had to find room in the fresh market, where the appetite for the bell-shaped fruit isn't as voracious as it is for a fuzzy peach.

John Smith and his daughter Jenifer had a sense that CanGro's end was nigh in 1994 when they set up a line to process peaches for freezing on their Vineland farm, Cherry Lane. The addition complemented the sour cherries they process for juice and for home and industrial bakers, at one time including McDonald's, which used them in its cherry pies. "There was the uncertainty of CanGro for many years, and we had acres of clingstones that we didn't want to be left in cold," Jenifer recalls.[16]

Their foresight made the Smiths heroes to growers who had a glut of those replacement peaches in 2013 and delivered two thousand tons of fruit to Cherry Lane for processing. It's the most peaches the Smiths have ever taken, but Jenifer was unfazed by the increase in demand for Cherry Lane's services. "If I had more peaches, I could sell them," she says about the popularity of their products.

Peaches and pears aren't the only Niagara fruits to fall victim to globalization. In the fall of 2007, just months before CanGro's demise, the Ontario government divvied up $3.8 million and sent cheques to 120 farmers to tear out their vineyards of Concord and Niagara grapes. Cadbury-

Inside the processing plant at Cherry Lane in Vineland. *Photo by Tiffany Mayer.*

Schweppes in St. Catharines, which made and distributed Welch's grape juice, was closing. It was the death knell for Canada's grape juice industry, save for a handful of local growers who spared some vines to bottle their own juice to sell at farmers' markets. A select few growers today also send their

21

John and Jenifer Smith in the peach orchard at Cherry Lane in Vineland. *Photo by Tiffany Mayer.*

berries to Westfield, New York, home of the National Grape Co-operative, which owns Welch Foods. It ensures that a small taste of Niagara can still be had in the famous grape juice, jams and jellies.

The hurt has been felt outside the tender fruit belt in south Niagara, too, where a former milling monolith sits as the gateway to the city of Port Colborne, a shell of its former self. The Robin Hood Flour mill, once buzzing with activity, is an almost clichéd reminder of more prosperous times in manufacturing, let alone food processing, in Niagara. Paul Laprise dropped out of high school in 1973 to work at the mill after spending a summer helping to deliver flour to pizzerias and bakeries in the region. Lured by the paycheque, Laprise, who was fifteen at the time, was certain he had a job for life. So was Fred Cronshaw when he joined Robin Hood's two-hundred-strong workforce in 1977. After all, the flour milling industry in Port Colborne was among the world's biggest at the time. Giving up an education for a job seemed like a safe prospect for Laprise because, as he aptly puts it, "everyone's got to eat."[17]

The Robin Hood mill had several large commercial customers. It turned out pancake mix for McDonald's and supplied flour to donut giant Tim Hortons and to the makers of the top-secret KFC and Mary Brown's Fried Chicken coatings. The plant also ground wheat to send to Russia and Cuba.

It worked with local bakeries and pizzerias to do custom blends, and of course, it filled countless yellow bags adorned with the Merry Man himself that are so ubiquitous in the baking aisle at the grocery store.

There was no task that Laprise and Cronshaw didn't do during their careers at the mill. Laprise found his forte grading grains that came to the mill by truck, rail or boat from Western Canada and Ontario farms. One look and sniff of a handful of wheat kernels and Laprise knew whether a load was good or bad. Meanwhile, Cronshaw proved his worth in labour relations, eventually becoming the president of the mill's union, United Food and Commercial Workers 416P.

But from the time they started, the mill's workforce was slowly whittled down to thirty-five employees as it switched to bulk flour shipping in the mid-1990s. Sensing what was to come, the union offered to buy the plant, but Robin Hood wouldn't sell. Fortunately, there was an uptick in employment when the line that turned out bags of flour sold at supermarkets returned a few years later, and staffing levels rebounded to seventy people.

"And then along came Smucker's," Laprise recalls, his voice foreboding. The mega-food manufacturer bought Robin Hood Multi-Foods in 2005, including its Port Colborne operation. On April 24, 2007, the mill's workers were locked out during labour negotiations. They would stay on the picket line until October 30, 2008, when the plant's latest owner, Cargill, closed it.

"I don't think anyone thought it was going to close," Cronshaw says about those early days on the picket line. "I think it was a shock to the community."[18]

The former Robin Hood Flour mill in Port Colborne. *Photo by Nathaniel David Johnson.*

But it was a relief nonetheless when it finally did happen, ending a bitter labour dispute. "I was glad it was over. After a year and a half, I could afford the Kraft Dinner but not the milk to put into it," Laprise says.

Today, Riverland Ag uses the seventy-plus-year-old mill for grain storage. It's considered a part of Port Colborne's Carbohydrate Valley, a new cluster of internationally owned biotechnology plants that convert carbohydrates into ingredients for pharmaceuticals and the foods that Michael Pollan and Mark Bittman rail against. Carbohydrate Valley is food processing's future in Niagara and marketed globally to attract complementary businesses to the area.

Meanwhile, every October 30, Laprise, Cronshaw and their former co-workers meet at Port Colborne's City Hotel to mark the anniversary of the Robin Hood closure. In one another's presence, they talk about anything other than careers cut short and the loss of a cornerstone of Niagara's food processing heritage.

"We don't talk about the plant," Cronshaw says. "We don't like talking about it."

To Market We Go

Torrie Warner's Beamsville farm is like a consumer research facility. It's home to trees bearing fruit that can't be found in most grocery stores. But at a farmers' market? If Warner is a vendor there, you might be in luck.

As a child, Warner remembers going with his father, Fred, to the Horticulture Research Institute of Ontario at Vineland to check out the tree fruit being bred and tested there with the intention of one day being the next big commercial crop. It was a formative experience for the farmer-to-be and is the reason the Warner farm is home today to German plums, Sheldon pears and several varieties of quince. They're niche fruits that Warner knows consumers want but chain stores can't be bothered stocking.

His willingness during his own career to experiment with new fruit varieties gives Warner the edge among gourmands looking for something new and different at farmers' markets. Other than selling to a handful of independent food stores, farmers' markets are the only place Warner sells his wares, including one five hours away in Ottawa that he attends weekly in the summer to sell peaches.

"At my markets, if I have something no one else does, they'll come to me," says Warner, who was once a member of the now-defunct Ontario Fruit

Testing Association. "But just because I try something doesn't mean it will be a success. I've tried five different varieties of grapes, and I'll plant maybe one of those."[19]

Farmers' markets have made a comeback in recent years, thanks to the increasing interest in eating locally grown, seasonal food. In Niagara, there are a dozen markets, giving locavores a place to get their fill five days a week. The markets are an avenue for smaller farmers, like Warner, who farms about sixty acres of orchards and vineyards, to get their season's work onto the plates of consumers because dealing with large grocery chains is virtually impossible as an individual, particularly one with such small quantities to offer.

Those who sell at farmers' markets often net two to three times what they would by selling wholesale, notes Len Troup, former chair of the Ontario Tender Fruit Producers Marketing Board. For guys like Troup, who is the largest pear grower in Niagara, farmers' markets aren't an option, however. The quantities of fruit they produce are just too big for them to market themselves. "If we need to sell five thousand to six thousand baskets a day, which we do for many months, it's hard to put your efforts into marketing," he says. "We were never retailers. We weren't oriented that way. You have to enjoy it."

Troup, like many large Niagara farmers, relies on Vineland Growers Co-operative to get his fruit to consumers by way of grocery stores. The one-hundred-year-old co-operative is a wholesaler and marketer of Niagara's tender fruits, getting baskets of peaches, nectarines, pears, grapes and other fruit into the produce section at national grocery chains, including retail monoliths Costco and Walmart.

While it takes the pressure off farmers to find a home for their harvests, it doesn't mean selling wholesale is a business model free of problems. Sometimes it means "getting caught up in a vicious cycle of doing more to make less," Troup laments. There's uncertainty surrounding the price those mega-retailers might be willing to pay on any given day. "The bigger you are, the greater the risk. They know they can break you. When they really want to get you down [in price] they can do it," he says. "They can also bail you out. If they really want the fruit, they'll do that."

Warner knows it, and that's why it's a game he'd rather not play. With farmers' markets, he has more control over his returns on a growing season. "I typically try to grow things that do well at the retail level," he explains. "I grow many things on my farm, which creates a management nightmare, but I have one thousand customers, I don't have one. If one of my customers closes tomorrow or dies, I don't notice. If my wholesaler closes tomorrow, where do I go?"

Niagara`s Farmers` Markets

Brock University Farmers' Market (June to September)
Fridays, 11:30 a.m. to 1:30 p.m.
Jubilee Court

Farmers' Market at the Village (May to October)
Saturdays, 8:00 a.m. to 1:00 p.m.
111 Garrison Village Drive, Niagara-on-the-Lake

Grimsby Farmers' Market (May to October)
Thursdays, 3:00 to 7:00 p.m.
Main Street West between Ontario and Christie

Jordan Village Farmers' Market (June to October)
Wednesdays, 2:30 to 6:30 p.m.
2789 Fourth Avenue (Jordan Lion's Park)

Niagara Falls Farmers' Market (Year-round)
Saturdays, 6:00 a.m. to noon
5943 Sylvia Place

Pelham Farmers' Market (May to October)
Thursdays, 4:30 to 8:30 p.m.
20 Pelham Town Square

Port Colborne Farmers' Market (Year-round)
Fridays, 6:00 a.m. to 1:00 p.m.
66 Charlotte Street

Ridgeway Farmers' Market (May to October)
Saturdays, 7:00 a.m. to noon
282 Ridge Road

St. Catharines Farmers' Market (Year-round)
Thursdays and Saturdays, 6:00 a.m. to 3:00 p.m.
91 King Street

St. Catharines Nighttime Market (June to August)
Tuesdays, noon to 8:00 p.m.
91 King Street

SupperMarket at the Village (May to September)
Wednesdays, 4:30 p.m. to dusk
111 Garrison Village Drive, Niagara-on-the-Lake

Welland Farmers' Market (Year-round)
Saturdays, 6:00 a.m. to noon
50 Market Square

Hired Hands

Every locavore has heard the saying "If you ate today, thank a farmer." But there are other people who deserve gratitude every time someone sinks his or her teeth into a Niagara peach, sips a glass of one of the region's wines or buys a loved one a plant that was grown at a local greenhouse.

Each year, Niagara welcomes more than 2,600 seasonal agricultural workers from Mexico and the Caribbean for up to eight months a year. They come to fill the void of labourers on local fruit farms, in vineyards and in greenhouses, doing work that many Canadians have no desire to do and that which can't be done by a machine. While corn, wheat or soybean farmers use heavy equipment to plant, maintain and harvest their crops, there's no shortage of manual work in horticulture, and no single farmer can do it alone.

Depending on the farm, the amount of hired help varies from a handful of workers to upward of one hundred. The labour pool drawn from over the years has changed, reflecting the social climate of the day. During the Second World War, local farms relied on students in Ontario's Farm Service Camp Program. Most of them were young women, dubbed Farmerettes, who did the work while the men went off to battle. Immigrants filled those jobs after the war as the number of students enrolling in the program declined until it was scrapped in 1953. These new Canadians brought with them a work ethic that enabled them to earn enough money to eventually buy their own farms and build new lives, and as they went on to live the Canadian dream, former soldiers, transients and students stepped in. Though the makeup of work crews was considerably different from one decade to the next, one consistency remained: finding reliable help wasn't easy because the work was—and still is—hard.

"I remember standing in a cherry orchard and my dad saying, 'I don't know if I'm going to have one hundred employees tomorrow or two hundred.' It was that unstable," recalls Art Smith, whose family owns Cherry Lane, a fruit farm and processing plant in Vineland. "You never knew if the help was going to be there or not. Farm work is not easy work, and our society evolved away from it. Industrial and manufacturing jobs started to open, and they paid considerably more. There wasn't that desire, as those jobs became available, to work on farms. And whether it's fifty or one hundred workers, you can't operate without a consistent, dependable workforce."[20]

Smith's father, Harold, figured out a solution to the workforce woes while on his annual winter getaway to Jamaica in the early 1960s. He noticed unemployment in the tropical island nation was high. Jamaica had the workers, and Niagara had the work.

Two years of meetings between growers and government officials ensued, and in 1966, the federal Seasonal Agricultural Workers Program launched, with the first Jamaican workers arriving that spring to work on Niagara farms. Farmers could hire from abroad only if they couldn't find Canadians to fill jobs. Hired help from Mexico, Barbados, Trinidad and Tobago and other Caribbean countries has since joined the seasonal farm workforce.

"This was an opportunity that was unbelievable to them," Smith says. "They've educated their children with the money they've earned, they've bought small farms and they've learned skills they can use back home."

The program has garnered its share of detractors, however. They argue foreign workers are vulnerable to exploitation because of how much they need the income, which is often ten times what they could earn at home.[21] The United Food and Commercial Workers union has opened outreach centres in farming communities to assist workers who feel they aren't being treated fairly by their farmer employers, though laws prohibit farmworkers from organizing. Academics have also come after the program despite stipulations that farmers who mistreat workers risk losing access to the foreign labour pool.

Whether a testament to how much the program has done for its people or an act of international diplomacy, the Jamaican government in 2013 presented its Badge of Honour to two representatives from Foreign Agricultural Resource Management Services (FARMS), which administers the agricultural workers program in Ontario.

Without the program, Smith says Niagara's tender fruit industry would be a fraction of the size it is today. Still, having to rely on hired help is costly for farmers, who must pay at least minimum wage. In 2014, that rate was eleven dollars an hour, an increase of 60 percent since 2004, while the prices growers received for their harvests rose only 9 percent in the same time.[22] Each wage increase poses a conundrum to farmers: it's in convincing the consumer to pay the true cost of Niagara fruit. Cheaper imports from countries that pay workers far less become a temptation for the consumer when grocery shopping and make it difficult for the local grower to compete.

Smith says growers faced with shrinking margins have contemplated "knocking their peaches out of the ground" to grow something less labour intensive and, therefore, gentler on the bottom line. "The industry isn't going to drop off tomorrow, but we are going to see a continuous decline of farmers doing it," he warns. "Do we want continued fruit and vegetable production in Canada? If the answer is yes, we need government and consumer support."

Growing Innovation

The solution to the tender fruit industry's labour woes rests partly in automation. Machines don't need to be paid to work after all, but can heavy equipment harvest a peach without bruising it? The Vineland Research and Innovation Centre is trying to find out. The mechanization of horticulture is on the to-do list of scientists at the latest incarnation of the 108-year-old research station, which was revitalized in 2006 after deep funding cuts saw research and extension services slashed through the 1990s.

The renewal of the centre, known in its early days as the Horticulture Research Institute of Ontario, included a mandate to tackle some of the biggest issues facing horticulture to the benefit of both the farmer and consumer. Since Vineland's rebirth began in 2006, scientists from throughout the world have come to Niagara to find ways to advance the horticulture industry here. They're breeding new varieties of apples that farmers can grow easily and that consumers will eat up. They've established a world crops program to determine profitable vegetable crops for farmers that will appeal to Canada's ethnic populations. The program has found that vegetables such as okra, Asian eggplants, bottle gourds and fuzzy

Jim Brandle, CEO of the Vineland Research and Innovation Centre.
Photo courtesy of Vineland Research and Innovation Centre.

melons grow well in Ontario and have the potential to create new markets for growers worth $36.6 million.

Researchers at Vineland are also on the case of breeding a greenhouse tomato with flavour rather than just a flawless appearance. They're working on developing a method to dry grapes for appassimento-style wines made in Canada and affordable to the average consumer. They're also developing new varieties of roses to find the next big selling bloom. The list goes on.

"Horticulture is a fashion business. You need to know the colour, the size that the consumer wants," explains Jim Brandle, CEO of the Vineland Research and Innovation Centre. "In the past, we'd often produce things for farmers that consumers didn't like even though they appealed to someone else in the value chain."

Innovation doesn't happen only in local research facilities, however. Farmers are known for being changelings when the industry demands it. Resilience and creativity are necessary in a business influenced by factors beyond human control, including weather and markets.

It was the latter that prompted brothers Jeff and Dan Tigchelaar to grow the kind of strawberries that made California the poster state for berry production. Growing up, Jeff and Dan's parents grew June strawberries and apples on one hundred acres north of Hamilton, but it was the berries that proved to be the most fruitful when the brothers delivered the family's harvests to the Ontario Food Terminal in Toronto as teens. There, a bushel of apples, roughly fifty pounds, would fetch about fourteen dollars at the time. A flat of strawberries, which is six quarts, netted eighteen dollars. The seeds were planted for a new business venture.

The brothers bought a farm in Niagara's Vineland in 1995 and, after a failed attempt with their first strawberry crop, found a cultivar and a method

Dan Tigchelaar (left) and brother Jeff are among the largest strawberry growers in Ontario. *Photo by Tiffany Mayer.*

for growing them that, twenty years later, would make the Tigchelaars one of the largest berry growers in Ontario.

The Tigchelaars plant hundreds of thousands of day neutral strawberry plants in the fall and cover them with plastic to protect them over the winter. By the time spring arrives, the plastic helps the ground heat up quickly, prompting plants to produce fruit weeks earlier than those that spend the winter under straw. It's not uncommon to see Tigchelaar strawberries—"a beautiful crunchy berry like a California berry," Jeff describes—in stores as early as May 15.[23] Traditionally, berries haven't shown up until June. Crop rotations of different varieties through the year also keep the Tigchelaars busy harvesting berries until Thanksgiving, months after most growers have called it a season.

The Tigchelaars harvest yields that are small by California standards, where drier weather and less pestilence help produce crops three times the size. Still, with sixty acres of strawberries in production, the brothers are two gutsy growers. Most berry farmers grow only one or two acres because of how quickly they need to get their harvest to market to avoid spoilage. If they can't find a home for their berries, the loss of investment for the year likely won't be crippling. That's not the case for the Tigchelaars, whose berries are stocked in national grocery chains and

Strawberries growing at Tigchelaar Berry Farm in Vineland. *Photo by Tiffany Mayer.*

farmers' markets. "The guys who really pay attention to what we're doing say, 'I would never do that,'" Jeff says. "It's the volatility of a tender fruit crop you need to move in a day."

That kind of courage and curiosity to do something unique resulted in another one of the sweetest ventures in Niagara agriculture. White Meadows Farms, the largest of the region's two sugar bushes and a bastion of agritourism, may never have come to be were it not for a family's openness to experimenting with different types of farming.

For most of the eighty years the Bering family has farmed in Effingham, dairy, grapes for juice and cash crops such as corn have been their bread and butter. That didn't keep the enterprising Murray Bering from trying out other ventures he hoped would be a cash cow. He tried raising veal, beef and chickens for eggs and meat but found the family's real niche in farming when he started tapping maple trees in the early 1990s as a hobby. It became an annual tradition that saw Murray set up an evaporator in the tractor shed, and he was soon selling some of his syrup to neighbours. Those same neighbours wanted to learn how Murray made the sweet elixir and started hanging around to watch. One of them suggested that a pancake house would be a great addition to the experience, and in 1994, the Berings set up a Quonset hut to serve pancakes. They also started offering sugar bush tours.

By 1999, people were lining up out the door for a table, and a year later, the Quonset hut was replaced with a permanent cafeteria-style pancake house for families to feast on flapjacks after an interactive walk through the sugar bush. Today, Murray; his wife, Ann; and their sons, Richard and Nicholas, tap five thousand trees for sap, serve countless pancakes to twenty-five thousand people every February and March and have an expansive line of maple products available year-round, featuring everything from candy and syrup to barbecue sauce and beans.

"Pretty much everything we've done has been inspired by a demand for it," Murray says. "Because there wasn't syrup being made here in Niagara, people were coming out here because they wanted to know about it."[24]

The success of White Meadows Farms' sugar bush has convinced Richard and Nicholas they have a future in farming. But there were other false starts along the way for the Berings, which only proved this farming family's resilience and adaptability, both essential to survival in agriculture. Their vineyard was rendered worthless with the 2007 closure of the St. Catharines plant that took the Berings' grapes to make juice. They unloaded their beef cattle herd in 2010, when prices for animals tanked while feed costs soared, and in 2013, after falling behind on planting at the end of maple season,

Richard Bering of White Meadows Farms throws another log on the fire while making maple syrup in the sugar shack during the sap harvest. *Photo by Tiffany Mayer.*

the family decided to give up growing corn and soy, which has also had tumultuous returns over the years.

"We were either going to have to go into cash cropping or maple syrup," Richard recalls about the decision to get out of corn and soy. "It was 'Look how many people have made the sugar bush their tradition. What are they going to miss more? Maple syrup or cash crops?'"[25]

The Big Boys

Ask a Niagara resident what the biggest farming sector is in the region, and chances are, most of them won't say greenhouses. It's what's growing under glass and plastic that has proven most profitable in Niagara agriculture, however.

Niagara's greenhouse industry was worth more than $244 million in 2011. Fruit, which includes grapes for the wine industry, was a distant second at $94 million.[26] Yet few think of greenhouses when they hear Niagara. It's an industry in which those driving it are most comfortable flying under the proverbial radar, focusing on growing potted flowers, bedding plants and nursery stock rather than calling out from their glass rooftops that they're the third-largest producer of floral crops in North America after California and Florida.[27]

"As a group, we're a little introverted," says Bob Martin, who grows garden-ready vegetable plants for sale in a national chain store and independent garden centres. "We're wholesale growers, so we don't need the publicity. We spend a lot of time in our greenhouses with a few people. The recognition for some, it's not worth breaking the privacy of others so people can know what we do."[28]

Martin comes from one of Niagara's oldest greenhouse families. His grandfather Leo built glass walls around his land, once used for a market garden, in the 1920s. Today, Martin Farms in Vineland is 18,600 square metres of greenhouse—small, he says, by Niagara standards, where the average operation is more than 28,000 square metres.

After the Second World War, Canada and the Netherlands came to an agreement that saw thousands of Dutch agricultural workers immigrate to the region. The war created a shortage of workers, and farmers desperately needed the labour pool refilled. Many left Holland willingly over fears of another war, a lagging economy and uncertain futures for their children. They brought with them a work ethic and knowledge of flower production from their homeland that helped turn the existing greenhouse industry into a tour de force.

"As a group of people, they work twenty-four/seven, they're really bright, focused and they have balls of steel," Martin says about his Dutch colleagues. "They'll take on anything where most other people are too scared to give it a try. They have really driven the industry."

Greenhouses in Niagara had their heyday from the 1970s through the 1990s. People gardened and bought indoor plants for their homes, Martin says. The value of the Canadian dollar was also low compared to its American cousin. That gave Niagara growers a sales advantage over those south of the border. American Walmart and Home Depot stores were regular customers of the region's largest greenhouses, buying potted plants weekly to stock their stores. Business was booming.

When the Loonie soared to parity, and Canada and the United States plummeted into recession in 2008, those sales vanished with a stable economy. The biggest casualty was the cut flower industry—a major part of floriculture in Niagara. It was lost to South America, where flowers can be grown more cheaply and are inexpensive to ship.

Big corporate buyers attempted to get through the lean years by scrapping annual traditions, such as purchasing a poinsettia for every employee at Christmas. Added to this was the growing trend of new homes built on smaller lots, which meant smaller gardens with less room for those bedding plants Niagara's greenhouses turn out each spring. Growers who had small operations and didn't diversify struggled to survive, and many were pushed out, Martin says. Even today, the 283 greenhouses dotting the landscape continue to be rigorously thinned out by market forces.

Through it all has been the debate about whether growing anything in a greenhouse is bona fide farming. Some argue that the glass and plastic structures are flower factories masquerading as farms to benefit from the rules and tax breaks that apply to agriculture when they should be classified as industrial plants. It's all farming to Martin, though. The only difference is that greenhouse growers have some protection from the elements and can reach for the thermostat in cool weather. "If I have a few weeks of really crappy weather, my crop is going to look as crappy as a peach crop would in the same conditions. I'm not the guy doing widgets that can go on a shelf," he insists.

The money that can be made in the industry makes a career in a glass house a tempting option, yet it's one of the hardest industries for a young person to enter into, with new construction of a greenhouse costing up to $1 million per acre.

That's not unlike another of the largest farming sectors in Niagara: poultry. West Niagara, particularly Grimsby, Lincoln and West Lincoln above the escarpment, is home to hundreds of long, windowless barns that house tens of thousands of chickens and turkeys. Birds for meat, eggs and breeding stock are big business in Niagara, where 164 farms generated $93.3 million in 2011, making it the third-largest agriculture sector in the region.[29]

Not unlike greenhouses, it's an industry dominated by Dutch and Greek farmers who arrived postwar and were beckoned to west Niagara by cheap land and a business that required hard work and determination more than experience. They entered into poultry farming at the right time, before the advent of supply management, a system in which farmers must own quota to raise and sell birds on a large scale.

Supply management puts a cap on the number of birds or eggs produced each year in Canada and sets the prices that farmers will be paid in order to keep business profitable. But it's a system with unintended side effects. Just as it's prohibitively expensive to build a greenhouse, it's the same to enter into mainstream poultry farming. Quota for one egg-laying hen, for example, costs between $250 and $300.[30] A farmer must buy quota to raise more than one hundred layers. The average industrial flock is twenty-five thousand birds, which means about $7 million is needed just to get to industry scale. For meat birds, also known as broilers, a farmer in Ontario can't raise more than three hundred birds a year unless he has quota.

Those who got in early landed the goose that laid the golden egg. "It was an industry you could progress in and make money, and a lot of these guys who came in the 1950s were millionaires by the 1960s," says Paul Kent, who owns Kent Heritage Farms, a processor in Niagara-on-the-Lake. Kent's father, Paul Sr., came to Canada from Hungary and started raising chickens in 1958. "But trust me, there's an easy way to make money and a hard way, and this was the hard way," he adds.[31]

Just ask Albert Witteveen, who spent twenty-five years raising broilers, following the career path of his father, who got into meat birds in 1977. At the time, it took eight weeks to raise a two-kilogram bird. Today, it takes thirty-one days, a number achieved through breeding for rapid growth and nutrition. The use of growth hormones in livestock is illegal in Canada.

When Witteveen started farming in Grassie in the early 1980s, he had quota for ten thousand birds per six-week growth cycle. Thanks to rented quota that kept him from needing a job off the farm to supplement his income, his flock grew to sixty thousand birds per cycle by the time he flew the coop in 2011. Witteveen decided that rather than raise birds to feed people, he'd buy grain to sell to farmers raising those birds instead. He also planted hops for craft beer production and now dreams of opening an on-farm brewery.

"I got tired of sucking dust and ammonia," says Witteveen, who doubles as the president of the Niagara North Federation of Agriculture. "My children were grown up and just finishing high school. My son wasn't interested. Farming, it's a lifetime commitment. If you want to make a living, you commit your life, meaning twenty-five years. Yeah, it would be nice if it took five years of work to pay off, but then we'd have a Tim Hortons on every corner and none of us would make any money because we'd all be sitting around drinking coffee. Niagara didn't get like this because we all sat around in coffee shops. It's like this because people worked hard."[32]

Today, Niagara's chicken industry accounts for nearly 12 percent of production in Ontario—the third-largest region in the province after Wellington and Huron Counties. But unlike the greenhouse industry, poultry farmers want residents to know just how big and important their farms are to Niagara's economy. Every June, as many as ten thousand people flock to

PoultryFest in Smithville, in the heart of Niagara's bird bailiwick. Witteveen is one of the event's founders.

"There are few venues where the industry can explain to the public how poultry is raised. You can see the barns, but you can't see into them," Witteveen says. "This allows the industry to respond to any misconceptions. There's a whole education aspect. When a kid gets to touch a chick, that's an imprint for the rest of their life. That's the connection you want to make. It's about experiencing your food. [Farmers] are 1.6 percent of the population, so we can be decimated pretty quickly. People have to feel good about what we're doing."

New Shoots

Ryan Thiessen felt so good about farming that he started making a career of it in 2010. "I have just always wanted to farm," Thiessen maintains. "I like to be outside and be with equipment. There are other jobs where you can do that, but I just want to farm. I guess it's in my blood."

Except it's not really. Thiessen didn't grow up on a farm. He doesn't come from a long line of people who successfully worked the land, and yet, he is. He grows heritage varieties of vegetables called heirlooms with his wife, Amanda, and their daughter, Sydney, in St. Catharines on two and a half acres they call Creek Shore Farms.

The Thiessens are two of several young farmers in Niagara born city slickers or to non-farming families who see farming as their dream job. While the common refrain among established farm families is that their children don't want to follow in their parents' footsteps, the new generation of food producer is blazing its own trail. These new farmers aren't taking over established orchards, buying quota or inheriting vineyards. They're renting land or buying a few acres to organically grow their dreams of feeding people sustainably.

They're reconnecting eater with farmer using Community Supported Agriculture (CSA) shares, selling directly to people hungry for food production that builds community. Their farms are small, but they're mighty, often producing fresh vegetables year-round, and they're growing in number.

Linda Crago was the first farmer in Niagara to offer a CSA when she began working nine acres of heavy clay land in Wellandport in 1997. Her farm, Tree and Twig Heirloom Vegetable Farm, is a virtual seed bank,

Amanda and Ryan Thiessen of Creek Shore Farms in St. Catharines check out the winter greens growing in their unheated greenhouse with daughter Sydney. *Photo by Nathaniel David Johnson.*

home to upward of seven hundred varieties of tomatoes and other unusual vegetables snubbed by large-scale commercial growers more concerned with the perfect appearance of their produce rather than taste. Without growers like Crago propagating some of these rare heirloom vegetables, they would cease to exist. Hers is a diverse, organic oasis in the middle of a genetically engineered countryside filled with soybeans and corn.

Crago, who did grow up on a farm north of Hamilton, opted for the CSA business model somewhat by accident. She still had her social worker job when she started her farm. All of her initial customers were her co-workers, and Crago delivered her harvests to their homes. "I just had the idea that I would grow food and deliver it door-to-door. I didn't even know what a CSA model was," she says.[33]

After seventeen years, she has a waiting list of people who want into her CSA, which is exactly how Crago would want to buy food if she wasn't the one growing it. "If I didn't grow vegetables, I'd like to be a member of a CSA because that's the way I eat," she says. "I don't go to the grocery store and buy for a certain dish. I look in the fridge or garden and see what I have."

Farmer Linda Crago grows hundreds of varieties of heirloom tomatoes and other vegetables that she sells through her CSA basket program. *Photo by Tiffany Mayer.*

Today, there are nearly a dozen farms in Niagara that have followed Crago's lead, often forgoing farmers' markets, which have been enjoying a renaissance recently, because of the security that comes with selling annual shares in their farms in exchange for a weekly delivery of vegetables. As they would with investments in the stock market, CSA members ride the waves of farming, experiencing the effects of Mother Nature, good and bad, in every basket of vegetables they receive. For the growers, though, it is money paid upfront, enabling them to do their jobs without having to take on huge debt to get through the growing season.

"It's the only way to make money. It's guaranteed sales, unlike a farmers' market," Amanda Thiessen explains. "Our customers are people who really love local food. At the farmers' market, people can say, 'Oh man, four dollars for tomatoes, that's expensive,' but when they come out here, they don't mind."

Jordan Brock Fowler smiles proudly as he runs his thumb over his Ontario Federation of Agriculture membership card. It is confirmation the young farmer is part of an exclusive club, counted among the less than 2 percent of the population of Canada that farms for a living. Fowler, who had intended to be a graphic designer but changed his mind after learning about farming's possibilities while working with a non-governmental organization, is now reclaiming eighteen acres of land his parents had been renting to a farmer growing corn, wheat and soybeans. He's healing the soil on his Jordan farm after years of what he calls degradation, which he says the previous farmer knew he caused "but yet you could tell he was trapped by the scale of the operation," Fowler explains. "Fuel prices were squeezing him. He was questioning whether he was going to re-sign with Monsanto. I was speaking with him for forty-five minutes about how oil determines how he farms."[34]

Fowler, like his other young colleagues who are trying to grow the farming population, focuses on land stewardship as much as ensuring genetic diversity with every old vegetable cultivar he grows. He doesn't use heavy machinery to plant his crops at his Forworld Farm. He raises sheep for meat and manure to nourish the soil. His chicken coop is portable, moving around the farm so the birds can forage and feel the sun on their wings, returning the favour with eggs. He partnered with another young farmer who grows leafy greens in a St. Catharines greenhouse to start a CSA in 2014. It's a positive cycle he wishes other farmers would try on for size.

"My type of agriculture doesn't negatively impact other farmers and the work they want to do, but conventional farms impact my farming," he asserts. "I can't certify my honey [as organic] because I'm ten kilometres from a Monsanto corn field."

Rick and Shirley Ladouceur had never heard of Monsanto, nor did they ever give much thought to where their food came from, when they gave themselves a crash course in Farming 101 in 2010 after acquiring some chickens for eggs and eventually decided to buy the whole farm. "I thought I might as well grow a few vegetables, and it just took off. I loved it," Rick says. "I would never have thought of doing this as a kid. I never saw it as a career or job."[35]

The Stevensville couple has made sacrifices to feed people with what they grow on their small organic farm that, like Crago's, is wedged between massive homages to monocropping. They made twice the salary by working half as much in their previous lives with Shirley as a child and youth worker and Rick as a millwright, but they don't care. What they make now, they put back into building their Chez Nous Farms, including paying the hefty cost of certifying it as organic. Early on during that process, they could barely afford to feed themselves, but they weren't willing to spare the expense of doing right by the land, Shirley recalls. "There was no question to do it any other way," she says. "We were doing something so good, we believed we can't fall on our faces. We had a belief it would pay off."[36]

There's a satisfaction that comes with feeding people that those who do it say they couldn't find in previous careers. "There's nothing like it. The fact that I can take my energy and put it into the soil, raise something from seed, which I've collected, raise it to something and feed it to my family, that's the ultimate to me," Fowler says.

There are also the secondary effects of the work these farmers do. They aren't just farmers; they're community builders, too. Part of that comes from a desire to give back. The other part is about paying it forward. The Thiessens donate 15 percent of their harvests to the local food bank because they believe everyone has the right to good food. Crago preaches the perks of growing one's own food with the Niagara edition of Seedy Saturday, an annual event she organizes for people to learn about growing heirloom vegetables in their own gardens. Green thumbs come in droves. If they can't make it to Seedy Saturday, they invade Crago's Wellandport farm every spring in search of the tomato plants she sells that will produce fruit in every size, shape and shade of the rainbow.

Rick Ladouceur is known as Farmer Rick at one local elementary school, where he has worked with students building gardens and teaching them how to grow vegetables. The crops they reap together are used in school meal programs. All the while, Ladouceur is mentoring people who may one day make the same career choice he did.

Raising a future farmer is certainly on the to-do list for the Thiessens. The couple hopes to rent more land. Five acres would be ideal because then Ryan could give up his job off the farm and the couple could become full-time food producers. In the process, they would give their daughter Sydney the childhood neither had and plant the seeds of possibility within her.

"We want her to grow up like this, to be outside all the time, to understand the importance of hard work and the importance of food and to not take things for granted," Ryan says. "I want her to be a happy little girl, but not because she has everything she wants. I think a farm is a great place to grow up."

....

Back at the table in Len Troup's kitchen, the farmer gets lost in reminiscing about his fifty-year career working the land. He goes off on tangents talking about the different people he has met in that time—all characters in a story filled with victories and losses, tragedies and good fortune.

Troup's story goes back 150 years to when his family first started farming in Niagara, landing here by way of Scotland. When he talks about buying the family farm with his brother when they were in their early twenties, he makes it sound like he had nothing better to do.

"No one knew where they were going in life," he recalls. But where he went is very telling. For much of his career, Troup has been a staunch advocate for local farmers, serving as chairman of the Ontario Tender Fruit Producers Marketing Board for fifteen years. In that time, he took on the powers that be to try to ensure there's as much of a future in farming for his children as their was for him as a young man. He has survived on account of his temerity, but so much is beyond his control. Will his sons, Ron and Brad, make it? Will his grandchildren even consider taking over the farm, seeing what their parents have to deal with? The hope is that they will, says Troup's wife, Judy.

"It's just so tenuous. You can't keep living on the edge," Troup interjects. "It doesn't mean we're going to quit. It's just hard."

Still, that's not a complaint. Complaining isn't Troup's style. He's simply matter-of-fact about the state of agriculture in Niagara. While he had nothing else on the horizon when he bought the family farm, it's clear fifty years later that fate had the right idea, and Troup wouldn't have it any other way.

"I think I'm addicted to it," he says. "In spite of all the moaning and groaning, we're proud we're still here. Most people aren't."

Chapter 2
Liquid Sustenance

If we sip the wine, we find dreams coming upon us out of the imminent night.
—D.H. Lawrence

Head west out of downtown St. Catharines, and in a matter of minutes, the city will feel like the distant past. The gateway to the rural periphery of the Garden City is marked by a modest bungalow surrounded by sprawling fields. They're taken up by vegetables, hay and a chicken pen, where, on a summer's day, a small flock of red sex-link hens busies itself foraging for insects.

There's no sign at all that Arden and Bill Vaughn's farm, also home to a herd of red deer, beef cattle and the Lake Land Meats and Farm Market store, was once three hundred acres of lush vineyards filled with rows of labrusca—Concord, Niagara, Agawam, Catawba, Elvira, Delaware and Dutchess—and French hybrid grapevines lined up like soldiers ready to serve. They're gone now, uprooted after having been a fixture on the Vaughns' farm since the turn of the last century, relegated vitis non grata by a 180-year-old wine industry built on their fermented juices. With them went some of the Vaughns' land, sold to a local construction company kingpin who now uses the vast swath to grow hay for his horses and store fill from his projects.

"It was a time of turmoil for everybody," Vaughn recalls about cutting ties with the industry that sustained her family for decades. "It was quite upsetting, having to tear out your vineyards, but what are you going to do? We just didn't see a future because the prices were dropping at the time."[37]

For a long time, there was a future in growing labrusca grapes, however. They were an important crop on local farms dating back to the early 1800s. One of the earliest references to grape growing in Niagara came compliments of the War of 1812 and a claim submitted by Thomas Merritt of Grantham Township. The father of Welland Canal mastermind William Hamilton Merritt documented the loss of grapevines among his other usual suspects of nineteenth-century wartime destruction and looting—buildings, crops, a horse, stoves and feather beds. Including his grapes in his claim hints that they weren't wild.[38]

In 1873, George Barnes established Niagara's first commercial winery, the Ontario Grape Growing and Wine Manufacturing Company Ltd., later renamed Barnes Wines Ltd., where he made native wines in St. Catharines. But it was the opening of Andrés Wines Ltd. nearly one hundred years later in 1970 that provided the wine industry with what has since become a bit of a running joke, keeping Canadian tipple from entirely shaking an unpalatable reputation despite earning world renown in the past twenty years. Andrés gave Canada Baby Duck, a sweeter spinoff of the sparkling Cold Duck. It was the quintessential bootleg at high school proms in the 1970s and '80s and served as inspiration for other local wineries to flood the market at the time with their own hangover-inducing, regret-filled bubbly renditions.

"The wineries came up with some crazy versions back in the '70s," remembers Vaughn, whose family was the largest grower for Brights Wine, which made President Canadian Champagne. "One winery at the time was making wine to taste like Coke. Can you imagine? Why would anyone want to do that? The wineries did nothing to help the industry."

Yet everything about Niagara made it ripe for a world-class wine industry. The peninsula boasts a climate that's comparable to Bordeaux and Burgundy.[39] That's thanks to the temperature-moderating effects of Lake Ontario and the rocky embankment rising from the earth that is the Niagara Escarpment. Together, they create a natural circulation system that helps to stave off extreme temperatures that would damage vines. The grapes are further helped along by deep, mineral-rich soil.

It wasn't until an Austrian winemaker walked into a local nursery in search of grapes that didn't "taste Canadian" or foxy that those in the industry started realizing they could use the peninsula's traits for so much more than making plonk that mimicked soda pop. Donald Ziraldo, a newly minted agronomist from the University of Guelph, fulfilled Karl Kaiser's request when he sold him American and French hybrid De Chaunac vines in 1973. Kaiser returned with a bottle of his homemade wine, and to

Pinot Noir grapes on the vine. *Photo by Tiffany Mayer.*

Ziraldo's astonishment, it was good. Like any decent bottle does, it spurred conversation, this one about a partnership to build a new cottage winery that wouldn't use labruscas in its vintages.

Ziraldo was convinced by his travels to European cool-climate wine regions growing vinifera grapes that the same could be done in Niagara, given the fruit the region produces. He had already been experimenting with grafting European vines on Canadian rootstock to prove his theory. He and Kaiser paired perfectly and found someone with a similar vision for wine in Ontario in General George Kitching, the head of the Liquor Control Board of Ontario (LCBO). As Ziraldo recalls, Kitching got a taste of good wine while serving in Europe during the war, and he felt that an industry could make such vintages here. Kitching donated ten old Portuguese oak barrels to the duo to age their wine and, in July 1975, granted Ziraldo and Kaiser one of the first licences to make tipple in Ontario since 1933, when the Wine Standards Committee recommended that the LCBO issue no new licences.

They called their winery Inniskillin Wines and turned out their first vintages made with hybrids: a Maréchal Foch, De Chaunac and a Vin Nouveau, which blended both with Chelois and Chancellor grapes. By 1978, Inniskillin was bottling Chardonnay, Riesling and Gamay Noir using berries from vines Ziraldo and Kaiser planted in 1974. The days of the labrusca's stranglehold on the industry were now numbered.

The idea that there were better grapes for wine production than the likes of Concord and Niagara wasn't new, though. In 1923, the grape breeding program at the Horticulture Research Institute of Ontario at Vineland abandoned using Concords and Niagaras as parents of new varieties. A report from the research station nearly twenty years later stated the program's objective was to produce cultivars more like vinifera varieties and less like labrusca grapes, which were high in acid and had to be watered down, used in fortified wines like sherry or tempered with imported vintages just to be drinkable.[40]

There were also pioneering grape growers who had already turned their vineyards over to vitis vinifera—European wine grapes—long before Kaiser showed up at Ziraldo's nursery. Bill Lenko and John Marynissen were two of the first growers to abandon labrusca grapes for the likes of Chardonnay and others. It was 1959 when Lenko followed the advice of a buyer of his Niagara grapes, which fetched a price that "wouldn't even pay the mortgage," and planted two thousand Chardonnay vines to be turned into Brights Pinot Chardonnay.[41] Four years later, his first harvest netted him a $3,000 paycheque and a new perspective on grape growing that saw him yank his labrusca vines by the late 1960s.

Still, labruscas remained the grapes of choice for most growers for decades to come. Concords accounted for nearly one-quarter of the region's grape crop in 1976, and half of the eighteen thousand tons grown that year went into wine.[42] Even though new "trendy hybrid cousins from North America and pushy immigrants from Europe" were growing in more vineyards, wines made from Concords still produced 90 percent of profits raked in by wineries, and Concords were being planted more than any other grape.[43] Those light-alcohol sparkling wines were one reason the Concord held fast and, ultimately, held back Niagara wine's evolution into tipple that would one day have its praises sung by the who's who of wine writers, including British critic Jancis Robinson.

The proliferation of the Baby Ducks in the local industry also may have given some growers a false sense of security about the future. Ronald Moyer, chairman of the Ontario Grape Growers' Marketing Board at the time, predicted that wine made from labruscas would one day be drunk elsewhere in the world, even though European wine appellation laws prohibited their production for wine, let alone being sold in any bottles of tipple, imported or otherwise. "Labrusca wines have a definite and sizeable future in North

Karl Kaiser (left) and Donald Ziraldo in the vineyard at Inniskillin Wines. *Photo courtesy of Inniskillin Wines.*

America and probably beyond North America as well," he said in 1978. "They have a fruitier flavour than the French hybrid and vinifera wines and I foresee a growing demand from processors in the labrusca classes."[44]

Not if Ziraldo had anything to do with it. When he tried to sell the French his Maréchal Foch in 1982, they wanted none of it because no one could prove the wine's provenance. Canada's wine industry wasn't helped by the fact that the Wine Content Act allowed for wineries to blend their local labrusca juice with imports, yet they could still slap "Product of Canada" on the label.[45] A determined Ziraldo knew that had to change if Canadian winemakers were to ever see their life's work gain access to the coveted European market. The only alternative was for the industry to continue lagging behind other wine regions in the world and, ultimately, perish.

"Labruscas were the scourge of the industry," Ziraldo asserts. "Those wines were not allowed in the European Union or OIV [the International Organization of Vine and Wine]. We'd never be able to sell wines to the Europeans if we didn't follow their standards."[46]

What comes next is years of turmoil and anger in the countryside as Ziraldo and a group of winemakers and grape growers, including Paul Bosc Sr. at Château des Charmes, Len Pennachetti of Cave Spring Cellars, Paul Speck of Henry of Pelham and Peter Gamble at Hillebrand Estates Winery, joined forces to elevate Niagara's wine industry to one that would excel at producing wines made from vinifera grapes. Together, they established the Vintners Quality Alliance (VQA), an appellation system to regulate the origins of local wine. But first, what to do about those labrusca grapes taking up valuable vineyard real estate that could be used to grow Riesling, Chardonnay, Cabernet Franc, Sauvignon Blanc or Gewürztraminer instead?

"The big paradigm shift was the farmers," Ziraldo recalls. "They had to go from labrusca to vinifera. There was a lot of gnashing of teeth."

And little incentive for growers to make the transition. Government money was doled out to pay growers to pull out their labrusca vines, but it amounted to about only one-third of what they would have needed to replace them with vinifera varieties, Ziraldo remembers. Five hundred of eight hundred grape growers were culled from the wine industry, though some continued growing labrusca grapes for processing into less-profitable concentrate for juice and jelly. "A lot of old guys—and I empathize—said we don't know how to grow vinifera, and we're too old to go back to school," he says.

The advent of the Canada-U.S. Free Trade Agreement in 1989, however, made the switch to vinifera grapes and high-quality wine that much more critical. The agreement would see the markups on imported wines whittled away, which meant that local wine would have go cork-to-cork with foreign vintages vying for wine drinkers' dollars in the liquor store. To better the tipple's chances of purchase, VQA rules stated that table wines could no longer contain labrusca grapes. The liquor board had a control lab to do tests ensuring no one tried to sneak any in.[47]

"It was a necessary evil to move us along," Vaughn recalls. "It was really hard for a lot of growers, but someone needed to make the push. Donald Ziraldo was behind that at the time, and he's not a hero to a lot of grape growers because of it. But he moved the industry forward and got us producing higher-quality European wines."

At times, the vitriol for Ziraldo knew no limits. He recalls attending a hearing about the creation of the Greenbelt agriculture preserve in Niagara with police escorts to protect him from being mobbed by angry farmers. Ziraldo, who was becoming the fedora-sporting champion of the Canadian wine industry abroad by peddling Niagara icewine to the world, didn't entirely understand it because he was trying to create a 100 percent Canadian product that would make Niagara and the nation proud. "It was kind of like—I hate to use the analogy—but like a militant union. The growers were great people individually, but they didn't see the big picture," Ziraldo says. "I was too busy flying around the world selling icewine, so I wasn't always here to hear it, but I was getting pretty beat up."

While Ziraldo was globetrotting with icewine in tow, one French oenologist had his head down in his Niagara-on-the-Lake vineyard, toiling in a less flamboyant but equally tenacious way to move the industry forward. Paul Bosc Sr. planted the first local commercial vineyard dedicated entirely to European grape varieties in 1978, when he opened his Château des Charmes winery. He has never looked back, despite detractors along the way.

"To improve the wine, you have to improve the grapes. I thought we had wonderful fruit here—the cherries, the peaches—but the crappiest ones were the grapes," Bosc Sr. says. "It wasn't going to be easy, but we sure could do better than what we were doing at the time."[48]

The Algerian-born Bosc Sr., who studied winemaking in Dijon, France, landed in Niagara via a stop in Quebec, where he worked briefly for the liquor board as a quality control technician. The issues he encountered with product from a Niagara Falls winery called Château-Gai were a sign to Bosc Sr. that the winery could use some help with fermenting grapes. He was hired a week after contacting the winery about the possibility of becoming a winemaker there, and while at the helm of the Château-Gai barrel room, Bosc Sr. made several experimental wines using vinifera grapes, including a Pinot Noir, Chardonnay

A worker harvests grapes at Inniskillin Wines in Niagara-on-the-Lake. *Photo by Scott Rosts.*

and Gamay. They got ink from American wine writers, who marveled that such wines could be produced in Canada. With that success in mind, Château-Gai started asking its farmer suppliers to plant vinifera varieties.

"In a very short time, I resolved their problems. They thought I was a genius," Bosc Sr. recalls. "It's not that I was. It was just how I was trained. People were educated here, just not in formal winemaking."

His success during his fifteen years with Château-Gai inspired Bosc Sr. to start Château des Charmes with his business partner, the late Rodger Gordon. Their first vineyard of exclusively vinifera grapes was sixty acres of risk in a labrusca-driven industry. "People thought, 'This guy has lost his head,' but we persevered and this is where we are today," Bosc Sr. says from his son Paul Jr.'s office on the second floor of the Loire-style château that houses his winery today. It's poignant that the auspicious edifice was built on unplanted land once owned by Brights Wines, which started selling off holdings in the late 1980s because it saw little future for a local industry beyond labrusca grapes.

Still, the dedication to only vinifera varieties was a gutsy move at the time, Paul Jr. recalls, mostly because there was no "Plan B" for the family. If his father couldn't make vinifera grapes work here, including his Aligoté vines—the only of their kind in Canada—he had nothing to fall back on for all the time and money invested. Fortunately, just a decade later, as the 1980s drew to a close, he would be proven right when free trade took effect and labruscas were banned from table wine production. As Paul Jr. notes, though, his father always remained humble and was never one to flaunt his foresight to his naysayers, even when he had a soapbox in 1988 as that year's Grape King.

"He was a very positive Grape King at a very dark hour for the industry. He said if the industry focuses itself on premium varieties, it has a very bright future," Paul Jr. remembers. "But he wasn't out there preaching from the pulpit. He went out and did it, and other farmers saw it with their own eyes. Farmers are show-me types and are more likely to do something when they see it can be done. And that's what my dad did."[49]

His expertise with European appellation systems was also why Bosc Sr. was tapped to help establish the VQA, which operated as a volunteer organization until 1999, when the VQA Act was passed in the Ontario legislature and the alliance became a provincially regulated body. Bosc Sr. opposed allowing any vinifera hybrids to be used in VQA wines, though in the end, thirteen were deemed permissible.[50] Today, Bosc Sr. has conceded somewhat to the hybrid in his 250 acres of vineyards. He has made room for the French hybrid Vidal, though the fruit is strictly for icewine production.

Bosc Sr. continued to eke out his legendary status in Niagara's wine world when he opened his château in 1994, which Paul Jr. describes as "a big step compared to what was around." It was an early example of agritourism in Niagara as one of the first wineries to beckon tourists with a tasting room and a production facility within the same building. The benefit was that tourists could see how the wine they drink is made. With its regional character, Château des Charmes stood in stark contrast to other wineries at the time, which existed in nondescript buildings in industrial parks. Others would follow Bosc Sr.'s example in the years to come.

Today, Niagara is the largest of Canada's wine-producing regions because of his vision, and that of Ziraldo, Kaiser and that group of rogue winemakers that came together to create the VQA. The region's vineyards boast thirty-two varieties of vinifera and hybrid grapes grown on more than 13,600 acres. There are more than eighty wineries ranging in size from producing a few hundred cases of wine a year to more than ninety thousand. Combined, Niagara's wineries make more than two million cases of VQA wines from two regional appellations and ten sub-appellations.[51]

What's more, sales of VQA wines increase steadily each year. In 1992, the wines rang up more than $16.6 million in sales. In 2012, that figure grew to more than $309 million, working out to about 13.8 percent market share.[52] In total, Ontario's wine industry is worth a whopping $3.3 billion and draws 1.9 million tourists, and that's largely due to Niagara alone.[53]

Sitting at a picnic table next to her meat store while a bulldozer and backhoe work in tandem to pile soil on land that was formerly owned by her family to grow grapes, Arden Vaughn notes there isn't the income in livestock that there was in her previous career. Still, there are no sour grapes. A pragmatic Vaughn, who has always been a proud advocate of Niagara agriculture, champions what the wine industry has become, even without her.

"We have the climate, we have the grapes," she says. "There's no reason why we can't produce world-class wines."

A Sweet Success Story

Niagara is the kind of place that could make a person love winter. However, it's not because the region boasts a cold season that plays out like eternal November, milder than much of the rest of the country.

It's thanks to the production of icewine—a viscid, sweeter version of fermented grapes than other table wines. The only catch is that, despite the region's predominantly fall-like winter, icewine needs truly cold weather to happen. Grapes destined for icewine production are picked frozen when the mercury dips to between negative eight degrees Celsius and negative fourteen degrees Celsius, making those few weeks a year that Niagara plummets into a deep freeze a necessary evil to get the most out of fruit left to linger on the vine long after fall harvest.

The three most commonly used grapes in icewine production are the white French hybrid Vidal, the white German grape Riesling and the red Bordeaux variety, Cabernet Franc. The freeze-thaw cycle that the grapes go through before it gets cold enough to signal harvest time concentrates the sugars in the berries, which are pressed while still frozen. Though it's not quite like drawing blood from a stone, the frigid fruit yields only 15 to 20 percent of the juice by volume that grapes harvested in the fall give.[54] The premium price—an average of fifty dollars—affixed to every 375-millilitre bottle of this liquid gold makes up for the difference, though.

Niagara's knack for making magic with frozen grapes has made Ontario the only wine-producing region in the world with a climate that, most years, can guarantee an icewine crop. It's a bragging right that not even Germany, where icewine originated in 1794, can claim, and it makes icewine a Canadian icon not unlike maple syrup or a double-double coffee.

But it took more than climate to make icewine a point of pride for Niagara and the nation. Founding Inniskillin Wines partner and winemaker Karl Kaiser was the one who set it on the path to becoming Canada's signature tipple. His 1989 vintage showed the wine world that the True North was a tour de force in icewine production when it was awarded the distinguished Grand Prix d'Honneur at the VinExpo wine fair in 1991. Other local wineries took notice and started making their own editions, while the large wineries, including Inniskillin, started making inroads into markets, such as Asia, that were previously impenetrable to Canadian wines.

One winery, Royal DeMaria in Beamsville, decided to hang its hat exclusively on icewine production, starting in 1998 and gaining notoriety ever since thanks to prices that make most people gulp. Owner Joseph DeMaria slapped one of the heftiest price tags on any bottle of wine ever produced when he listed his 2000 Chardonnay icewine at $250,000, a markup of more than 800 percent after a Saudi prince purportedly bought a bottle in 2006 for $30,000.

Inniskillin has also had a major influence on how people enjoy their icewine, working with Austrian glassmaker Georg Riedel to design new stemware for the sweet wine. The tulip-shaped bowl, launched in 2001, holds eleven and a half ounces and brings out that tension between acidity and sweetness that aficionados say keeps icewine from being cloying and makes it a perfect match for everything from foie gras to fresh berries.

By 1998, Inniskillin was turning out 360,000 bottles of icewine and had become the largest producer on the planet. It's a torch that has since passed to another Niagara-on-the-Lake winery, Pillitteri Estates.[55]

Gary Pillitteri's ambitions weren't to become the patriarch of the largest estate icewine producer in the world, however. The farmer and hobby winemaker tried out politics first, running as a federal Liberal Party candidate under leader John Turner in 1988. When voters handed him a loss, Pillitteri recovered by spending the next five years building a winery. (Pillitteri won over the electorate in 1993, the same year Pillitteri Estates Winery opened.)

The wine business proved just as unpredictable as the polls, though. In 1995, the Liquor Control Board of Ontario (LCBO) delisted a Pillitteri Estates Chardonnay. Its $12.95 price was considered steep and blamed for slow sales. Pillitteri, whose passion was making sweet wines, had several vintages of icewine to his name, so his son Charlie convinced him to put them in a container bound for China to sell on consignment.

Frozen grapes destined for icewine production in the vineyard at Pillitteri Estates Winery in Niagara-on-the-Lake. *Photo courtesy of Pillitteri Estates Winery.*

They took the gamble with the foreign market after a Taiwanese visitor to the winery pitched selling Pillitteri icewine back in his homeland. There was trepidation, but there was also too much to gain after the LCBO incident. Six weeks after the Pillitteris packed up their precious cargo, Chinese consumers with a nose for the finer things in life bought every bottle, and as promised, the money came. Cue the adage about the rest being history.

"It was a new market in a new place. Canada was only just being recognized," Charlie remembers. "Would he do it now? No. But then? We hadn't sold it yet so it was 'Let's give it a try.'"[56]

Today, Pillitteri Estates makes thirteen styles of icewine, including Chardonnay and Pinot Noir, both by far the most difficult of the bunch to produce, Charlie says. The winery ships its sweet vintages to thirty-two countries, including Germany, Japan and Korea and still to China, where it operates more than twenty-five wine retail stores. The wine has also made its mark in political circles, much like Gary Pillitteri had. More than one thousand souvenir-sized bottles of Pillitteri icewine went to Washington in 2013, a gift for each guest attending U.S. president Barack Obama's inauguration. The family's handiwork has also been served at the Kremlin. And in 2009, the winery teamed up with former Russian hockey great Igor Larionov to produce a vintage.

The world loves Niagara's icewine, Charlie says. "It's a very Canadian product. It's sweet and lush and crisp and has all of these Canadian traits. We knew we had something special with what Inniskillin and Mr. Kaiser had been doing for years."

The sweet story of Niagara's icewine has its share of sour, though. In 1998, cheap counterfeit versions made using grapes frozen after harvest or by adding sweetener to table wine started to appear on the market, diluting the Canadian icewine brand. Knockoff versions account for half the sales in some countries, according to the Canadian Vintners Association.[57] Sixteen years later, it's still a problem that plagues wineries like Pillitteri Estates, which produced forty-five thousand cases of icewine in 2013 and pegs its success on overseas sales.

Deep in the winter of 2014, the Canadian government introduced a national standard for icewine production that would be included in international trade agreements. It would limit the use of the "icewine" name to tipple made exclusively from grapes naturally frozen on the vine. The standard is meant to assure those all-important international markets that icewine from Canada is authentic.

Pillitteri Estates protects its reputation by using a tamper-proof seal, virtually impossible to replicate, that links each bottle of icewine it produces to a database for authentication.

While the rest of the world knows a good thing—and is willing to either spend money on it or imitate it—icewine is a tougher sell in Canada. Price aside, it's a misunderstood wine, often mistaken for a dessert wine, a course that Charlie notes few Canadians take time to enjoy. That's something he hopes to help change with every sample of icewine poured in his winery's tasting room in Niagara-on-the-Lake.

"It's the fast-food mentality. We need to slow down and enjoy our food," he says. "We're a culture that eats to work. Asians work to eat a great meal. That's why icewine doesn't sell at home. We just don't make time for it. The next generation that comes through, we need to train to get the importance of food back."

Red, White and Green:
Niagara's Organic and Biodynamic Wines

Jens Gemmrich shuns all the trappings of conventional grape growing. As the proprietor of Ontario's first certified organic winery, Frogpond Farm, Gemmrich refuses to spray, over-mechanize or do anything against the forces of nature for the sake of his livelihood.

Being the first to do without those chemical helpers in Niagara, however, meant that it took some convincing for others to get on board with his earth-conscious crops in those early days. "The first crop I grew, there was no interest in bottling a separate organic wine," he remembers. "There was a lot of resistance."[58]

Some doubted Niagara's climate would be conducive to organic grape growing. The heat and humidity would leave the berries vulnerable to disease and needing to be doused with a chemical remedy. However, Gemmrich, who certified his vineyard in 2001, never bought that story. "There are challenges with everything. It's not harder than growing conventionally. You have problems, and you have to come out with creative solutions for it," he says.

His most intensive work comes at the beginning of the growing season, as he sets up his vines to prevent issues from arising later in the crop cycle. Gemmrich uses compost instead of artificial nitrogen as fertilizer to produce strong, healthy vines. He keeps the canopy of leaves open to keep molds at bay and let in life-sustaining light and air. It's survival of the fittest in his

Jens Gemmrich of Frogpond Farm winery, Ontario's first certified organic winery. *Photo by Tiffany Mayer.*

vineyard, disease prevention rather than treatment. "If you have a problem with fungus, it's because the plant is weak, so nature recycles it," Gemmrich explains. "We try to keep [the vine] strong so nature doesn't recycle it."

There were those who refused to buy into organic because they felt threatened by it, he recalls. They worried about the potential edge it could give Gemmrich's wines with consumers thirsty for a good wine but also one that didn't take a serious toll on the environment. "We don't do this for marketing," he says. "We do it because we actually think it's the right way of doing things."

Now, nearly twenty years later, Gemmrich can be considered a trailblazer instead of an oddball. In 2014, Niagara was home to a handful of organic and biodynamic wineries, forgoing modern methods for older wisdom. For some, that includes paying attention to new moons and old moons, as prescribed by biodynamic agriculture, which couples spiritual principles with organic's ecological approach.

Sheep in the vineyard at Featherstone Estate Winery in Vineland. *Photo by Tiffany Mayer.*

While some wineries have gone to the labour-intensive and expensive efforts of becoming certified, others merely pick and choose holistic or homeopathic tactics to limit chemical intervention. That could mean employing a flock of sheep halfway through the growing season to eat low-hanging leaves, exposing fruit to more sunlight and boosting its flavours. It can also entail fermenting cow manure in buried cow horns to create compost. Others take the environment into account by simply cutting back on the frequency of spraying and the amount they apply.

Going green also applies to the facilities where the wines are made. Niagara is home to the world's first Leadership in Energy and Environmental Design (LEED)–certified winery building at Stratus Vineyards. It was a designation achieved thanks to incorporating recycled materials in the winery's construction, using geothermal heating and cooling and landscaping with native plant species, among other features.

At Niagara-on-the-Lake's Southbrook Vineyards, proprietor Bill Redelmeier is a passionate proponent of producing biodynamic wines. He grows sixty acres of grapes according to the rules of Rudolph Steiner, biodynamic agriculture's founder. Taking his cues from the earth below his feet and the planets in the sky above has paid off. Southbrook was named Canadian winery of the year in 2012 by the InterVin International Wine Awards.

Vineland's Tawse Winery, also certified biodynamic, was named Canada's winery of the year three years running—in 2010, 2011 and 2012—by the Canadian Wine Awards.

Those producing organic and biodynamic wines say their vintages are a truer reflection of terroir—that sense of place that comes through in a wine's taste—compared with their conventional counterparts. Not spraying grapes with chemicals spares the natural yeasts on the fruit's skin so they don't need to be added during fermentation.

Redelmeier compares it to baking bread with a homemade starter versus store-bought yeast that anyone can use. "The really interesting bread, the really artisanal bread with the sourdough, if I make bread like that, it's going to be different than my neighbour's," he explains. "The yeast that comes on the grapes that most people kill [by spraying their grapes] is like the sourdough. I want to make wine interesting. I don't want to make wines that my neighbour is making. I want to make something different. The whole point of biodynamics is to make the best, most interesting wine possible."[59]

Having been the grandfather of the movement locally, Gemmrich is just happy to see such production methods finally taking root here, let alone the success of those who have adopted them. "It makes me proud of myself sometimes," he says. "It's like you stepped on a stone, it became loose and it started rolling downhill and you had a movement happening."[60]

Niagara's Organic and Biodynamic Wineries

Frogpond Farm (Certified organic)
1385 Larkin Road
Niagara-on-the-Lake
frogpondfarm.ca

Ravine Vineyard (Certified organic, uses biodynamic methods)
1366 York Road
St. Davids
ravinevineyard.com

Reimer Vineyards (Certified organic)
1289 Line 3
Niagara-on-the-Lake
reimervineyards.com

Southbrook Vineyards (Certified biodynamic)
581 Niagara Stone Road
Niagara-on-the-Lake
southbrook.com

Tawse Winery (Certified biodynamic)
3955 Cherry Avenue
Vineland
tawsewinery.ca

The Future: The Glass Is Half Full

From his office at the top of the tower at Vineland Estates Winery, Allan Schmidt has an eagle's-eye view of his sprawling vineyards on the cusp of the Niagara Escarpment. Schmidt's vantage point as president and managing partner of the mid-sized winery in west Niagara has also given him valuable perspective on the region's wine industry as a whole.

In 2013, Schmidt brought those insights with him to the Wine Council of Ontario when he was elected board chair of the organization tasked with supporting and promoting the production of 100 percent Ontario wines and their vintners. He plans to use that wisdom during his tenure to successfully work through an ambitious to-do list that he has been compiling for more than twenty-five years. It's filled with issues dating back to when he first arrived in Ontario, via the wine industry in British Columbia, to serve as winemaker and general manager at Vineland for its founder Herman Weis.

Turn the clock back to that time in the late 1980s, and it was the advent of the Canada-U.S. Free Trade Agreement—that "catalyst for waking the industry up." Free trade did away with preferential markups on wines from Ontario's twenty-five wineries at the time and forced them to compete with cheaper imports at the province's government-run liquor stores. The agreement also saw labrusca grapes—Concord, Niagara, Catawba and Delaware, among others—banished from wine production, with the Ontario

The Niagara Wine Festival in Montebello Park in St. Catharines celebrates the grape harvest every September. *Photo by Nathaniel David Johnson.*

government giving $145 million to grape growers to yank their vines and replace them with vinifera or European varieties, such as Chardonnay, Riesling and Cabernet Franc to make high-quality wines. It was a time that also bore the Vintners Quality Alliance (VQA), which worked to differentiate pure Ontario wines from the blends of imported and domestic grape juice and catapult local wines to the world renown they have today.

Despite all that free trade did to bolster the industry, it's the reason why Schmidt's task list as Wine Council chair is as long as it is and his goals as lofty. "Free trade began a split in the industry, which exists today and is probably one of the biggest irritants in the industry today," he explains.[61]

Here's what happened: The provincial government, which holds the monopoly on booze sales through its Liquor Control Board of Ontario (LCBO), put a moratorium on new wine stores when free trade came into effect. But it grandfathered those that already existed and were owned by two major wine conglomerates, Vincor Canada Ltd., now part of Constellation Brands, and Andrés Wines Ltd., now Andrew Peller Ltd. At the time, Schmidt recalls the province said the moratorium wouldn't last, but twenty-five years later, it's still in place, giving the big wineries access to even bigger market share thanks to their nearly three hundred additional retail outlets often located in busy grocery stores. Meanwhile, every other Niagara, and Ontario, winery has to rely on sales in their tasting rooms and fight with one another for limited shelf space at LCBO stores to reach consumers outside Niagara.

So tops on Schmidt's to-do list is to loosen the LCBO's grip on the liquor market and open up retailing to include a combination of government-run and private stores. Not only would it give wineries more—and perhaps easier—access to thirsty consumers, Schmidt and the Wine Council figure that the creation of private stores operating in tandem with government outlets will create 5,600 new jobs in Ontario. "There's not a program in Ontario proposing 5,000 new jobs, so if we want new jobs, here you go," Schmidt says.

Having both types of stores while keeping the LCBO as the importer and distributor of wine to all retail outlets—similar to the system in British Columbia—could rake in $290 in markups and taxes per capita versus the current $120. That's money that could go toward new hospitals, roads and other important infrastructure, Schmidt notes. "We don't have an issue with the LCBO. It's the best big-box retailer of liquor in the world," he says. "They do it very well. They just don't have enough shelves for all the VQA wines now available. What I'm not for is $120 per person in provincial profit on liquor when we could bring in more money like in British Columbia if we partnered with private stores."

Next on Schmidt's list: ensure that International-Canadian Blend wines are clearly labelled. The cheaper blended tipple that sees Canadian and imported juice mixed together in the same bottle—or in most cases is 100 percent foreign content—only serves to confuse wine drinkers about what is truly a Canadian wine while diluting the Niagara wine brand. International-Canadian Blends account for 73 percent of all wine sales in Ontario, while VQA wines make up 27 percent.[62] That's a sign it's high time to do more to get more VQA, or 100 percent Niagara, wines into consumers glasses, Schmidt says.

"The future of Ontario wine lies in VQA and not blended wine," he asserts. "People think that when they buy a blended wine, they're supporting the Ontario wine industry. News flash: You're not. You're largely supporting the Chilean grape grower, or Bulgarian or Argentinian."

Ideally, Schmidt and the Wine Council want to see VQA wines account for at least half the vintages sold at the LCBO. So why has that been so difficult to achieve? When the North American Free Trade Agreement came into effect in 1993, all new winery licences were granted on the condition that they could use only Ontario grapes in their vintages and not blend with imported varietals. Meanwhile, the Constellation and Peller wineries, which existed pre–free trade, could still top up local grape juice with foreign editions and continue to do so today. Those wines are found in the LCBO, and those nearly three hundred grandfathered wine stores operated under the Constellation and Peller banners.

Doing the math, Schmidt points out that the twenty wineries between Constellation and Peller have access to 100 percent of Ontario's wine-buying market, while VQA wineries, which best represent Niagara, Ontario and Canada, reach only one-third of the market because of the limited outlets where they're allowed to be sold: the winery, LCBO and, as of 2014, farmers' markets.

And yet, there are more than two thousand VQA wines in Ontario, but only three hundred are listed at the LCBO because of a finite amount of shelf space. If a vintner lucky enough to get some of that space doesn't sell $150,000 of tipple a year, it loses its coveted spot, making the winery the only place consumers can purchase that wine. It doesn't help that in order to list one new VQA wine at the LCBO another has to be delisted. As a result, the growth of post–free trade wineries is stifled, and Schmidt predicts fewer new wineries will open in the years to come.

"The problem isn't that we have lots of wine to sell. We have limited shelves," he explains. "There's no winery that's opened in the last ten years that's selling at more than twenty thousand cases a year. Antiquated regulations are forcing new wineries to remain small on a world scale. There's a lot of people who got into the industry with their eyes wide shut. They go, 'Wow, what a great lifestyle.' We have a lot of Bay Street winemakers who come into winemaking as a second career. I often say, if you want to end up with $1 million in the wine industry, start with $2 million."

The disparities that have been created by free trade proved so fractious around the Wine Council board table that, in 2009, Ontario's largest vintners—Constellation, Peller and Colio Estate Wines—split from the council and formed their own lobbying group, the Winery and Grower Alliance of Ontario, to protect their stores and blended wines. They were joined soon after by three other major Ontario wineries: Diamond Estates, Kittling Ridge and Magnotta. Combined, these mega-vintners buy as much as 80 percent of the province's grape crop and produce 90 percent of wines made in Ontario, including VQA vintages.[63]

The parting of ways was prompted in part by the province's plans at the time to increase taxes on wines sold through the private wine stores to pay for the

Oenophiles sample and learn about Riesling at the Riesling Experience hosted by Brock University's Cool Climate Oenology and Viticulture Institute. *Photo courtesy of Cool Climate Oenology and Viticulture Institute.*

Wine Council's marketing of Ontario vintages and a VQA subsidy program at the LCBO while cutting grants that supported International-Canadian Blends.[64] "It caused a huge rift in the industry and made it difficult for government to work with the industry because there were two factions now," Schmidt recalls.

Schmidt speaks with so much conviction and determination that, even though he is clamouring for change as some of his predecessors and other industry advocates previously had done without success, one can't help but believe he will be the guy to finally get the job done. He's as optimistic as he is certain that one day government will look back on the current state of the industry and wonder what took it so long to make these long-awaited changes. If not, there's only one way Schmidt will sum up his tenure with the Wine Council of Ontario.

"Hopefully before my four years is up as Wine Council chair, I'll accomplish that," Schmidt says. "Otherwise, I'll consider my term a failure."

The future of the industry rests with others, too. It's in the hands of up-and-coming winemakers, viticulturists, the researchers supporting the industry and, of course, the wine drinker.

At Brock University, the Cool Climate Oenology and Viticulture Institute (CCOVI) plays a strong role in helping to grow Ontario's wine industry

Scientist Jim Willwerth from Brock University's Cool Climate Oenology and Viticulture Institute tests grapevines for cold hardiness to help growers protect their vineyards. *Photo courtesy of Cool Climate Oenology and Viticulture Institute.*

while raising its profile as well. With three core researchers led by director Debbie Inglis, two additional scientists and a team of fellows and professional affiliates, the thirty-six-member CCOVI team fills a void of outreach services for growers. The institute shares its research findings with those in the vineyard and wine labs to ensure the best vintages possible. CCOVI labs can test juice and wine for critical factors, such as fermentable sugar, acid and finished alcohol levels. The institute monitors fruit development as harvest time nears to help growers decide when they need to get picking. It focuses on protecting vines from winter injury through its VineAlert program, which tests grapevine bud hardiness throughout the cold season so farmers can take steps to mitigate any damage.

CCOVI dedicates researchers to the most pressing issues facing the industry, including preventing the tainting of wine by certain chemical compounds, sparkling wine production and the impact of climate change. Expert tastings to educate wine writers, sommeliers and restaurant staff about highlighting the quality of Ontario tipple is also part of its directive. "Our mandate always from the start was to build up our research expertise to address the priorities of the wine industry," Inglis says.

Brock is also home to an oenology and viticulture program that graduated its first class of future winemakers and viticulturists in 2000. Similarly,

Niagara College established Canada's only fully licensed teaching winery in 2002 and later followed with the Canadian Food and Wine Institute in 2010 to integrate its food and beverage programs. Both were created in anticipation of the growing need for skilled workers in the wine industry. The college's two-year winery and viticulture technician and wine business management programs have turned out winemakers, vineyard managers, retail marketers and players in wine importing and exporting. Its graduates have gone on to produce award-winning vintages in Niagara and throughout the world's old and new winemaking regions.

Niagara is fertile ground for the entrepreneurial winemaker. Though one might need big bucks to build a winery, one only needs a vineyard to make wine and a website to sell it. Virtual wineries are becoming the avenue of choice for talented winemakers to ply their trade without huge investment. Instead, they rent vineyards, free to move to different locations and sign new leases each year in their quest to find and grow the best grapes to make wines of the highest quality. They rent space and equipment from established wineries to crush and ferment the fruits of their labour while the host winery ensures compliance with VQA and other production regulations.

"It's really the only way if you don't have money to buy a winery. This isn't an industry for people with no money," says Kevin Panagapka, a Niagara

Kevin Panagapka, owner and winemaker at 2027 Cellars, a virtual winery. *Photo by Nathaniel David Johnson.*

College graduate and proprietor of 2027 Cellars, one of Niagara's first virtual wineries. "If I had the money, I'd buy a winery, but it's a very long-term business. Nothing in the wine industry moves quickly, and the general rule is that it takes eight years to break even and ten to start turning a profit when you own a winery."

It's the young and the resolute, like Panagapka, who will write the next chapter for the industry—and a more pleasant one at that, industry pioneer Donald Ziraldo predicts. The new generation of winemaker and grape grower is coming to the industry with fresh eyes and free of battle scars.

"The younger generation, that's where you're going to see real progress," surmises Ziraldo, who was instrumental in establishing the industry programs at Brock and Niagara College. "They're going to be confident and cocky because they don't have to deal with the past, which, for a lot of us, is still lingering on."

The future is also in the glass of the young wine drinker, Paul Bosc Jr. of Château des Charmes winery notes. As with older winemakers and grape growers, the former incarnation of the Niagara wine industry as labrusca-driven is still too fresh in the memory of the baby boomer wine drinker.

"They left our industry behind when they got a taste of decent wines from France and Italy. They'll say, 'Yeah, I've heard Ontario wine has improved…but I've been drinking this wine for years. I've visited this winery,'" he explains. "But the young consumer, are they being served Baby Duck? No, it's VQA. In the entire time they've been consumers, the message has been more positive. They don't have the hang-ups their parents have about the industry."

Paving Niagara's Ale Trail

Visit a wine region and the people with the secret to making great vintages aren't just the grape growers and winemakers. In the footnotes of every bottle, kudos could also be given to the local brewmaster. "[There's an] old winemaker's proverb that it takes a lot of beer to make good wine," says Matt Swan, who owns Silversmith Brewing Company in Niagara-on-the-Lake with business partner Chris Pontsioen.

So it was only a matter of time before breweries started to pop up in Niagara wine country, creating an unofficial ale trail running parallel to the Niagara Wine Route, which leads tourists and backyard day-trippers from one local winery to the next.

Cian MacNeill of Niagara Oast House Brewers in Niagara-on-the-Lake. *Photo by Mike DiBattista.*

Since 2012, three craft breweries—Silversmith, Niagara Oast House Brewers and Brimstone Brewing Company—have opened to tap into what the region has to offer as a culinary destination. Fundraising efforts to build another bastion of beer called Brothers Brewing Company got underway in early 2014. Together, they join three other brewpubs and one teaching brewery in pouring heady options for beer aficionados and the curious. At the same time, they're relegating as passé beer's reputation as the gateway booze to more refined wine drinking with every small-batch milk stout, farmhouse ale and black lager they sell.

"People's eyes are really opening to beer's diversity and how well it does at the dinner table," explains Cian MacNeill, a partner in Oast House, which, like Silversmith, is located on the main artery into Niagara-on-the-Lake, now nicknamed the Beer Funnel. "That craft beer made with quality ingredients can do as well at the table as wine can, sometimes better. It's coming out of its reputation as a low man's drink."[65]

By definition, craft beer is made by breweries producing fewer than 2.8 million cases of cold ones each year. It was introduced to Niagara when Jon Downing opened the Atlas Brew Pub in Welland in 1986. That was before local wines started winning any major accolades. More than twenty years later, Downing would set up Niagara as a suds centre when he lobbied for a

Inside the Niagara College Teaching Brewery. *Photo by Luke Gillett.*

teaching brewery at Niagara College to fill the void of professionally trained brewers in Canada.

He succeeded, and the 1,500-square-foot Niagara College Teaching Brewery opened in 2010. The program is flooded every year with hundreds of applicants vying for one of thirty-five spaces that open each September. The popularity of studying suds prompted a partnership with Olds College in Alberta to launch a sister program there in 2013, taking some of the pressure off Niagara to turn out the only pro brewmasters in the country.

Students at Niagara ferment one-off experimental beers and also keep the brewery store stocked with a regular repertoire of six styles of brew under the college's First Draft label. The students' handiwork has garnered provincial, national and international awards, including nods at the U.S. Open Beer Championships and the Dublin Craft Beer Cup.

More than learning how to operate a mash tun, students will also grow their own hops to use in their ales, lagers, pilsners and bitters. Oast House also plans to contract local farmers to grow hops, demonstrating that terroir can be reflected as much in a growler as in a wine bottle.[66]

Downing credits the college's program with the growth of craft brewing in wine country. These days, rather than being like oil and water, beer and wine seem to be a perfect pairing, making Niagara a culinary destination

Matt Swan (left) and Chris Pontsioen of Silversmith Brewing Company in Niagara-on-the-Lake. *Photo by Bob Tymczyszyn.*

with broader appeal. In the spring of 2014, the region was the backdrop for three busy craft beer festivals: the Real Canadian Craft Beer Festival, Niagara College's Craft Beer and BBQ Festival and the Albino Rhino Beertuberoolapolooza Festival held at Brimstone in Ridgeway.

"As Niagara attracts more and more attention for the growing culinary culture in addition to its wine, locals and visitors alike deserve a locally produced, high quality, small batch, fresh beer," Swan says. "We look to offer the opportunity to enjoy beer made with the same care and effort that our chefs and vintners are working hard providing."[67]

Niagara's Breweries

Brimstone Brewing Company
209 Ridge Road North
Ridgeway
brimstonebrewing.ca

Merchant Ale House
98 St. Paul Street
St. Catharines
merchantalehouse.ca

Niagara College Teaching Brewery
135 Taylor Road
Niagara-on-the-Lake
firstdraft.ca

Niagara Oast House Brewers
2017 Niagara Stone Road
Niagara-on-the-Lake
oasthousebrewers.ca

Silversmith Brewing
1523 Niagara Stone Road
Niagara-on-the-Lake
silversmithbrewing.com

Syndicate Restaurant and Brewery (Niagara's Best Beer brand)
6863 Lundy's Lane
Niagara Falls
syndicaterestaurant.ca

Taps Brewing Company
4680 Queen Street
Niagara Falls
tapsbeer.ca

Niagara Distilled

Niagara is no slouch with hard stuff, either. The proof is in the award-winning whisky and gin being poured into a growing number of highball and old-fashioned glasses in high-end sipping rooms and hipster hangouts throughout Canada and into the United States.

That success is relatively recent, however, despite the region's modern commercial distilling history going back to 1971, when Swiss eau-de-vie maker Otto Rieder opened a distillery bearing his name in Grimsby to make schnapps with Niagara cherries or pears and brandy with grapes rejected by wineries. The problem was that while he had what undoubtedly would have been a recipe for success with his spirits in Europe, Canadians weren't taken with the potent liqueurs. Rieder stepped away from his stills in 1992, when he retired and sold his operation to veteran winemaker John K. Hall, who added steel tanks for winemaking to Rieder Distillery's copper pot collection.

In an interview with the Grimsby Museum in 2009, Hall recalled Rieder "actually made some excellent, excellent eau-de-vie out of Ontario-grown fruit but his only problem was the marketing of it because people in Canada drank whisky and vodka and rum...so he had limited success and unfortunately the company was ailing."[68]

In 1993, winery licence in hand, Hall relegated Rieder to a handle in the history books and renamed the company Kittling Ridge. He began making handcrafted single-grain whisky, launching the Forty Creek Whisky brand soon after. The move kick-started a renaissance in Canadian whisky production, which had been faltering with distillery closures and consolidations.

Wine accounted for 85 percent of Hall's sales in the beginning, but when his distilling handiwork became the fastest-growing premium Canadian whisky, his artisanal amber elixir eventually traded places with tipple for prominence in the Kittling Ridge portfolio.[69] That shift was formally recognized in 2012, when Kittling Ridge underwent an identity change, marked when Hall switched the sign on his orange brick headquarters overlooking the busy Queen Elizabeth Way to read Forty Creek Distillery. That was also the year Forty Creek won the coveted Canadian Whisky of the Year title for the third time at the Canadian Whisky Awards. Hall's list of other gold and silver medals at national and international competitions for his spirits is as long as a proofing parrot's beak.

His success was enough to pique the interest of big-time investors, and in March 2014, Forty Creek, with sales hovering around $40 million annually, was sold to Italy's Gruppo Campari for $185.6 million. The sale ended Hall's reign as the only independent whisky maker in Ontario, but it was necessary to achieve his dream of taking Forty Creek global.

At the same time, Niagara's new Otto Rieder was working diligently on building his distilling empire down the road in Beamsville, one stylishly labeled bottle at a time. Geoff Dillon opened Dillon's Small Batch Distillers in December 2012 after falling in love with the art of craft distilling while working on his biochemistry degree in university. That curiosity-turned-passion was ingrained in him by his father, Peter, who collected spirits from around the world when Dillon was growing up in Ontario's rugged Muskoka region.

Still, the cherubic proprietor of Niagara's latest line of liquor wasn't convinced there was a career in distilling until he saw an explosion of craft

Geoff Dillon of Dillon's Small Batch Distillers in Beamsville. *Photo by Nathaniel David Johnson.*

distilleries stateside, where the number of small spirit makers doubled between 2010 and 2012 to more than two hundred.[70] Dillon travelled to the United States and United Kingdom to learn more about the business by working at distilleries there. The experience was enough to convince him to put his own name on a booze factory, though it was a tossup between doing it in Niagara or in the Distillery Historic District in Toronto. The small-town boy wasn't keen on creating a life in the hustling, bustling metropolis, however. He was further wooed away from setting up shop in Toronto by a highly visible winery storage building with room for a new tenant that abutted Niagara's stretch of the Queen Elizabeth Way, a highway that gets clogged with tourists every summer.

Then there was Niagara's fruit to further add to the equation for Dillon, whose flagship ferments include a vodka and gin made from grapes. "The big plan was to do something so different that the people in Toronto would want to serve us in their bars," Dillon explains. "Grapes make this beautiful, sweet, smooth viscous base. That sealed the deal."[71]

Dillon buys his grapes from growers after they have thinned their crops or if they've lost contracts with one of the mega-wineries that once bought their fruit. Sometimes Dillon will even purchase excess wine stock from local vintners to turn into his Method 95 vodka or Unfiltered Gin 22, the latter of which took him and Peter four years and the addition of twenty-two botanicals, including hibiscus and lavender, to perfect. An herb garden at the distillery keeps him in supply of some of those ingredients that helped land his gin double gold at the 2014 San Francisco World Spirits Competition.

"Niagara is an absolutely perfect fit," Dillon explains. "We've got the fruit, we've got the farmers as neighbours, and we've got the tourists coming for wine."

These days, they're also coming for the spirits, sampled in a bright tasting room filled with natural wood, white paint and clean lines that make it look like the setting of a photo shoot for *Kinfolk Magazine*. Dillon reached his goal of wowing those Toronto bars he wanted so badly to dazzle and then some. His spirits can be sipped as far away from Niagara as Florida and Alberta. The biggest retailing coup may be landing the fruit spirits he and his father developed on the shelves of the bon vivant's Shangri-La, Williams-Sonoma.

Dillon and assistant distiller Dave Dickson set to work each day with custom-built copper equipment to keep up with the mounting demand. Since opening, they've added a rose gin, absinthe and pear eau de vie to their repertoire. The first ever "ultra-local" rye made with 100 percent Ontario rye and aged in Ontario oak will be released in 2016. For now, the distillery sells its unaged White Rye, which is void of the whisky's usual warm caramel hue imbued by toasted oak barrels.

At all times, there are at least twenty potential products in the research and development stage—experiments headed up by Dillon's dad, Peter. Dillon's father-in-law, Gary Huggins, minds the drier details of the distillery as business manager.

"I still can't believe we have a distillery here and we're making it. Once you have it in a bottle and have a label on it, it's like, 'Wow,'" Dillon says as he pauses in his swoon-worthy sipping room to take stock of his success. "The plan is to keep making new things, making exciting things that keep people coming back."

Dillon's Small Batch Distillers
4833 Tufford Road
Beamsville
dillons.ca

Forty Creek Distillery
297 South Service Road
Grimsby
fortycreekwhisky.com

Chapter 3
From Farm to Table to Curb

The Evolution of Wine Country Cuisine

Cooking demands attention, patience, and above all, a respect for the gifts of the earth. It is a form of worship, a way of giving thanks.
—*Judith B. Jones*

There was a time when tourists flocking to Niagara came for one reason: to check out some water spilling over a cliff, perhaps buy a tacky souvenir and head home. They certainly weren't coming for the food.

The fine dining establishments of the day in the 1970s and for much of the 1980s served frozen vegetables and sauces made from powder to accompany the protein du jour. Starters were tomato juice or fruit cocktail from a can. It left Emil Rinderlin, a classically trained chef who hails from a German wine region, with a bad taste in his mouth. "It was atrociously simple and safe, and there wasn't much knowledge involved," Rinderlin recalls. "Cooking, per se, or chefs, did not exist in Niagara. They were mainly brought in from abroad."[72]

Skills were self-taught among local cooks. Apprenticeships in kitchens and culinary programs were nonexistent in Niagara at the time. Worse yet, chefs working in a region with some of the most unique farmland in Canada weren't taking their cues from local farmers by cooking seasonal fare. "I was shocked because we, in this particular area, had such diverse farming, and we could not get fresh vegetables," Rinderlin laments.

It wasn't always this way at Niagara's dining establishments. One hundred years earlier, long before farm-to-table cuisine became a staple in the foodie's lexicon and modern-day chefs were listing their suppliers on menu cards, it was just the way things were done. A menu from a dinner for the Prince of Wales in 1860 noted that the peaches served were from the farm of Joseph and John Brown, owners of Niagara's first commercial orchard.[73]

Sometime between then and Rinderlin's arrival to Niagara in the late 1960s, using locally grown food in restaurant kitchens was traded for what came from abroad and in a package. There was a certain prestige to using imports over the local bounty, even if the quality of the food suffered as a result. "We got away from the basics, the ability and understanding of what the basics are about and where things came from," he says.

Rinderlin, like other European chefs who came to work in Niagara around the same time, wanted to get back to those basics. He opened Rinderlin's Dining Room in Welland in 1981, bringing in young cooks to be his apprentices. He'd warn them they were about to work in the worst kitchen ever because Rinderlin demanded meat be cooked to order, no vegetables would languish in a steam tray and all sauces would be made from scratch. He taught his staff butchery, bringing in game meats just to expose his team to something different.

By the late 1980s, when Niagara was overhauling its identity as a wine region, he hosted tasting dinners to showcase the local vintages that were fast becoming more palatable. It's true he had to ensure his plates looked full rather than artistic when they left the kitchen so locals wouldn't stigmatize his restaurant as expensive yet leaving one needing a pizza after dinner to feel sated. But everything was made to order. "Nothing hit the pan until the waiter said, 'Pick up table so and so,'" Rinderlin recalls. "Of course, the stress factor is highest, but the satisfaction was higher. Did people appreciate it? I didn't really care. I wanted to do it right."

A decade later, Niagara would beckon another group of classically and internationally trained chefs wielding the same philosophy. They were young and media savvy, their talents giving rise to a culinary brand that became known as Niagara wine country cuisine. They laid the foundation for the region to become a dining destination one plate of bespoke fennel seed and juniper-crusted venison loin with Pinot Noir sauce at a time.

So what exactly is wine country cuisine? It's a philosophical question to those in the industry with answers as varied as how to poach an egg from a locally raised hen. The consensus is that it's food starring local produce, made to order, and it goes well with the wines of the region, making it distinctly Niagara.

The combination of local food and wine were what piqued Michael Olson's interest when he accepted the invitation of Len Pennachetti, president of Cave Spring Cellars, in 1993 to check out the winery in Jordan. Pennachetti wanted Olson to run the kitchen in the café he planned to open alongside Cave Spring. Olson, who was working in Ottawa at the time, came at the most uninspiring time of year. It was mid-March, yet he still saw the potential in turning the village of Jordan into a polestar for the palate. "I thought, 'This is really cool. It's a food-producing area and it could be a food destination,'" Olson recalls.[74]

He took the job and "put my head down like an idiot to build the place. Of course, all the experts said we were stupid for trying to open a restaurant in the middle of nowhere."

Still, Olson got behind the burners with sous-chef Mark Hand at a time when people were starting to be less impressed with every ingredient on their plate being imported from far-flung corners of the globe. The young chef noticed a "complete turnaround" in diners who were growing more interested in dishes featuring food grown nearby. Admittedly, it was a struggle finding local ingredients at first. Most farmers, passed over by Niagara chefs for years, had been selling their harvests to the Ontario Food Terminal in Toronto, where other restaurants and grocery stores would pick it up. As Olson got to know the area, he got to know who was growing what and began curating menus based on what he found driving around the countryside. After his first season at On the Twenty, named for its location in Niagara's Twenty Valley, farmers began lining up at the kitchen door to sell Olson their produce. The media weren't far behind, with big city food writers leaving their comfort zone of Toronto to report on what was happening in Niagara.

By 1995, when Olson's future wife, Anna, joined the team in the kitchen, the restaurant was serving 220 people on a good day. The lineup for a table started forming at 5:00 p.m. "You'd see six bushels of tomatoes coming in and think, 'Oh my God,' but they'd be gone in a day," Anna remembers.[75] Most days, there wasn't time to put produce in the fridge. It would arrive at the restaurant and be used right away or set out in the dining room to ripen while customers marvelled that it wasn't made of wax.

"There almost wasn't a trust in food, but we put the trust in food," Michael Olson says.

Two years later, he would be joined by two other innovative chefs who had been given the reins in winery kitchens to do with food what was being done with the region's wine: make it authentically Niagara while elevating it to world-class standards.

Tony de Luca and Mark Picone built their kitchens in opposite corners of the region: de Luca was the inaugural chef at the restaurant at Hillebrand

Estates Winery (now Trius Winery at Hillebrand) in Niagara-on-the-Lake; Picone helmed the line at Vineland Estates Winery.

De Luca brought with him experience gleaned from stints at Canadian culinary cornerstones, including Toronto's Windsor Arms Hotel, and abroad at the Michelin-starred Chewton Glen in southern England. De Luca had also worked under some of Canada's biggest names in cheffing: Michael Bonacini and Marc Thuet. That experience would help him shake up a dining scene dominated by "very English" menus of thick steaks and lobster tails. The focus of most local fine dining establishments in Niagara-on-the-Lake, often adjoining swanky hotels, was on feeding three hundred tables quickly rather than innovatively, de Luca recalls.

Shortly after de Luca's arrival in Niagara, he got a call from Olson, who offered to share his farmer contacts. De Luca, who cut his teeth in cutthroat kitchens where backstabbing was served up daily, was caught off-guard by the gesture—suspicious, even. Still, he accepted Olson's offer and got an even clearer sense of what he was to achieve at Hillebrand after seeing ripening vegetables posing as a centrepiece in Olson's dining room. "I realized that was wine country cuisine, the provenance," de Luca says. "Michael Olson is such a genius in conviviality."[76]

The camaraderie that phone call and subsequent meeting created only helped to further a common goal of making Niagara a gourmand's Garden of Eden.

One of de Luca's own contributions to Niagara wine country cuisine was imparting the concept of a forager as a way to source local ingredients. He got the idea during a stint he did in Napa, where restaurants had runners to find the freshest foods from farms and market gardens in the area. De Luca secretly put John Laidman, the father of his pastry chef, Tara Laidman, on the payroll to roam the countryside in search of daily culinary inspiration. Laidman often sent Tara to work with offerings from his garden, but his fate as forager was sealed after he and de Luca shared a flat of local strawberries Laidman delivered one day to the Hillebrand kitchen. "It was gluttony. I told him bring me this stuff. I'll pay for it out of pocket," de Luca remembers.

Eventually, the chef convinced his bosses to consider Laidman staff, offering up his own job as collateral if the arrangement proved too costly or failed. Today, Laidman's foraging enterprise has grown to include several restaurants.

De Luca also put ads in the local weekly asking farmers to bring him their goods. "I had this old woman come to me with a jar of pansies, and I said, 'OK, here's ten dollars.' I wanted to be the guy who bought everything. It wasn't just about the food but about terroir in the full sense. It encapsulates the producer, the earth, the weather," de Luca explains. "My costs weren't always in line. They could have fired me at any time, but they didn't."

There was little reason to come down on the chef because his unorthodox ways earned the restaurant at Hillebrand four stars in the esteemed *Toronto Life* magazine, a glossy devoured by potential culinary tourists. He was the first chef in Niagara to achieve such a review.

Meanwhile, in Vineland, an exacting and meticulous Picone was cooking up the recipe that would turn the restaurant at Vineland Estates Winery into a culinary crown jewel for the region. Picone, who hails from a food family—his grandparents started Picone's Fine Foods in Dundas, Ontario—spent five years in kitchens in France and Italy when he was asked by John Howard, then owner of Vineland Estates, to cater the Cuvée gala wine awards in 1996. It ended up being his audition to head up the restaurant at the winery, which he would go on to do for nine years. In that time, he and his team—"It's always about the team," Picone stresses—made the five tables at Vineland vessels for world-class dining at every service. He had a level of autonomy in the kitchen that enabled him to "put us on the culinary map." That success was rooted in relying on the farms surrounding the winery to provide Picone with his muses in the kitchen. It's local agriculture, he maintains, that enabled wine country chefs to give Niagara some culinary cachet.

"If we don't have farmers, if we don't understand it begins with the farmers, the suppliers dedicated to working the land, foraging, sourcing, we would not be able to do what we do," Picone asserts.[77]

Though local gastronomes readily credit him with being one of the culinary masterminds who helped create Niagara wine country cuisine, Picone is uncomfortable with such a notion. He sooner points to chefs like Rinderlin and Mark Walpole at the Prince of Wales Hotel for starting the movement.

"I would never say we're the fathers of Niagara cuisine. That would be erroneous," Picone humbly maintains. "We're the grandsons or sons of Niagara cuisine. We capitalized on the media attention at the time. We also capitalized on the wineries having food service."

The hotels in the area started to take notice. In 1994, the posh Queen's Landing in Niagara-on-the-Lake landed Stephen Treadwell in its kitchen. The British-born chef cooked up major media buzz while he was at Toronto's Auberge du Pommier, considered one of the best French restaurants in the country. He did the same for the Tiara Dining Room at Queen's Landing, staying until 2006, when he opened Treadwell Farm-to-Table Cuisine, a culinary mecca unto itself, first on the waterfront in Port Dalhousie and then in a return to Niagara-on-the-Lake in 2013.

Chef Mark Picone is one of the pioneers of Niagara wine country cuisine and helped make the region a culinary destination. *Photo by Nathaniel David Johnson.*

Meanwhile, the Prince of Wales Hotel had already been putting its trust in a local chef, Mark Walpole, to make its name synonymous with more than just opulent lodgings. Walpole's early days of cookery were in some of those kitchens pushing out those plates of frozen vegetables that made Rinderlin cringe. Walpole, a formally trained chef, was twenty-nine when he was tapped in 1984 to take over the hotel's kitchen. Owner Henry Wiens told his young culinarian to "do what you do best within these four walls and don't worry about what the rest are doing," Walpole remembers. "We looked inward, not outward, so we were constantly improving."

Wiens wanted the restaurant to embrace the local wine industry. Walpole did that by hosting wine dinners before they were popular, he says. He had his own gardener to grow herbs and bartered with backyard gardeners for their harvests. Walpole purchased game from Arden Vaughn at Lake Land Meats. His trout came from a fish farm in Fonthill. Word got out among farmers that they should bring their wares to Walpole because he was open to using them in the Prince of Wales kitchen. When he left in 1996, Walpole witnessed a sea change in fine dining in Niagara.

"There was a difference in the product available. When I started in the business, vegetables were frozen," he explains. "When I worked at the Skylon

Tower [in Niagara Falls], we weren't cleaning vegetables. We were thawing broccoli and serving 1,200 people a night."

He was grateful when Olson, de Luca, Picone and Treadwell arrived to further propel local dining into its own prestigious brand. "It was nice to be joined. I knew a lot of other chefs in the area, but they were not as forward-thinking," Walpole says.

There's no denying the effect this quintet of cuisiniers had on Niagara, taking some of the burden off the Falls as the main tourist draw. "We created a culture here in Niagara that made it a destination people come to for the food," Picone says. "It was always a world-class destination, but now that we have people making great wine and great food, it attracted more people."

Emil Rinderlin was just happy to see kitchens finally eschew tomato juice appetizers and start doing scratch cooking with what has always been here: farm-fresh ingredients. "They said, 'Oh, this is regional now,'" he says with a wry grin about the movement that was afoot at the time. "But anything that improves the cuisine in a region is good. It was for the betterment of all."

Second Course:
The Next Generation of Wine Country Chef

The fathers of Niagara wine country cuisine continue to leave their indelible mark on the region's culinary culture today. Play a game of six degrees of separation in a local restaurant kitchen and odds are someone has been taught or mentored by one of them. Today, Olson, de Luca and Picone pass on their expertise in culinary labs at Niagara College's Canadian Food and Wine Institute rather than their own restaurant kitchens.

The new generation of wine country chef is using the knowledge gleaned from its predecessors to not only carry on their legacies but also to push the dinner plate a little further.

Ryan Crawford, who apprenticed under de Luca at Hillebrand, went on to win awards and praise from some of the best-fed critics in the industry as he built a hole-in-the-wall eatery in a Niagara-on-the-Lake strip mall into one of the most coveted reservations in the region.

Today, animal husbandry has become part of his job description. Crawford has ventured out on his own in search of some land upon which he and his wife, Beverley Hotchkiss, hope to build a restaurant that combines gastronomy and farming in the same location, similar to an Italian

Chef Ryan Crawford is one of the new generation of wine country chefs helping to shape Niagara's culinary identity. *Photo by Nathaniel David Johnson.*

agriturismo. As they search for their "gastrohomestead," Crawford contracts out his culinary talents seasonally to local wineries that offer al fresco dining. He has raised heritage breed pigs for house-made charcuterie and entrées starring all parts of the animal. He also makes his own wine and grows his own vegetables. Crawford's goal is to not just make Niagara a food region but also to create a food movement here.

"We go out the morning before service, pick things and figure out what we're going to do, then go for it," Crawford says. "It makes you respect things that much more when you plant the tomatoes, you weed the tomatoes, you rototill the tomatoes. There's less waste, which is what we need."[78]

At Ravine Vineyard in St. Davids, chefs Paul Harber and Nathan Young are making and serving the food they like to eat. Both have worked overseas and with some of the most influential Canadian chefs—Harber with Michael Stadtländer and Young with Anthony Walsh. Harber has also worked with de Luca at Hillebrand while Young was executive sous-chef to Frank Dodd, de Luca's successor at the winery. "You work with all these different chefs and you get different philosophies. You get to a point in your life where you want to do what you want to be doing," Young says.[79]

For both, that includes keeping the menu small, focusing on local ingredients, including homegrown ones they preserve so they can have local bounty to get them through winter. Add to that one of the most serene settings in Niagara overlooking a vineyard in a rustic yet polished dining room, and Ravine Vineyard has one of the most successful recipes for a dining experience.

Young and Harber fed more than 50,000 people in 2013. When they started, they figured they'd feed 70 people a day at lunch. Soon they were

Chefs Paul Harber (left) and Nathan Young of Ravine Vineyard. *Photo by Nathaniel David Johnson.*

hosting 300 diners, but they scaled back to "control the experience more," serving a maximum of 140 people for lunch and dinner. Harber explains, "It's a small profit margin to bring quality to the table that we don't want to scrimp on."[80]

Though a winery restaurant, Ravine Vineyard stands in stark contrast to those where wine country cuisine really started to take shape in the 1990s. Many in the industry argue the big winery restaurants, whose existence is as much about selling wine as feeding people a gourmet meal, are no longer the calling card for culinary adventurers that they used to be.

"Local chefs today are not lionized as they once were," Picone notes. "As much as for what the chefs do, it also reflects that people now do not have the same disposable income. Lobster bisque may have been super premium once but it is no longer about prestige."

As a result, the winery restaurant model of the Olson, de Luca and Picone era has become outdated, depending on whom you ask. People are choosing to forgo white linen and jaw-dropping tabs for something more relaxed and regularly attainable.

At The Good Earth in Beamsville, owner Nicolette Novak turned her family's orchard into a destination, starting with a cooking school in 1998 when agritourism was nonexistent. The concept threw the municipality for a loop. There were no zoning bylaws to deal with it, but Novak persevered, eventually adding a restaurant with an al fresco kitchen where you won't find a stitch of tablecloth or servers dressed in formal black-and-white uniforms. "It started with the idea to invite select people to suspend their disbelief and drive down this laneway to spend three hours enjoying themselves with laughter," Novak explains.[81]

In 2008, she added a winery to "bring the fun we had on the food side to wine" and create that *agriturismo* feel in Niagara wine country. Novak isn't convinced she would call what she does wine country cuisine, however. Nor is she convinced the concept of wine country cuisine actually exists in Niagara. "We talk about it a lot and pretend, but I'm not so sure. Vineland Estates, On the Twenty and Treadwell have done a great job," she explains. "I sometimes get discouraged by the food scene, though. It's food, kids. That's all it is. This stuff about how it comes from John Smithers' garden and his dog Al peed on it—it's gotten precious. It's disingenuous really. Len Pennachetti put it best when he said we suffer from affluenza. What we do here, we really just focus in on providing fresh, well-made, honest food for people. Whether that's leading edge or pioneer, I don't think so."

Chef Justin Downes of Vineland Estates Winery, part of the new generation of wine country chef. *Photo by Nathaniel David Johnson.*

If the winery restaurant that Picone refers to has become an unappetizing anachronism, no one has told forager John Laidman. He's still busy with regular deliveries to his Niagara-on-the-Lake chefs. "In the summer, we're delivering a huge amount of food for them to not be selling," he says.[82]

Still, there's a difference between the wine country cuisine being cooked up in Niagara-on-the-Lake wineries and that of west Niagara, notes Justin Downes, chef at Vineland Estates Winery, which is located in the latter. "Twenty Valley wine country cuisine is more comfortable. Our philosophy here is simple. Our food speaks for itself, and our menu reads that way. It's well balanced and a little bit of everything. The food also goes with the wine. It's good, it's elegant."[83]

Downes started as a dishwasher at the winery restaurant with no real interest in cooking until the chef at the time, Mark Picone, saw something in him and "pushed and guided" him to be the thoughtful, talented culinarian who continues to keep Vineland on the dining map. Downes has embraced the same philosophies as his mentor: teamwork and turning out high-quality food made with local fare in a world-class setting. Yes, there are tablecloths at Vineland, but white linen and the relaxed dining that people crave today versus twenty years earlier when wine country cuisine was just getting its bearings don't have to be mutually exclusive, he says.

"One thing you can't take away is that we're still a winery restaurant. I don't think we'll ever get away from that. They're very much a staple in this region."

Wine Country Cuisine Hits the Streets

A new way of dining rolled into Niagara in 2010. It eschewed the white linen of winery restaurants, even renouncing plates, unless they were compostable. That summer, Ontario's first food truck, El Gastrónomo Vagabundo, pulled into the peninsula to serve up fresh, made-to-order fare in a way that had previously been reserved for hot dogs and pre-fab finger foods: at the curb.

The proprietors of El Gastrónomo, Australian-born chef Adam Hynam-Smith and his Canadian partner-turned-wife, Tamara Jensen, came for the comestible inspiration that Niagara's farms offered and stayed for the culinary revolution that ensued, thanks to their meals on wheels.

They invigorated local dining by bringing gourmet food to a more casual setting that, with the help of social media to announce menus, hours and locations, beckoned the young, hip and hungry with cleverly named tacos filled with five-spice Berkshire pork belly, deep-fried mozzarella or cod dressed with habanero and pineapple hot sauce. Salads and soups inspired by the formally trained Hynam-Smith's travels in Asia and Africa rounded out the day's offerings, scrawled on a scuffed chalkboard.

Their approach appealed to a new kind of culinary tourist who might otherwise have bypassed Niagara's more formal—and typically more expensive—gourmet settings where the menus might change seasonally rather than daily. The duo also inspired other chefs and entrepreneurial gourmands to trade a stationary kitchen for a mobile galley in the back of a converted courier cube van. It's safe to say the filterless Hynam-Smith and his foil Jensen are the patriarch and matriarch of Ontario's gourmet food truck movement and, with it, a new kind of wine country cuisine that's more about rubbing shoulders with fellow diners than staying tucked in at a table to interact only with one's date and server.

Tamara Jensen and chef Adam Hynam-Smith of St. Catharines–based El Gastrónomo Vagabundo, Ontario's first gourmet food truck. *Photo by Tiffany Mayer.*

"There's the idea that in wine country, you're going to have dinner at a table with a white tablecloth, and sure, people are going to do that," Jensen says. "But people want variety."

"Food is more about the overall experience of who's there with you," Hynam-Smith adds. "It's a celebration. You're sharing company, you're experiencing a new environment. It shouldn't be repetitive."

Still, operating a food truck in Niagara—or Ontario, for that matter—hasn't been an easy ride. The concept of fresh food being peddled out of the back of a truck was so foreign here when Hynam-Smith and Jensen showed up that existing health and food safety regulations were a major impediment to doing business. Rules only allowed for the sale of food prepared or packaged off-site, which was the antithesis of El Gastrónomo's modus operandi.[84]

Municipalities weren't prepared for roving kitchens, either. Bylaws allowing trucks to pull up to a curb in a city centre or park and serve bespoke lunches or dinners were either nonexistent or prohibitive. For its first few years in Niagara, El Gastrónomo could park only on private property to which it had been invited. Wineries that didn't have a restaurant attached to them willingly rolled out the welcome mat, seeing the truck as a magnet for tourists who wanted a bite and a bottle of wine to go. They were especially keen on drawing the upwardly mobile twenty-somethings with money to spend, who were starting to take an interest in wine.

There have been other bumps in the road. Bricks-and-mortar restaurants have railed against the presence of food trucks, fearing curbside eateries will take a bite out of their customers and bottom line. The result has been heated fights at city halls, with food truck owners on the defensive as they try to convince the powers-that-be not to trounce on their entrepreneurial endeavours over unfounded fears that diners will cancel restaurant reservations at the sight of a mobile eatery. Other restaurants, unafraid of the perceived competition, have come out in support of food trucks, seeing the roving kitchens as complementary, offering small bites to whet appetites for what else the region's dining scene has to offer.

In 2012, the City of St. Catharines became a model for other municipalities with the launch of a pilot program that would license a limited number of trucks, establish clear boundaries for where they could operate in proximity to restaurants and reevaluate how it worked. So far, El Gastrónomo and others in the growing convoy of food trucks here in Niagara have only proven critics wrong.

Niagara is now home to one of the largest food truck festivals in Ontario—Food Truck Eats at Peller Estates Winery—where thousands come over three days in May to step up to truck windows for orders of oysters, pulled pork in umpteen incarnations, smoked meat poutine, vegan tostadas, burgers topped with peanut butter, fish tacos and cupcakes. In addition to El Gastrónomo, Niagara now boasts trucks proffering pies, both sweet and savoury, oysters, wood-fired pizza and a solar-powered model offering classic farm-to-truck fare.

Now that other municipalities have decided yea or nay to allowing trucks, food trucks from other cities want the opportunity to feed people in a region with a reputation as a culinary destination. While Hynam-Smith and Jensen can pat themselves on the back for helping to pave the way for food truck culture to thrive, they aren't celebrating their coup. They're more concerned about one bad truck spoiling the whole bunch now that Niagara is a food truck beacon. They don't want to see trucks pulling up at wineries with little concern for health regulations.

Some industry stalwarts see food trucks as fleeting, nothing more than a food fad. But Hynam-Smith and Jensen maintain that the new generation of wine country chef is doing "courageous things with food, and as a result, customers are more adventurous." Those chefs also know that people are

Mike Langley of Niagara's Tide and Vine Oyster Co. serves up oysters at Food Truck Eats at Peller Estates Winery, one of Ontario's largest food truck festivals. *Photo by Tiffany Mayer.*

"crying out for more places to eat" and are even recommending a stop at the food truck. The diner only stands to benefit from this type of cooperation, the food truckers say.

"We all need to work together to drive [dining] standards up," Hynam-Smith says. "If we don't, we're all going to suffer together."

Chapter 4
Food Fighters

The Quest for Change at the Dinner Table

When we eat together, when we set out to do so deliberately, life is better, no matter what your circumstances.

—*Thomas Keller*

For all its beauty, Niagara has its share of scars. As a region whose driving economic force had been manufacturing for many decades, Niagara got walloped in late 2008, when the economy tanked and the world was dragged into a full-blown recession.

Early 2009 became Niagara's winter of discontent, with the local economy hemorrhaging good-paying factory jobs. The region's jobless rate rivaled only Windsor, Ontario, for worst in Canada at 9.5 percent.[85] By that summer, it lurched toward 11.0 percent.[86]

Manufacturing monoliths, including John Deere and one of two General Motors plants, shuttered and became symbols of urban decay. Niagara's historically low family incomes and literacy levels left little in the way of resilience to temper the economic crisis.

The dinner table, once a place where family and food provided refuge from a day's hardship, had now become a stark reminder of the dire situation in which some found themselves. People's abilities to feed themselves had eroded with their income security.

Food banks felt the pressure of mounting food insecurity and continue to do so in the years since the recession started. They are faced with growing client lists and a greater need than ever to help those chewed up and spit out by an economy whose pulse is still weak five years after it crashed. By early 2014, Niagara had the worst unemployment rate in all of Ontario at nearly 9 percent.[87] More than twelve thousand people, about one-third of whom were children, used food banks—a number that has only swelled since 2008.[88]

All levels of government have poured big money into major construction and cultural projects in the region with the hopes of rebooting the local economy. Meanwhile, local social organizations and residents with bigger hearts than budgets have stepped up to ensure that not only is there room at the dinner table for everyone but that there is also enough to eat.

Setting the Table

Scott Ritchie sips a cup of coffee at a bar-height table occupying a parking space on St. Catharines' main drag, St. Paul Street. Across the road, a wall of blue scaffolding marks the spot where several buildings have been razed to make way for a city-run performing arts centre that will feature dance, film, concert and recital halls. Since being hinted at in the mid-2000s, the centre has been championed as a cornerstone of revitalization efforts for a downtown long neglected by councils and bypassed by residents on their way to the box stores and chain restaurants that sucked the soul out of the city centre.

The table occupied by Ritchie, a young urban design planner with the city, will be gone in a few months, along with the simple deck structure upon which it and two other tables sit outside a Korean restaurant, sandwich shop and café. But as easily as the entire arrangement disappears, it—and others like it along St. Paul—will reappear in the spring.

They're called pop-up patios, an idea Ritchie borrowed from San Francisco, which turned pavement into parks with temporary structures called parklets. St. Catharines' versions are fleeting setups stretching from the edges of sidewalks into on-street parking spaces, enabling eateries to have the outdoor seating otherwise absent from St. Catharines' downtown streetscape.

The structures are sponsored and maintained by local businesses, mainly restaurants, allowing diners to spill onto sidewalks instead of being squirrelled away indoors. Pop-up patio users don't even have to be customers of the restaurant maintaining the space. They can bring their bagged lunches, thermoses of coffee or water and become a part of something more meaningful through the act of eating at a shared table and breaking bread with friends, co-workers, neighbours and even strangers.

It's a low-cost way of creating public space where people want to be, Ritchie says. At least one café owner has noticed increased business thanks to the people converging outside, who are drawing in passersby for a bite. "The last thing we wanted to do was get in the way of making downtown more hospitable. We had business owners who kept coming to us saying they wanted sidewalk cafés, and we kept saying, 'Sorry guys, the space is too tight,'" Ritchie says.[89] "If there's not room on the sidewalk, why not the street? It puts the onus on the business and what they value. Do they value the parking spaces or twelve more customers for lunch?"

Really, Ritchie notes, the communal tables are placeholders until St. Paul Street is rebuilt to include wider sidewalks that can accommodate proper patios and more people—something that will be done in tandem with the art centre's construction. "People attract people. This makes downtown dining more sociable," he says. "You're going to run into people you know on the sidewalk, watch the traffic go by, meet the characters. Even if you're just having coffee, it makes you feel part of the community more instead of being huddled in a corner inside."

Meal Preparation

Some of the newest titles at the Grimsby Public Library sound like the makings of a gripping read. There's Bull's Blood, Black Valentine, Tom Thumb and Bountiful, but they don't come from any bestselling authors and aren't shelved under the genres they conjure. Despite their names ranging from mysterious to cute, they all share similar plots, however: achieve food literacy through gardening.

The titles are part of a seed library. In 2012, the Grimsby library expanded its collection to include heirloom vegetable seeds, lending them out to patrons on the condition that they return them at the end of the gardening season after growing them in their own patch of soil and harvesting the seeds their crops produce. To help budding growers along the way, the library offers a series of gardening workshops rather than pointing seed borrowers to how-to titles on the shelves so they can figure out the art and skill of growing food on their own. Recipes are also posted to a blog to inspire green thumbs with their harvests of green zebra tomatoes in the kitchen.

Librarian Colleen Lipp shows off some of the vegetables grown using seeds from the Grimsby Public Library's seed library. *Photo by Tiffany Mayer.*

Former deputy chief librarian Adrienne Charette saw seed libraries sprouting up alongside book lending services in the United States, and having one in fertile Niagara only made sense. The only of its kind in the region, the Grimsby seed library is galvanizing other book depositories keen to stay relevant and attract new patrons.

"It was a natural progression for us and [producing food] is what the Niagara region does well," says chief librarian Colleen Lipp. "From a librarian's perspective, we're always looking for ways to get people in the door, that we're not all about books and shushing people when they walk through the door."

Lipp and her staff even test out their own gardening prowess, planting a few tomatoes, peppers and beans in pots on the library's underused patio. She laughs as she points out how the control plant, a grocery store garden centre tomato, thrives compared to those library seeds staff sowed and nurtured through the season. Still, the scraggly stems with spent leaves now curling in the early fall sun have turned out some decent harvests that were quickly devoured and have given staff and patrons new perspective on both food and their local library.

Fruit grower Torrie Warner picks apples in his Beamsville orchard. *Photo by Tiffany Mayer.*

Every year, Niagara welcomes more than 2,600 migrant workers from the Caribbean and Mexico to work on local farms. *Photo by Jane Andres.*

Lake Land Meats proprietor Arden Vaughn feeds her hens on her St. Catharines farm. *Photo by Tiffany Mayer.*

Wine country chef Tony de Luca helped to establish Niagara as a culinary destination. *Photo by Tiffany Mayer.*

Peaches are the largest stone fruit crop grown in Niagara. *Photo by Nathaniel David Johnson.*

Paul Bosc Sr. (left) and Paul Bosc Jr. in the vineyard at Château des Charmes winery in Niagara-on-the-Lake. *Photo courtesy of Château des Charmes.*

Chef Nathan Young from Ravine Vineyard barbecues ribs at the Niagara-on-the-Lake SupperMarket. *Photo by Melinda Cheevers.*

Harvesting corn in Wainfleet. *Photo by Tiffany Mayer.*

Above: Shirley and Rick Ladouceur of Chez Nous Farms in Stevensville. *Photo by Tiffany Mayer.*

Right: Mario Pingue (left) and brother Fernando of Niagara Food Specialties, which specializes in prosciutto. *Photo courtesy of Niagara Food Specialties.*

Above: Bacon and eggs with house-cured prosciutto and fresh egg mousse by chef Ryan Crawford. *Photo by Nathaniel David Johnson.*

Left: Michael Wasyliw, a volunteer with Start Me Up Niagara, harvests corn at the organization's garden in Vineland. *Photo by Nathaniel David Johnson.*

Peach blossoms. *Photo by Nathaniel David Johnson.*

Sorting grapes during harvest at Inniskillin Wines. *Photo by Scott Rosts.*

Shoppers check out the produce of Campden farmer Tom Neufeld at the St. Catharines Farmers' Market. *Photo by Nathaniel David Johnson.*

Research scientists Valerio Primomo (left) and David Liscombe are trying to create a better-tasting greenhouse tomato at the Vineland Research and Innovation Centre. *Photo courtesy of Vineland Research and Innovation Centre.*

Simon Kelly and Angela Peebles of The Regal Diner in Niagara Falls. *Photo by Nathaniel David Johnson.*

Ruth Anne Schriefer of The Pie Plate Bakery & Café in Niagara-on-the-Lake. *Photo by Nathaniel David Johnson.*

Scallops and quail breast prepared by chef Mark Picone. *Photo by Nathaniel David Johnson.*

Chocolatier Rebecca Nigh of Nigh's Sweet Shop in Stevensville. *Photo by Nathaniel David Johnson.*

Charcuterie at Ravine Vineyard. *Photo by Nathaniel David Johnson.*

Fresh produce at the Welland Farmers' Market. *Photo by Nathaniel David Johnson.*

A student harvests grapes for icewine at Niagara College. *Photo by Luke Gillett.*

At the pass at Benchmark Restaurant at Niagara College's Canadian Food and Wine Institute. *Photo by Luke Gillett.*

Celebrating icewine at the Niagara Icewine Festival in Niagara-on-the-Lake. *Photo courtesy Niagara Wine Festival.*

German plums growing in Torrie Warner's Beamsville orchard. *Photo by Tiffany Mayer.*

A harvester moves through the vineyard at Pilltteri Estates Winery in Niagara-on-the-Lake, collecting grapes for icewine. *Photo courtesy of Pillitteri Estates Winery.*

Vineyards in the summer sun. *Photo courtesy of Pillitteri Estates Winery.*

Kevin Echlin of the Smokin' Buddha in Port Colborne. *Photo by Nathaniel David Johnson.*

"It makes the library a little more approachable. People like to think of librarians as the experts, and clearly we're not. I think people like to come in and tell us what they know," Lipp says. "If you're going to the effort of growing what you're preparing to eat, you're certainly humbled by it and you make the effort to enjoy it a little more."

If seeds have the power to change the perception of a library's role in a community, they can also alter how one sees their own community. Not only do they grow into food that nourishes bodies, seeds—and the places they're planted—nourish neighbourhoods, too.

Jane Hanlon has seen pride grow in some of Niagara's most underused, ignored and downtrodden corners. Spurred to action in 2006 after watching Al Gore's environmental zeitgeist, *An Inconvenient Truth*, Hanlon formed the group Climate Action Now (CAN). The group set out to tackle climate change through community projects focused on such issues as energy conservation and waste reduction. Members, including artists, gardeners and seniors, were also hungry to include food security on the group's to-do list. Some years, it was the group's primary concern, and in 2013, CAN morphed into Greening Niagara, taking on the role of community garden and fruit tree trail builders in Niagara's urban centres. The goal: show communities how to feed themselves.

"We're seeing crop losses globally, sometimes entire crops from a country, taking down the economy with it," Hanlon says, referring to the 2008 rice riots, brought on by shortages and subsequent price hikes of one of the world's most important food staples. As a result, rice became unaffordable for many of the world's hungriest people.

"What does that do for people who want to stretch a dollar and then have to use a food bank? Then there's the quality of food out there. What would you call it? Quasi-food? It fills children's bellies but doesn't provide health."[90]

So Hanlon, whose brusque ways shatter the stereotype of the gentle tree hugger, convinced the City of St. Catharines to let her carve up a barren corner of Centennial Gardens in 2009. At the time, Centennial Gardens was a tired greenspace in one of the city's most beleaguered neighbourhoods. The park had become the backdrop for crime, with dark, overgrown corners for addicts and prostitutes to duck into for a hit or trick. Meanwhile, longtime residents fought with the municipality, police and even one another to restore their desperate corner of the city to its former glory as a safe, inviting refuge from the hustle and bustle surrounding it.

Thanks to Hanlon and Greening Niagara, Centennial Gardens is now home to a twelve-thousand-square-foot community garden, growing from

Jane Hanlon of Greening Niagara in the Centennial Gardens community garden. *Photo by Tiffany Mayer.*

seven thousand square feet when it started. Annual waiting lists fill with names of the area's new Canadians, seniors and low- and middle-income earners eager for a small swath of soil to call their own. For twenty dollars a season, gardeners can grow their own food, and with it, a sense of pride and ownership in their community. Harvests of tomatoes, peppers, chard and crinkly kale mixed with nubbly bitter melon, ground cherries shrouded in paper husks like Chinese lanterns and ginger reflect the diversity of those growing them.

"What we see now is potluck lunches here in a park that used to have high crime," Hanlon says. "It's a family-friendly place now. We have competitions over when to harvest zucchini, who has the best arugula. We have community work days to pull weeds and do transplanting."

More gardens under the Greening Niagara banner have since sprung up in St. Catharines, Welland and Fort Erie. In all, seventeen parcels of land have been set aside to provide food for people of all backgrounds and income levels, "even those from ritzy areas who don't have room for a garden." Centennial Gardens remains Greening Niagara's flagship growing space, however—an example of revitalizing a neighbourhood one tomato plant at a time. "The first thing we do is bring in the community when we want to start a garden and see what they'd like to grow, how they'd like to grow it, how they want to govern it. Then we help design the garden and get it established," Hanlon says.

Workshops on composting and seed saving are often held in conjunction with a potluck to beckon participants, teach them to be more confident gardeners and, in some cases, have them graduate to become sole stewards of the space. "The gardeners want to have a say in things and be part of something, not be listed as followers," Hanlon says. "The gardeners, they're the ones who tell us what needs addressing, and it's in everyone's interest to listen to them."

For as much as Hanlon sees neighbourhoods revitalized by people growing food, Debbie Sexsmith sees renewal in the people themselves. As the garden facilitator for Start Me Up Niagara, the Ridgeway farmer has witnessed how corn, beans, lettuce and eggplant can heal people, and not just because of the nutrition they pack.

Start Me Up Niagara opened in 1999 to help people surviving with mental health issues launch their own businesses. Three years later, the organization added a drop-in centre and, as executive director Susan Venditti recalls, meaningful relationships with clients formed over coffee. "Food was always a way for us to connect with people. In the early days, we had coffee on, and it was a way for people to relax," Venditti recalls.[91]

Start Me Up Niagara's mandate changed over the years as demands for its services grew. These days, its mission is to simply help people who are experiencing difficulty in their lives, be it homelessness, unemployment, mental health issues or drug problems. Meal programs have been added to its list of services, particularly on weekends when neighbouring soup kitchens, serving lunch to hundreds each weekday, close to give staff the chance to recuperate for the next busy week ahead.

To supplement donations Start Me Up Niagara was receiving to fill bellies, the organization struck up a relationship in 2009 with the Vineland Research and Innovation Centre, an agriculture research and plant breeding hub. The centre is equipped with orchards that serve as living labs for growing new varieties of tree fruit, and Start Me Up began sending crews to harvest excess peaches, apples, pears and plums no longer needed for study by scientists. In some cases, the fruit was so new and far from being grown commercially that it didn't even have a name. There was, however, a moniker for what Start Me Up Niagara's clients were experiencing: purpose.

"We have a lot of people who are not overly busy. Why don't we get them in cars and go get food to augment our food program and go get the best food you can get?" Venditti explains.

The relationship blossomed into something bigger when the research station offered Start Me Up Niagara a quarter of an acre of unused land in 2010. It was a blank canvas to turn into a garden to grow fresh food, life skills, reprieve from the hardships Start Me Up's clients might be facing and self-sufficiency for the organization itself. In the years since, and under Sexsmith's leadership in the soil, the plot has grown to two acres, with plenty of social enterprise opportunities coming with it, including selling excess produce to restaurants. It also provides jobs paying above minimum wage for Start Me Up clients wanting to work in the garden.

The priority, though, is growing food for the kitchen back at the organization's headquarters in the Queenston Street neighbourhood of St. Catharines. It's a part of town, not far from where Greening Niagara's Centennial Gardens community garden has flourished, that's known more for its faults of crime, prostitution and poverty than its attributes as one of the city's older, established neighbourhoods.

In 2012, Sexsmith, with the help of Start Me Up clients and volunteers, produced ten thousand pounds of food for as many meals served throughout the year. They're meals that clients help prepare in the kitchen with the organization's Red Seal chef Susan Stevenson. Harvests are also used in

Staff and volunteers at Start Me Up Niagara prepare meatballs for the organization's monthly spaghetti dinner fundraiser. *Photo by Nathaniel David Johnson.*

cooking lessons or sold at a stand in front of Start Me Up's home base in the heart of a food desert with no grocery store nearby. Prices are geared more toward affordability than profit. As a goodwill gesture, volunteers deliver some of the fresh fruits and vegetables to neighbours who will likely never need to tap into the organization's resources, raising Start Me Up Niagara's profile among those living nearby.

"It really has strengthened our organization because people in the community like to see others taking care of themselves," Venditti says. "It's also helped people in the community see our clients in a different light, and we're seeing that by the number of people wanting to volunteer with us and the media coverage we're getting. The people doing this, their self-esteem is growing, their pride is growing and it spreads to this community."

Back at the garden in Vineland, Sexsmith watches as regular helper Michael Wasyliw, rumoured to be the best weeder Start Me Up has, darts in and out of towering sweet corn stalks, picking the freshest ears. He moves nimbly between the crowded rows before emerging with his harvest and hopping on a golf cart to shuttle himself to another plot with snake-like long beans and chard the size of canoe paddles. Nearby, board member Bob Hillier takes a moment to reflect in the garden's labyrinth, equipped with a bench, trellises and tangled vines that provide a lush shroud to those who visit. It's a meditative oasis for anyone needing a quiet moment away from the realities they face back in St. Catharines or a rest from weeding in the garden.

One night a week, the volunteers come here to feast, celebrating their harvests with barbecues and homemade pizza made on site. It gives them the chance to connect with one another while sampling the vegetables they grow and learning how to use them in their own kitchens. The meals draw about twenty-five people, who are there as much for the social outlet as for food that's "a really healthy meal," Sexsmith notes.

The rosy-cheeked farmer has no shortage of stories about the healing that has happened in the garden. She recalls the story of a man nicknamed Farmer Roy, who spent much of his life institutionalized in a group home. He wasn't well liked, "a crotchety old fart," who barely uttered a word to anyone when he walked through Start Me Up Niagara's doors. "When he came out here, he started talking. He started communicating, and from that we discovered he had worked on a farm," Sexsmith says. "People have never seen him be able to express himself. He still comes, and he's hilarious, and he'll leave with food on his face."

"[The garden] is about contributing to something," she adds. "You have a place, you belong. With some, that's key. A lot of folks are on the street or in that world so being able to give and be a contributing part of society is really important. It's therapeutic, really. Now you've got a place to come to, where you belong and can be part of this. Sometimes the people who come here can't really put it into words, but they know they feel better."

Waste Not, Want Not

In an act of what I can describe only as shameless self-promotion as a food blogger, I signed up for a Twitter account in 2009 to broadcast what I hoped would be click bait and draw traffic to my site, Eating Niagara. Soon after, my forays on the social media site provided me with so much more than blog hits. It's where I found inspiration to change something that had been eating at me as a resident of the buckle of Ontario's fruit belt.

Through 140 characters, I discovered a Toronto group called Not Far from the Tree. It was an organization that harvested tree fruit grown in big city backyards and delivered it to local soup kitchens and food banks rather than have it fall to the ground and rot.

I tweeted that they should come to Niagara, where neglected urban fruit trees abound, and establish a chapter here. I had witnessed frustrated homeowners shovelling fallen pears into yard compost bags rather than enjoying the bounty. I walked by homes where the limbs of fruit trees in the yard hung heavy with ignored harvests and wondered if I could help myself. Instead, I watched year after year as the trees went through their cycles of blossoming, fruiting and waiting, unfulfilled, for their season's work to be savoured. I was struck by how we could afford to waste food yet have food banks constantly struggling to meet the needs of the hungry.

In the fall of 2009, I founded The Garden of Eating–Niagara, an organization of one that would put out the call to others to be weekend warriors and rescue unwanted fruit from its fate as compost. I had no idea what I was doing, but it started with a knock on the door of a home with an ignored pear tree, my ladder and a few baskets. Soon, we had our first harvest and our first donation. We collected 550 kilograms of fruit—mostly pears— that autumn and have grown in harvest size and demand for fruit-picking services and donations ever since. As volunteers with full-time jobs and other commitments, our biggest challenge is keeping up with the trees we're offered.

By 2013, we had a career harvest of four thousand kilograms of mulberries, apricots, plums, apples, grapes, berries and pears that were delivered to shelters

Volunteer Ian Watson harvests pears for The Garden of Eating–Niagara to donate to local social organizations. *Photo by Tiffany Mayer.*

and soup kitchens grateful for a fresh alternative to their usual boxed and canned donations with dubious nutritional value. Harvests have been used in canning workshops, helping to resuscitate the art of home preserving. Fruit has also been used in cooking and baking demonstrations, serving up greater self-sufficiency with each sauce or pie produced. I found a champion in a local chef turned high school teacher Michael Gretzinger, who had his students can pears and make crab-apple jelly to donate to local food banks.

Volunteers have also learned the work it takes to get fruit from tree to table and have seen staples of their diet in their natural settings, far removed from the cherry-picked supermarket shelf. It's a small dent, given the tons—I'm not using that term metaphorically—of fruit that still go to waste, but a small contribution has to be better than none.

Irrigating the Food Desert

Something is noticeably absent from downtown St. Catharines. There isn't a single food store to be found. There hasn't been one since 2004, when the last supermarket in the city centre closed. Its departure left residents in need of groceries to rely on a farmers' market, expensive corner stores with limited variety and a discount department store selling sodium-packed canned and frozen foods.

Those with cars could drive the few kilometres to a giant box store, the kind of place where one can buy a new wardrobe with their kale, but those with transit and mobility issues—and often financial ones, as well—were left to cope with a drought of fresh, healthy edibles in a downtown that would remain a food desert for at least the next decade.

A food desert is an area—urban or rural—where access to healthy and affordable food is limited. They are the backdrop against which discussions about food security happen, and in St. Catharines, that conversation began among residents, social organizations and churches in 2011. They were determined to bring more and better food options to downtown dwellers who had gone so long without. They contemplated a grocery bus to shuttle residents to stores or a delivery service to bring food downtown, but the ideas gained little traction. Instead, the goal to irrigate St. Catharines' food desert became more ambitious. Residents decided to build a co-operative grocery store, one that featured local food priced fairly for both farmer and consumer, a community kitchen and a place where customers can be dividend-earning members, enabling them to feel a sense of ownership in their community food store.

"There were a lot of cold, hard realities we had to face," says Karrie Porter, project manager overseeing the development of the Garden City Food Co-op. "We can't have healthy, local food and pay farmers and workers fairly and have cheap food. We realized the benefit to the community would be a store that offers a lot of local food that will pay workers fairly and offer food as cheaply as we can, realizing we can't compete with Walmart."[92]

Porter's motivation for seeing this project through is as much personal as professional. As a St. Catharines resident with two young children and a member of a one-car family living in the city's midtown, she has experienced the frustrations of trying to shop with limited time in an area with equally sparse amenities. Shuttling herself and her children to a supermarket in another neighbourhood still left Porter hungry for more. "When you could buy local apples because they were in season and the store only has one variety of local apples—and I know we grow more varieties—I just think we could do better," she laments.

Modelled after Buffalo's Lexington Co-operative Market, home to a bakery, kitchen, extensive bulk foods section and a rate of return to the local economy of fifty-two cents on every dollar spent, the Garden City Food Co-op began selling memberships in early 2014 with hopes of opening a store in 2015.[93] It's a four-year process to open a co-op, Porter explains, with that time spent fine-tuning financial projections and getting a supply chain in place that will include a ten-year plan to boost local content annually while keeping prices in line with what customers have said they're willing to pay for local food. That's no more than 5 percent above the price for imported equivalents, Porter says. She and her board also aren't naïve to the fact that bananas make up 10 percent of a grocery store's produce section and such non-native foods need to have room on store shelves, too.

Though food co-ops have become symbols of gentrification and, as a result, sources of resentment in some U.S. neighbourhoods where they've opened, Porter emphasizes the Garden City Food Co-op will be a store for everyone.[94] She envisions moms shopping there, single people and students, too. Staff will get to know customers on a first-name basis to keep channels of communication between store and shopper open. She sees a space for Start Me Up Niagara to sell some of what it grows at its Vineland garden and employment training for some of its clients. There have been talks with other social organizations about selling them food for their programs or providing space for them to teach classes about cooking on a budget. Farmers could come in to talk about their crops and offer samples of the food they grow, building a stronger connection to where food comes from. Really, it won't just be a place to shop for food, but for a community to grow.

"It's a project that will create employment for people downtown, create a sense of community and support the economy downtown," Porter says. "I see this as a place where we can talk about food and food issues whereas I can't do that at other stores."

Inviting Our Guests to Dinner

Every spring, Niagara sees an influx of temporary residents arrive to live on its farms. More than 2,600 seasonal agricultural workers come from Mexico and the Caribbean to toil in our orchards, vineyards, nurseries and greenhouses, doing the delicate manual labour of pruning trees, potting plants and picking fruit and vegetables that many Canadians have no interest in doing themselves.

For years, under the advice of some of Niagara's year-round residents, local bed-and-breakfast owner Jane Andres avoided those workers on her walks through her hometown of Niagara-on-the-Lake. Ditto during trips to the grocery store, where every week, busloads of the foreign workers would be dropped off to buy essentials for themselves and to send to family in their homeland. People told her the workers were dangerous, the fear heightened by language barriers built up by every Spanish or patois word overheard when sharing lineups at banks and supermarket checkouts in Niagara's most affluent municipality.

In Canada for up to eight months of the year, foreign farmworkers are critical to local horticulture's success. But the ignorance that can prevail in their host communities, in part because of consumers' disconnect from food production, results in many workers feeling marginalized—feelings that have led to depression and suicide—during their transitory tenure.

In 2006, Andres was forced to challenge her own preconceptions about Niagara's interim inhabitants when she was invited to help with the music at a nondenominational church service for the workers. Driven more by curiosity than feeling compelled to help, Andres attended the service hosted by the Caribbean Workers Outreach Program, a local outreach ministry, and found herself sticking around to sip coffee afterward with the two dozen men and women who attended the evening worship.

It was an a-ha moment for Andres, who saw that not only was the service in desperate need of her musical abilities, but also her ideas about the

Jane Andres (centre) visits with seasonal farmworkers Erroll Wright (left) and Clive Brown in Jamaica. *Photo by Jodie Godwin.*

workers were just plain wrong. "I was so shocked at the misconception I had of them, and I think I represent the average person here," Andres recalls.

With her newfound outlook, Andres agreed to help with music at the services. That came with the task of tracking down a guitar-playing farmworker named Winston to join in harmonizing the worship sessions. With little to go on, the tenacious Andres started knocking on doors of farms in her neighbourhood, an opportunity that came with another realization: Andres discovered there were about one hundred workers living within a ten-minute walk of her front door. That's as many as she thought came to all of Niagara-on-the-Lake every year. It turns out four of them were named Winston.

She eventually found her guitar player, but Andres also came upon something else in her search: friendship. In the years since providing those spiritual musical interludes at church, she has shown unyielding acceptance and has worked to make the rest of her community more welcoming, too.

She has emotionally and financially supported permanently injured and terminally ill workers, fighting with reluctant governments to get them access to Canadian employment insurance or healthcare that exceeds what's available to them back home. This despite foreign workers paying taxes on the wages they earn here—the same taxes that provide Canadian citizens access to universal health care.

Andres drives workers to medical appointments and plans social events for those who arrive to Canada early or stay late in the season, long after their friends and colleagues have returned home. She also invites workers to her home for Easter dinner. For some, Andres's invitation represents the first time in decades of labouring to feed Canadians that they have ever been invited into a local's home to share a meal. Andres calls her actions "random acts of food, fellowship, friendship and family."

"That's what's so painful for the guys. It's the burden of missing their families," she explains. "For a lot of men and women coming up here for years, this is the rhythm of life. For the workers in their thirties leaving their young children for the first time, it's hard. So for these guys to be around families and young kids is huge."

Andres has sent point-and-shoot cameras home with workers over the winter on the condition they return them the following year, the photos to be used in exhibits to show Niagarans that people who live as virtual invisibles here are important and loved elsewhere.

Patois, the native Jamaican dialect, has become like her second tongue now, thanks in part to her wintertime visits with workers and their families in

A scene from the annual Workers Welcome Concert, held for seasonal agricultural workers and farmers at Orchard Park Church in Niagara-on-the-Lake. *Photo by Joel Hannigan.*

their homeland. Her compassion and desire to make Niagara more inclusive culminates every spring with the Workers Welcome Concert held at a local church. Farmers are encouraged to attend with their crews, too, and the event is now seen as a town function with participation by Niagara-on-the-Lake's Lord Mayor. Everyone—resident, worker, farmer—is welcome.

Andres's efforts have helped some residents change their perceptions and workers to feel more at home in Niagara, but the Seasonal Agricultural Workers Program, which brings foreign labourers to the area, still polarizes many. Some equate the program to modern-day slavery, while others see it as essential to the survival of local horticulture. Advocacy groups "stemming from academic work rather than relationships" have formed to help workers who lack recourse when unable to access government programs, such as employment insurance, or to assist if workers feel they are being mistreated on the job. Andres has heard harrowing tales about labourers treated with little regard, but she hears the good stories, too. Her empathy runs deep for both employer and employee.

"Some people are very quick to blame farmers for exploitation, but this is very expensive help for farmers and the majority of farmers have strong relationships with their workers," Andres says. "I just pray for new eyes to recognize opportunities in creating a more welcoming community. For me to be able to help bridge any communication gaps unofficially—it's just wanting to be a support for both farmer and worker."

Andres shakes her head when she thinks back to how she used to be. "I was really afraid of them, which is so silly now. Maybe not afraid, but cautious," she says. "It just comes down to a lack of opportunities to converse with people face-to-face. To have such a wonderful time with them, you think, 'Wow, so many people are deprived of such good friendships.'"

Chapter 5

This Niagara Foodie Went to Market

Niagara, with all its thundering water, its backbone of an escarpment and expansive orchards, vineyards and grain fields, can inspire a person to greatness. The diverse landscape and fresh local food that it provides make the region a land of opportunity for entrepreneurs with a passion for good eating, a marketable idea and a knack for turning both into a business. The "foodpreneur's" role in Niagara has become that much greater in recent years, following the closure of Niagara's canneries, juice factories and flour mills as the multinationals that own them caved to their vice of cheap labour and raw materials overseas. Niagara's food artisans have found a way to turn local agriculture into a cash cow, making a name for themselves and the region in the process, and all the while pleasing the discerning gourmand's palate.

Niagara Food Specialties

Niagara Falls
pingueprosciutto.com

Every parent has hopes and dreams for his or her children. Mario Pingue Sr. pinned his on his two sons, Mario Jr. and Fernando, making and selling the kind of prosciutto crudo that was reminiscent of his birthplace but eluded the Italian immigrant in Canada.

Like many children, the young Pingues didn't listen to their father. Both opted to work in restaurants and bars instead, using in their kitchens the cured pork that the elder Pingue had been making himself since 1975 to fill a void of porcine proportions. After all, why would the sons buy the pig when they could get the ham for free?

Still, Mario Sr., who purchased fifty hogs every January to turn into the quintessential Italian cold cut that he would share with friends, family and a few local chefs, felt strongly that his Old World, artisanal ways of dry-curing ham legs had a bigger place among New World deli meats made without such care. That same understanding finally dawned on Mario Jr. and Fernando in 2000, when they decided to become provisioners of the pork that customers ate up at their respective eateries. They were also nudged along by legendary wine country chef Michael Olson, whom Mario Jr. credits with defining what the Pingues' meat business would eventually become.

"I remember him saying 'Niagara cuisine,'" Mario Jr. recalls. "And I said, 'What's Niagara cuisine?' He told me, 'This prosciutto, the way it's handmade, local, is Niagara. If you're not doing it, shame on you.'"[95]

Mario Jr. got affirmation in 2002 that he was not only creating Niagara cuisine, but also he was doing it well when he fed his prosciutto to fellow Italian Michael Bonacini, the chef-partner in Oliver & Bonacini (O&B) Restaurants. O&B operates several upscale, starred Toronto eateries, including Canoe and Auberge du Pommier. Two of Bonacini's executive chefs at the time, Anthony Walsh and Jason Bangertner, counted among the who's who of Canadian haute cuisine creators, were also part of the tasting that would ultimately put Mario Jr. on the path to becoming a professional prosciuttai.

"They got it. I was in shock. I spilled on the prices, and they didn't blink," Mario Jr. says. "I called my brother Fernando and said we're getting out of the restaurant business and doing something with our dad's cottage business."

To bone up on prosciutto production, Mario Jr. spent four months in 2003 as a protégé at Prosciutto di San Daniele, a prosciutto consortium in northeastern Italy. Soon after returning to Canada, he and Fernando hit their first snag in mastering the art of meat curing. The capicollo they made didn't taste right, a problem eventually traced back to the source of their pork. Mario Jr. figured out that if Niagara Food Specialties was to succeed at making cured meats, he needed to pay more attention to how his muses were raised. Today, his pigs come from a Quebec pork co-op that raises the animals in open-air barns without pens. The animals are allowed to live twice as long as what Mario Jr. calls "commodity pork"—animals

butchered at five months old for the sake of profit, their cuts winding up
in everyday supermarkets. The Pingues' more patient approach to pork
production results in Rubenesque hams with darker meat, more marbling
and flavour. The pigs are also raised free of antibiotics or genetically
modified feed.

"We didn't make the decision knowingly to use commodity pork to do an
artisanal product. We just thought everyone raised their pigs like my dad
did," Mario Jr. says.

A Pingue prosciutto is sea salt–cured for up to four weeks and aged in a
drying room on average eighteen months. During that time, it loses up to 50
percent of its weight in moisture before being sliced for sale. The brothers
also cure other cuts, including guanciale (pork jowl), pancetta (Italian bacon)
and peameal bacon. Their meats appear on tony menus in Toronto, in
gourmet food stores and in Niagara restaurants—everything from white
linen establishments to pizzerias. Getting that local buy-in took years of
educating consumers about the difference between those Old World values
instilled by Mario Sr. and what could be found at most grocery store deli
counters, the younger Mario recalls.

"It's a cultural learning curve," he explains. "Some people say our
prosciutto is too fatty. Fat is what identifies prosciutto, preserves it, flavours
it. I say people have lost their cultural anchor to food when they cannot
understand and appreciate that."

ACETO NIAGARA

Niagara-on-the-Lake
acetoniagara.com

Imagine spending a season tending to a grape crop, waiting patiently for
winter's deep freeze to set so the grapes could be harvested for coveted
icewine and then fermenting the sweet juice only to have it turn into vinegar.
It's enough to make a winemaker wake up in a cold sweat.

But one winemaker's nightmare is two Niagara-on-the-Lake farmers'
dream. Martin Gemmrich and Wolfgang Woerthle pride themselves on
turning icewine into the kind of vinegar that's good enough to drink.

The German-born grape growers could have opened a winery to add
value to the fruit they grow in Niagara. Instead, they opted to carve their

Wolfgang Woerthle (left) and Martin Gemmrich of Aceto Niagara. *Photo courtesy of Aceto Niagara.*

niche with wine's antithesis, showing Canadians that there was more to vinegar than white, malt and balsamic.

Walk into any grocery store in Germany, and the vinegar section is an abundant array of fruit essences used to enhance the flavour of food rather than merely be a major player in salad dressing. Gemmrich and Woerthle wanted to re-create that selection here when they founded Aceto Niagara in 2004 and set to work producing peach, apricot, cherry, tomato and icewine vinegar. The endeavour would also provide a market for other farmers to unload undersized fruit that couldn't be sold fresh because consumers would snub it.

Icewine vinegar is Aceto Niagara's flagship ferment. Woerthle uses his frozen grapes to make icewine before Gemmrich adds a vinegar mother to turn the sweet tipple into a condiment. He then ages it for three to five years, after which the vinegar is hand-bottled for sale or siphoned into a French oak barrel for another five years to mellow and become drinkable. With only 3 percent acetic acid by the end of the process, the vintage vinegar, known as Icewine Aceto, becomes an apéritif that can stimulate the appetite or be served as a post-dinner drink marketed to stimulate digestion. Given vinegar's well-documented though unproven medicinal benefits, the duo's creation brings the apothecary to the kitchen.

Admittedly, getting the concept to catch on in Canada has been a mother of a challenge. People aren't always sure how to use Aceto Niagara's specialty vinegars, so about half of Gemmrich and Woerthle's inventory is exported to Germany, Switzerland, Korea and China. Neither has soured on the idea of making small-batch fruit vinegars for a local market, though. "We came a bit blind to that business," Gemmrich admits.[96] "It's part of the European tradition that's focused on making meals, and this was a fast-food society. But if we wouldn't have believed in it, we would have closed [the business]."

MOYER'S CANDY APPLES

Beamsville
paul@candyapples.ca

Paul Moyer remembers 1976 fondly. Back then, the Beamsville farmer could fetch twenty-four dollars for a bushel of apples from his family's farm, in operation since 1799. Today, that same bushel is worth only eighteen dollars.

Faced with the reality that money wasn't growing on his apple trees like it used to, the entrepreneurial Moyer stopped sending his fruit to the Ontario Food Terminal, a distribution hub in Toronto, where farmers sell their goods to retailers and restaurants. He started moving it to his barn instead, where, with the help of a cauldron full of melted sugar, he transformed his pickings into candy-coated concoctions and started asking people how they liked them apples.

The response was sweet. By 1998, Moyer's Candy Apples, cloaked in red candy coating, were drafted to the big leagues. They sold at what was then the Toronto SkyDome, home to Major League Baseball's Toronto Blue Jays. Theme parks signed on to carry the sweet treats soon after, as did some large entertainment farms elsewhere in Ontario. But with the candy apples having only a two- to three-day shelf life, Moyer's window of opportunity to recuperate the losses on his fresh apples was far narrower. That prompted him to expand his offerings, adding homemade caramel and chocolate to the mix.

It proved a winning combination, landing his candy apples on the shelves at Loblaw, a national grocery store chain, and in Western New York supermarket mainstay Tops.

Doing everything by hand in his barn, Moyer and his small staff were able to turn out about 180 candy apples a day. That wasn't enough for long, particularly after a 2008 appearance on a primetime business pitch-for-cash

Paul Moyer of Moyer's Candy Apples in Beamsville. *Photo by Nathaniel David Johnson.*

investment TV show catapulted Moyer to a level of fame that earned him the moniker "the Apple Guy."

Moyer was forced to move to larger digs and mechanize his operation, devising an octopus-like apparatus that clicked and clacked as it dipped locally grown Crispin apples, known for their crunch, sweetness and girth, through a vat of chocolate. It was a like a scene from Willy Wonka's Chocolate Factory, both comical and magical, but it worked. More candy apple production meant more opportunity, and today, Moyer's operation is housed in an even larger factory in Beamsville, where the smell of sugar and vanilla collide to create the sweet smell of success.

Moyer now ships his candy apples coast to coast in Canada and farther afield in the United States. At their busiest, Moyer and crew, including business partner Amber Gulbis, can turn out as many as five thousand chocolate-covered Crispins per shift or about ten thousand smaller caramel- and peanut-coated Empire apples. Before the gussied-up fruit completes its journey down a conveyor belt to be packaged for shipping, it's adorned with a band that tells the customers their treat was made for them in Niagara, putting the region on the map as a candy apple capital. Still, no matter how far his apples travel, they haven't strayed far from their humble origins in a Beamsville barn.

"Everything is stainless steel now. It's not made on my grandma's wooden table anymore, but the apples are still made with the same care and attention," Moyer says. "We're still small batch. We just do more small batches."

Nigh's Sweet Shop

Stevensville
nighs.ca

Rebecca Nigh could rewrite the adage that the way to a man's heart is through his stomach. Based on the chocolatier's experience, it's actually through his mother's home-based chocolate business.

Roxena Nigh started creating Easter chocolates in her Stevensville home in 1958. The wife of a local pastor named Ross, the business-minded Roxena had cultivated a network of women in her husband's church to sell hundreds of chocolates, some of which were molded into everyone's favourite comic-strip canine, Snoopy. Hairdressers, storekeepers—they'd all offer up samples to their customers, and the orders would start rolling in. When Rebecca came on the scene in 1974 to lend a hand with growing the seasonal production, the shy sixteen-year-old wasn't interested in learning the art of chocolate-making so much as gaining the interest of the chocolate maker's son, Richard.

Roxena assigned Rebecca fail-safe jobs at first: decorating and packaging the finished product. It was a few years before she was trusted to pour molten chocolate into molds, but the girl who didn't like to cook proved her aptitude in that, too. In the end, Rebecca got the guy and, eventually, a career as chocolatier, running Nigh's as a year-round business in the barely there hamlet of Snyder within Stevensville in south Niagara.

Those early years on the job for Rebecca were a time of major growth for Nigh's. Roxena's sales network helped the cottage chocolatier outgrow her kitchen, even her home. The family incorporated the business and moved it and themselves into Nigh's current storefront, an old farmhouse that's a Turkish delight's toss from Snyder's only intersection. At the time, that four-way stop was the second-busiest intersection in the municipality, and while some today might deem it the middle of nowhere, Rebecca pragmatically calls it "on the way to somewhere."[97]

Nigh's Sweet Shop opened officially in 1980, a week before one of the biggest chocolate holidays the calendar is blessed to contain: Valentine's Day. From an upstairs bedroom, today an office, Rebecca remembers seeing the throngs of Nigh-philes who gathered out front on opening day.

"We were so unprepared. It was just a spiral of people through the store, and the lineup was out into the parking lot," she recalls. "It was actually daunting to unlock the door and have so many people waiting. It could have just completely flopped, but because of the way [Roxena] started the business with her salesladies and network of people, people knew the name. We were just amazed people came."

Nigh's became synonymous with chocolaty goodness, and in 1990, the family converted their living quarters into more space for making and selling confections. Roxena, who died soon after, marvelled at how the business became Niagara's sweet spot.

Walk into the store today and the smell of chocolate is instant aromatherapy. There's also the eye candy of four walls filled floor to ceiling with bars, bonbons and molded treats in milk, dark and white chocolate. Visitors can catch glimpses of Rebecca and her staff working away at new batches in the kitchen. It all makes stepping into Nigh's a little like falling down the rabbit hole and ensures that more than half a century after Roxena created her first Easter chocolate for sale, Nigh's remains a place of pilgrimage for those with a sweet tooth and sense of tradition.

"We're so blessed people come. People like to have a special shop they go to for their meat or their flowers or their chocolate. It just seems to work," Rebecca says. "There's something special about coming to where it's made."

DE LA TERRE BAKERY

Vineland
delaterre.ca

It's a relationship Jan Campbell-Luxton can't do without. Like a maddening lover who can break your heart one minute and then woo you back the next with her seductive charm, sourdough just won't let Campbell-Luxton quit her.

Together, they've made it work, building the success of Campbell-Luxton's de la terre bakery slowly and steadily, much the way a sourdough starter works to leaven flour and water to become a loaf of bread. What began in 2007 as an operation turning out no more than 250 loaves a week at a small storefront that doubled as a café in Fonthill has risen to 800 loaves and 1,200 pastries, just on weekends alone, baked in a larger commercial space on Vineland's main street.

Campbell-Luxton had to shed the café business, which he always figured would be his bread and butter, as the demand for his multigrain,

Jan Campbell-Luxton puts the finishing touches on cinnamon buns at his de la terre bakery in Vineland. *Photo by Tiffany Mayer.*

spelt, honey-walnut and plain sourdough loaves with their beguiling tang outpaced requests for the trained chef to turn them into daily sandwich specials. His bread has become a staple at nearly a dozen farmers' markets in Niagara, Hamilton and into Toronto. De la terre loaves can be found at health and gourmet food stores in Niagara and the Greater Toronto area and, for the lucky few who arrive early enough, at the bakery's Vineland headquarters.

The direction Campbell-Luxton's bakery has gone suits a guy who studied international relations at university. Farmers' markets are the social side of food, he says, using public space to introduce consumers to the people feeding them and developing an "alternative black market," where carrots and garlic are traded for a loaf of bread. It drives Campbell-Luxton's accountant crazy, but it's all part of the baker's unconventional business plan.

"De la terre is slightly chaotic, slightly alternative marketing, but we manage to have personality and do what we do without a slick ad campaign," he says. "We're able to do it because we can talk to people."[98]

De la terre's sourdough loaves are a nod to the bread-making of old. It's slow food production that eschews commercial yeasts and grains from monolith mills that promote homogeneity with every sack of flour they sell. Campbell-Luxton's loaves take three days to make, the sourdough brooding all the while only to reveal when it's too late whether the baker has made a mistake with his muse or nurtured its nuances and their relationship into something beautiful.

He looks to local farmers first for his spelt and red fife wheat. His father recently bought one hundred acres of farmland east of Toronto where he'll try growing grains to supply the bakery starting in the autumn of 2014. Campbell-Luxton goes to these lengths because he believes that the role of bakeries and restaurants is to foster sustainable agriculture and fair pricing for farmers. Hence the five-dollar price tag on each of his loaves and why he'll stick with baking rather than try his own hand at working the land.

"We desperately need farms to be viable, and I've never been fond of chefs doing vanity projects [by growing their own ingredients]," he says. "I would much rather support local producers than have a photo op buying up land and taking one more farmer out."

Niagara Essential Oils & Blends

Niagara-on-the-Lake
neoblavender.com

It's remarkable what can happen when you put your head down and work. In Melissa and Robert Achal's case, when you finally look up, you see an entirely new business opportunity.

In the mid-2000s, the young couple had ambitions to make a dent in the cut flower market, growing blooms in their Niagara-on-the-Lake greenhouse. Lavender was among the many stems taking root, and soon, it was the only one. "We just fell in love with it and started propagating more and more," Melissa says. "And they just grew up and became bigger and bigger and it was like, 'Wow, we have a lot of lavender.'"[99]

The husband-and-wife team started reading up on the benefits of the herb, learning about its calming and soothing powers. Soon after, they abandoned cut flowers to start steam-distilling their lavender for its oil and a secondary product, floral waters, to go into a line of bath items and

Melissa Achal of Niagara Essential Oils & Blends in Niagara-on-the-Lake. *Photo by Tiffany Mayer.*

massage oils under the Niagara Essential Oils & Blends name—NEOB, for short.

That was in 2009. Today, the niche product line has expanded to 150 items, including several edibles. There are lavender teas and syrup that's perfect for pancakes, as an ice cream topper and even in brownies. There's also honey, shortbread, popcorn and plain lavender buds to join other herbs on home spice racks. Many of the culinary creations are dreamed up by Melissa and showcased at NEOB's annual lavender festival held the second weekend in July, where people often marvel at how the perfumed plant can be so palate perfect.

The couple grows twenty varieties of potent French and more subdued English lavender. They even came up with their own variety by crossbreeding English and French strains and aptly naming it Niagara lavender. NEOB's purple perennial is grown on twelve acres locally, either in the Achals' fifteen-thousand-square-foot greenhouse or three-acre field, and by four backyard growers, doing it as much for the aesthetics as the business opportunity.

Even with such a large, established product line, the wheels don't stop turning for this couple. In 2014, they unveiled a trio of sparkling waters that was two years in the making, infused with lavender and two other botanicals they've added to their repertoire: East Indian lemongrass and rose geranium. Plans are to get it on local restaurant tables, bottle it for mass retail sales and export it. The Achals have also discovered a bitter orange that bears a striking resemblance to a kumquat and can withstand Niagara's non-tropical climes. Its blossoms will be harvested for perfume. In 2013, they planted a crop of tea, ready for picking in 2018, to provide black and green leaves for their lavender-infused blends. Contracts are also in the works with farmers in Fiji to grow vanilla and eucalyptus, their oils to be channelled into more NEOB creations.

"There's a market out there for natural products," Melissa says. "It's filling a void in the marketplace. It's high-quality products that people know and come back for over and over again."

Greaves Jams and Marmalades

Niagara-on-the-Lake
greavesjams.com

Long before artisanal, small batch and handmade became part of the arsenal against big, corporate food, there was Greaves Jams and Marmalades.

William and Mabel Greaves weren't out to revive the art of home preserving in a world of processed foods with questionable ingredients when they started their jam business in 1927. The Toronto couple, who traded city life for a more bucolic one in Niagara, put the manual labour into their jams and jellies because that's how things were done at a time replete with family matriarchs whose canning skills hadn't yet been usurped by a hunger for ready-made foods.

That competition from the capable home cook, however, didn't stop the entrepreneurial Greaveses, who used Mabel's personal recipes for pectin-free fruit preserves to build a business that would hold its own for decades to come. The couple eked out their legacy in a humble storefront that still exists on Queen Street in Niagara-on-the-Lake's Old Town, where it beckons tourists and locals seeking a taste of Niagara tradition. Home was the apartment above the shop, where the couple lived with their five children, each assigned jobs in the business ranging from bookkeeping to door-to-door sales, including into Toronto, to build a loyal customer base.[100]

While some of the young Greaveses eventually forged their own career paths, William Jr., who also served as the town's Lord Mayor from 1950 to 1961, took over the business after his father's death in 1980. He continued to grow the Greaves enterprise with the help of his daughter Mary Ann and several nieces and nephews, though none wanted to take the reins when William Jr. hoped to pass them a few years later. Selling was the only option, but he was particular in his search for new owners, whom he finally found in 1989, when he met Angela and Lloyd Redekopp and Rudy and Giesela Doerwald.

The couples were looking to run a business that would keep their families in Niagara-on-the-Lake. That suited William Jr., who was determined that Greaves would stay a local family business rather than be swallowed up by a large corporation that wouldn't maintain the company's traditions.

Even in today's mechanized world some twenty-five years after the Redekopps and Doerwalds purchased Greaves, fruit for their jams is still prepared by hand, though now it's done in an industrial park rather than on Queen Street, where the scent of stewing fruit once spilled onto the town's main street. Ingredients are hand-measured and stirred by the staff of eight, which swells to a dozen people during the busy marmalade season. "There are no computers adding ingredients in. It's all done manually," Angela Redekopp notes.[101]

Greaves has built a loyal following in its more than eighty years of existence, even making the rounds in high-profile political circles. John Diefenbaker, Canada's prime minister from 1957 to 1963, was known to put in regular orders for Greaves black currant jam.

Today, the business continues its posh associations, appearing on breakfast plates at high-end hotels in Montreal, Winnipeg and Toronto. Angela is also determined to jam national grocery chain shelves with Greaves products, padding out existing sales at small, independent retailers who have long carried the company's most popular flavours of strawberry, raspberry, blueberry, peach and marmalade.

Some varieties have disappeared from the Greaves line, a sign of the times in local agriculture more than consumer taste. Gone are the jars of quince jelly because the small supply of the heritage fruit dried up. But Diefenbaker's beloved black currants, along with sour cherries, grapes, crab apples and apples continue to be sourced in Niagara. As much as Greaves tries to preserve the tradition of buying Niagara fruit, it's increasingly hard to do, says Angela, who grew up on a Niagara-on-the-Lake farm that's now the site of an elementary school.

"As the industry is changing and farmers are ripping out trees in the area, it becomes a challenge," she says. "It will always be a challenge as farmers retire and sell to larger farmers who rip out trees."

To ensure longevity for Greaves, the current owners are focused on finding ways to market the historic brand to twenty-something shoppers, a demographic into which the Redekopps' own children fall. "I'm hoping the local community does know of us and that we continue to be top of mind when they think of a high-quality processor," Angela says.

Marinelli Pasta Sauce

Niagara Falls
marinellisauce.com

Niagara is hundreds of kilometres away from Canada's tomato capital in Leamington, Ontario, but one local businessman is determined to build a pasta sauce empire in a region synonymous with fruit and wine.

Adriano Marinelli spends upward of sixteen hours a day crushing, cooking and jarring tomatoes in a dreary industrial mall off a busy highway in Niagara Falls as carloads of American tourists zip past en route to the best view of roaring water or to sip local vintages. There are few weekends off for Marinelli—certainly no vacations—as he; his wife, Lisa; and their small staff churn out sauce that's eating into

Adriano Marinelli, owner of Marinelli Pasta Sauce in Niagara Falls. *Photo courtesy of Marinelli Pasta Sauce.*

Canadian and American market share once monopolized by big brands with national name recognition.

Marinelli got his grounding in business with a wood flooring outfit he operated until it went bankrupt in the late 1990s. Rather than take that as a sign he didn't have the chops for successful self-employment, Marinelli, who couldn't even afford a pair of decent sneakers at the time, decided to build a livelihood out of a hobby instead. Every year for Christmas, he and Lisa would give gifts of their homemade tomato sauce to grateful friends and family. They eventually realized they were the ones with the gift—a knack for making a food product that would appeal to more than just the Marinelli clan.[102]

In the early 2000s, Marinelli set up a bottling line in a 370-square-metre warehouse off that busy highway and began jarring pasta sauce that sold at $3.99 a pop. That price tag at the time elevated Marinelli's sauce to the higher end of the sauce spectrum, and the pasta topper bearing its creator's name was only available in select independent food stores.

Then came the Italian invasion in the mid-2000s. Grocery stores started stocking more expensive sauces from Italy, fetching upward of ten dollars or more per jar, and amazingly, it sold. To compete at that premium level, Marinelli spent years researching and sourcing top-of-the-line ingredients, from a consistent supply of vine-ripened tomatoes to certified extra virgin olive oil.

In 2011, he introduced the Marinelli True line of ten sauces, made with a list of ingredients that reads like something from an Italian nonna's treasured recipe collection. The sauce, made in 950-jar batches to ensure consistency, is certified non-GMO, Kosher, gluten-free, vegan and by the California Olive Oil Council—all additional expenses Marinelli refused to spare to woo the customer willing to spend money on store-bought sauce that could easily be mistaken for homemade.

By 2013, Canada's second-largest grocer was carrying Marinelli True nationally. Other big chains started showing interest in adding the sauce to their offerings. The high-end sauce was also available in stores in most U.S. states. That warehouse nearly doubled in size, and that sauce empire? With a capacity of four thousand jars per day, it's coming along, just as Marinelli had hoped.

"Really, the future of the brand, what we're more about, is reflected in the True brand," Marinelli says.[103]

Sweet & Sticky Ice Syrup

Niagara-on-the-Lake
icesyrup.com

Steve Murdza loves to punch holes in the idea that maple syrup is quintessentially Canadian. He's certain anyone tapping trees for a living in Vermont would have a different opinion. Before anyone on this side of the forty-ninth parallel starts fearing a national identity crisis or a fallout in Canada-U.S. relations, however, the Niagara-on-the-Lake grape grower has a solution for a truce: ice syrup.

Simply put, ice syrup is grape syrup. Murdza, a second-generation grape grower, makes ice syrup with the juice of his Vidal and Cabernet Franc grapes, hardy grapes suited to Niagara's cooler climate and once destined for icewine.

Like he did for icewine production, Murdza harvests his grapes when they're frozen on the vine. The several freezing-thawing cycles they go through before being harvested cause the grapes to dehydrate, concentrating the sugars and bringing flavours to a peak. He then presses them, but instead of shipping the juice to a winemaker, Murdza sends it to an evaporator. The result toes the fine line between sweet and acidic and has the consistency of maple syrup, but unlike that other cold-weather elixir, ice syrup is made only in Canada thanks to a climate enabling consistent annual harvests of frozen grapes.

"We tout maple syrup as Canadian, and it's not. It's North American," Murdza asserts. "We tout icewine as Canadian, and it's not. It's German. Ice syrup is 100 percent proudly Canadian, Niagaran."[104]

Murdza unveiled his first batch of ice syrup in the winter of 2008–09, six years after accidentally discovering it while harvesting his grapes for icewine. He and his work crew had been pressing the frozen berries for nearly fifty hours when it got too cold to continue. So the crew took a break and had a snack—cheese, of course. Murdza, a self-professed "foodie," put a slice under the press to taste the juice, and while his work crew remarked how great a vintage 2002 would be, Murdza had other ideas.

"Everyone said, 'Jeez, that's going to make good icewine.' I'm thinking that's going to be good on pork," he recalls. The wheels started turning to create a food product rather than a libation. Murdza took the juice to a maple syrup producer to boil down but found the results too pruney. Undeterred, he worked on developing an evaporation method in a Guelph laboratory, perfecting the technique until he was ready to bottle and sell ice syrup under the Sweet & Sticky banner.

Ice syrup is high in glutamate, a natural flavour enhancer and the reason why Murdza can rhyme off a long list of foods and recipes it pairs with perfectly. Soon after releasing it, the tenacious Murdza got a bottle into the hands of renowned Canadian chef Susur Lee. Lee became so stuck on the concept that he endorsed it and uses it regularly in his kitchens—"the coolest thing," Murdza says. In 2012, Canada's largest grocery chain, Loblaw, added Murdza's ice syrup to a private-label gourmet line and started carrying it nationally.

Today, the farmer's entire 34-acre Vidal grape crop goes into ice syrup rather than icewine. He recently started buying grapes and juice from other farmers to keep up with demand. If he could tap into just 10 percent of the maple syrup market—which is nearly forty million litres strong in Canada[105]—he would need an extra 2,250 acres of grapes, he says. That means more opportunities and job security for his fellow grape growers.

"If I reach my goal, farmers can rely on a sustainable living because food products don't go away," he says. "They become a priority item."

Upper Canada Cheese Company

Jordan Station
uppercanadacheese.com

Salt and pepper, peanut butter and chocolate, strawberries and rhubarb. There are just certain foods meant to be together, so it makes sense that a wine region like Niagara would have its own creamery, making cheese with local milk to enjoy with a glass of top-notch tipple.

It wasn't Wayne Philbrick's intention, however, to find Niagara wines a soul mate in locally made cheese when the construction company owner started to make his own washed-rind wheels in 2004 after a visit to the Fromagerie du Pied-de-Vent in Iles-de-la-Madeleines. He took his new hobby seriously, though, researching sources of milk before finding the Comfort family in St. Anns in west Niagara. They were raising Guernsey cattle, a dairy breed vastly outnumbered by Holstein cows, those ubiquitous black-and-white dairy industry heavyweights producing nearly twice as much milk in one day than a mature Guernsey milker could.

Philbrick was sold on what a Guernsey could do, though. Each week, he bought from the Comforts about twenty litres of the rich milk that has more butterfat and protein than Holsteins pump out, and he would use it to experiment as a cheesemaker. He'd share his efforts with friends and family and at his wine club meetings, where it didn't take long before he couldn't attend without a wheel of cheese in tow. It all started pointing to the potential for a side business, and as with some of Niagara's other successful local food artisans, Philbrick got the final push he needed from Homeric wine country cuisine chef Michael Olson.

In 2005, Philbrick opened the Upper Canada Cheese Company on a main artery in the quaint hamlet of Jordan Station, in the centre of west Niagara wine country. Staying true to how he began, Philbrick continues to buy his milk from the Comforts, who have one of only five Guernsey herds in Ontario. As a nod to the family that provides him with his raison d'être, Philbrick and Upper Canada make a Brie-like cheese named Comfort Cream, a moniker that elicits exactly what such a cheese is: creamy comfort food.

Today, Upper Canada offers six cheeses, including two made with goat's milk. Its flagship is Niagara Gold, a firm Oka-style cheese that can now be found in major grocery stores in addition to being scooped up by wine country tourists and locals at the creamery. To keep up with demand,

Wayne Philbrick, owner of Upper Canada Cheese Co. in Jordan Station. *Photo by Nathaniel David Johnson.*

Philbrick has started sourcing additional Guernsey milk from a herd north of Niagara. The creamery converts as many as one thousand litres of milk a day into its cheeses.

Upper Canada also goes with flow of the milk's production, letting the nuances of its seasonality come through in every wheel of cheese. There's no balancing the star ingredient by adding or removing butterfat to achieve homogeneity. That makes Upper Canada cheese much like its soul mate, Philbrick says.

"We're like a small winery. We take what's given to us every day, so there will be some difference," he explains.[106]

Philbrick has no plans to follow the trajectory that Niagara's other famous father of fromage, J.L. Kraft, did, growing to multinational proportions. Given his devotion to Guernsey milk and the physical size of his small red-brick creamery, there's only so much he can and wants to do.

"My philosophy is that we don't want to be all things to all people," he says. "If we had two to three cheeses branded across the country, that's the biggest we want to get. It's never going to be Kraft."

Chapter 6
Local Legends

Niagara is a tourist hotspot, with the Falls alone beckoning upward of ten million visitors a year. For the people who live here, though, it's home. Part of what makes Niagara a place to call their own are the joints they like to tuck into for a bite or treat, off the tourist trail that's dotted with indistinguishable chain restaurants filling up empty-bellied visitors with overpriced grub made with little care.

The locals' favourite place to refuel and reconnect isn't serving up gimmicks. It's the bakery with the wraparound porch where people eat quiche of the day and watch tourist traffic zip past en route to the next stop on a packed itinerary. It's one of Ontario's first pizzerias serving pie in a city badgered by the bad luck of lost industry and an unfair reputation. It's the diner where farmers show up at the back door offering their harvests to the chef, then pull up a seat at the counter to enjoy it. It is the place that has become the local's favourite, the local legend.

Avondale Dairy Bar

461 Stewart Road, Niagara-on-the-Lake

With its terrazzo floors and oldies spilling from speakers, the Avondale Dairy Bar seems like an anachronism to the uninitiated, though it's a nod to simpler times for its regulars. The ice cream parlour, surrounded by corn fields and greenhouses in rural Niagara-on-the-Lake, remains virtually unchanged from when it opened in 1956. It has been deliberately kept free of slick modern trappings, like the milkshake mixing machine that was unplugged after a brief tenure in the 1970s because it nearly caused a revolt among customers used to hand-stirred versions.

The lineups of people snaking out the door as they wait to be served nostalgia with their favourite ice cream flavour, sundae, milkshake or banana split signal to owner Ray Sheehan that the Avondale is exactly as it should be.

It's a place of first dates, where couples come to fall in love on the swing sets over a scoop of mint chocolate chip. It's where those couples return years later, children in tow, to find reprieve on a hot summer's day with a peach sundae. And it's where they will one day bring their grandchildren to instil the same traditions.

Sheehan sees himself as much a guardian of Niagara history as the proprietor of one of its most treasured food landmarks, where ice cream is handmade daily and served up by a crew of employees virtually the size of a Major League Baseball team. "I feel I'm here to protect it," Sheehan says. "There's a magic to the place you can't re-create in another location. There's tradition and history to the place."[107]

The Avondale Dairy Bar opened in 1956 as an extension of the neighbouring dairy farm run by Bob Stewart and his family. It offered fresh milk and ice cream to those who weren't on the Stewarts' horse-drawn, home delivery milk runs at the time.

In 1963, the dairy plant that still exists on site today was opened, offering tours to those curious for a glimpse into how their cow's milk went from farm to glass. Six years later, Stewart sold the operation to dairy processor Beatrice Foods. The transition from family to corporate ownership was seamless, with Stewart still running the place. Many customers never clued into the change even as the family began its exit strategy by opening its chain of convenience stores, also bearing the Avondale name, that continue to anchor plazas and street corners in Niagara today.

Sheehan got his start at the plant in 1974, working his way up to the manager in charge of the dairy bar and ice cream production by the early 1980s. Beatrice had been buying up other dairy plants, many fronted by dairy bars, which it systematically shuttered to focus solely on milk production. Seeing the opportunity for business and historical preservation, Sheehan bought the ice cream parlour business in 1986, leasing the space

Deb and Ray Sheehan, owners of the Avondale Dairy Bar in Niagara-on-the-Lake. *Photo by Nathaniel David Johnson.*

from Beatrice and, today, French dairy conglomerate Lactalis. Despite what it's attached to, the Avondale is the "anti-factory," Sheehan says.

"Everything is handmade. We don't make a month's supply of product. If we make ice cream on Tuesday, people are eating it on Thursday, which in the ice cream world is high-speed," he explains. "We've always taken the approach where we're not in the business to make product that's cheaper than grocery stores. We're trying to make it better. How can we make our customers like it more? That's always motivated me and the people who work for us."

The Avondale's vanilla, chocolate, strawberry, Death by Caffeine and English Crumb Cake flavours have won national awards, but its chocolate–peanut butter, pralines and cream and chocolate chip cookie dough are the three most requested scoops. Nods are given to Niagara with seasonal sundaes, made with local strawberries or peaches, and ice creams blended with grapes and pumpkin.

"We love the tie-in. The strawberry patch is down the street. Everyone on staff learns how to peel a peach," Sheehan says. "We want to do that stuff because we always have, we always should and people love it."

The Regal Diner

5924 Main Street, Niagara Falls

More than just greens grew when Angela Peebles and Simon Kelly planted lettuce seeds on their small farm in British Columbia's Kootenay region. The couple wasn't convinced they were getting paid a fair price when they tried to sell their harvests at the local farmers' market, so they revamped their business plan, adding value to their leafy greens by souping them up to become Caesar salad and selling them out of a trailer they converted into a kitchen.

The Bistro a-GoGo was born and with it a homestead-to-food trailer business that saw the couple creating fresh, homemade food for school lunch programs and those hungry for street—or rural route—food in their backcountry locale. Orders came in via Skype, and the couple, who became known for their hamburgers, would bake buns, source local beef and make accompaniments from scratch for every curbside service.

"Because we were homesteading, we were very innovative, so it was a matter of putting those qualities together with what we like doing," Kelly remembers. "I like working with food, and it gelled and all came together organically."[108]

In 2011, Niagara called. It was a homecoming of sorts for Kelly, who grew up in Grimsby in the region's western corner. The couple opted for the opportunity that touristy Niagara Falls offered, and the Bistro a-GoGo headed east. Peebles and Kelly parked the Bistro in the Honeymoon Capital's nearly vacant downtown. Life had long been sucked out of it by the tourist trap of nearby Lundy's Lane, with its wax museums and cookie-cutter chain restaurants that survive on a captive market and little effort. Peebles and Kelly settled on the beleaguered city centre because they were keen to be part of neighbourhood revitalization efforts that were just getting underway.

There were challenges to their new surroundings, not the least of which was sourcing the local supplies that were the raison d'être for their business back in British Columbia. They relied on grocery stores, lamenting the lack of control they had over their ingredients. Still, they did what they could with what they had, and soon, nine-to-fivers started walking up to their trailer window to order the Bistro's trademark burgers. Loyal followings formed, even in temperatures of negative fifteen degrees Celsius.

In 2012, a regular tipped them off to the shuttering of a longtime coffee shop in the Main and Ferry neighbourhood, on the fringe of the city's tourist district. The Regal Coffee Shop, with its counter griddles and line of vinyl stools forming coffee row, had existed in various incarnations since 1936. Stepping into its narrow, dated digs, with room for only a handful of tables and a dining counter as its centrepiece, is like stepping into a time machine. Peebles and Kelly saw the potential for breakfast and lunch service in the throwback, signed the lease and, a week later, traded the trailer for bricks and mortar and hung on to history by calling the place The Regal Diner.

They've since developed a network of local suppliers, providing them with eggs, potatoes and meat that they smoke themselves. They remain committed to baking their own bread and buns. Peebles, who dons vintage polyester waitress uniforms, preserves local fruit for jams and jellies served with breakfast. Making omelettes is considered an art form, done only when time allows so there's no assembly line approach to moving meals from kitchen to table. As a result, The Regal exists in stark contrast to the nearby all-you-can-eat restaurants with their feedlot feel that appeal to culinary agnostics.

More than providing local diner fare, Peebles and Kelly see The Regal as a part of a neighbourhood renaissance. The restaurant draws people to an area once avoided by many because of a seedy reputation that's changing with the help of municipal investment in the area. The couple's efforts to do food differently while surrounded by dining generica have also landed them a spot on *You Gotta Eat Here*, a Canadian version of the Food Network's venerable *Diners, Drive-Ins and Dives*.

"Every piece of food that comes out of the restaurant is a reflection of us," Kelly says. "We like feeding people."

"But we like feeding people good food," Peebles adds.[109]

The Rex Hotel, Restaurant & Lounge

346 King Street, Welland

An important slice of culinary history exists in Niagara, cooked up in the kitchen of Welland's Rex Hotel. It was there, in the 1950s, that the Carusetta family started selling pizza pies, making The Rex one of the first pizzerias in Ontario.

Sixty years later and owned by the same family, The Rex Hotel is still known for its pizza-making prowess, drawing respect and loyalties from all corners of Niagara. But before there was pizza, there was ice cream and the determination of an Italian immigrant named Bruno Carusetta to build a better life for himself and his family on this side of the Atlantic Ocean.

Carusetta landed in Niagara via Ellis Island in 1909. Family history has it that he toiled in local factories before returning temporarily to Italy to marry. Niagara beckoned him back in 1914, this time with his wife, son and five dollars to his name. A year later, he opened an ice cream shop called The Tripoli on what was then South Main Street in Welland.

Business boomed, and the entrepreneurial Carusetta, with expansion on his mind, bought up neighbouring properties with his profits. By the early 1920s, The Tripoli morphed into an Italian restaurant called The Napoli, but by the late 1930s, with Europe about to descend into the chaos of the Second World War, Carusetta changed the name to The Marine to help keep the peace locally. "It wasn't cool to be Italian," Carusetta's grandson and current owner Bruno Aldo explains.[110]

In 1947, the family closed the restaurant to convert it to a hotel that opened a year later. The move would allow for beer and wine service, though the laws of the time meant hosting separate drinking areas for men and women. On the day of the ribbon cutting, the family hadn't anointed its new business with a name, so the mayor, H.W. Diffin, took it upon himself to do the honours before breaking out the scissors. He called it The Rex, a moniker inspired by the restaurant's location on King Street, which South Main Street had since been renamed.

Growing up, Bruno Aldo was at the hotel every day helping his father, Aldo, run the place. Rooms were rented for twelve dollars a night in those early days—"It wasn't the Royal York," he jokes, comparing The Rex to the swanky Toronto hotel. By the 1970s, hotels like The Rex became antiquated. Restaurants were allowed liquor licences, and many inns, which once existed for the sole purpose of serving alcohol, were mothballed and closed.

The Rex was the only Welland watering hole of its kind to survive—its hotel rooms were converted into apartments in the 1980s—and it continued to exist because of the food. Aldo and his wife, Phyllis, developed a menu of home-cooked Italian dishes, including handmade pasta, still served today following Phyllis's original recipes.

The pizza offerings were expanded with gourmet varieties topped with bold brick cheese rather than mundane mozzarella. It was a deviance from tradition but a crowning glory that put a Rex pie into a category all its own and contributes to its continued popularity. Even the famous are counted among The Rex's fans. Paul Beeston, president and CEO of the Toronto Blue Jays, grew up in Welland and served beer at The Rex before making it big in baseball team management. He's been known to order a Rex pizza for the ride back to Toronto when he comes to town for a visit.

Bruno Aldo Carusetta (centre) runs The Rex in Welland with his sons Bruno (left), Gregory (right) and Peter (not shown). *Photo by Nathaniel David Johnson.*

To Bruno Aldo, it's those endorsements that are a testament to The Rex's approach to food. "We're not a roadhouse that serves food out of a box," he says. "I can go to five places in this town, and they'll be serving the same soup that came frozen in a box. Not to put other places down, but they'll get frozen dough that's already shaped, and they put sauce and cheese on it."

Today, the fourth generation of Carusettas have come into the business with two of Bruno Aldo's sons, Greg and Peter, taking over the kitchen, and a third son, Bruno Jr., managing the dining rooms and lounge.

Despite its storied past and resilience, The Rex's future worries Bruno Aldo. The landmark is located in a city that was pummelled by the 2008 recession and hasn't been able to catch a break since. Major industry has left, taking customers with it. The family continuously strives to keep the old hotel relevant with those who remain, but admittedly, these are uncertain times.

"I hope we can maintain this place," Bruno Aldo says. "I hope for my sons' sake…I hope Welland can turn around so they can enjoy it and provide a good life for their kids."

The Pie Plate Bakery & Café

1516 Niagara Stone Road, Virgil

Door-to-door sales can be a cruel, demoralizing venture. Ruth Anne Schriefer could probably lead seminars on how to do it successfully, though. Rule number one would probably go something like this: show up bearing pie.

People willingly forked over cash for Schriefer's fruit-filled pastries when she proffered pie on their doorstep as a teen. In time, the tenacious and talented baker graduated from ringing doorbells to a constant stream of people coming to her door at her Niagara-on-the-Lake shop in search of pie.

Still, it would be years before Schriefer opened The Pie Plate Bakery & Café in an old house on a busy artery funnelling people into and out of town. In the meantime, there was no doubt among her fans that her calling was to become a baker.

Schriefer grew up in Niagara-on-the-Lake at a time when she would have been the oddball if she didn't bake or sew. Extra motivation to find her way with measuring cups and flour came when her dad bought a hobby farm and small orchard when Schriefer was a teen. She discovered greater joy in making peach cobbler than helping out in the barn, and fortunately, her brothers, who benefited from her baking, never begrudged her choice of chores.

The door-to-door sales happened soon after, more as a way to prove her business mind to her parents, but Schriefer was also tipped off to Niagara's need for more homemade pie while waitressing at a local hotel dining room at the time. It was before the advent of Niagara wine country cuisine and the emphasis on creating menus with local food. Schriefer was coached to serve Sara Lee pie, warmed in the microwave and call it homemade. She refused to lie whenever someone hopefully asked if the desert was made with Niagara's bounty. People were inevitably disappointed in her answer.

Smelling the opportunity, Schriefer approached local markets, which guffawed at the idea of selling fresh baked fruit pies, doubting anyone would buy them. So she opened her own bakery, not far from where The Pie Plate Bakery & Café exists today, hawking her crusty creations filled with seasonal fruit to tourists. "People would come in after buying a strawberry pie and say, 'Do you have meat pie or lemon pie?'" Schriefer recalls.[111]

She started thinking about growing her bakery, but the demands of parenthood put expansion on hold. By the late 1990s, opportunity knocked again when she invited her new neighbour over for coffee and pie. He was

Toronto transplant Tony de Luca, and he had moved to Niagara to helm the kitchen at what was then Hillebrand Estates Winery. Schriefer welcomed him to the neighbourhood with an apple pie.

Her gesture struck her as a half-baked idea once she learned de Luca's identity. The next day, though, he surprised Schriefer by putting in an order for five pies to serve at Hillebrand. Soon after, Schriefer's pie became a fixture on the dessert menu, but de Luca saw even greater potential in her pastry and encouraged the baker to make a career out of it.

"What he was doing with local food—I always had those roots in me—but they really came alive when I saw what he was doing," Schriefer says. "Tony was the one who said, 'I don't know why you don't have a place.' He really pushed me."

In 2003, Schriefer opened The Pie Plate Bakery & Café, selling baked treats and café fare made with what's in season. She'd start her day at 4:00 a.m., sifting, mixing and baking, and sneak moments with her son Noah, now a chef at the bakery, by passing cinnamon buns to him at recess through the fence that separated Schriefer's store from the school he attended. At one time, all five of her children worked together in the bakery. Today, three of them remain on staff, and her husband, Kirk, helps out.

Baking is a science, but for Schriefer it's about more than getting the measurements right. It's also about nailing the ingredients themselves. "We actually go to Froese Farms and buy our peaches and lay them out so they're all equally ripe and roll out our crusts," Schriefer says. "We do that for our customers, and they appreciate it and come from far and wide. After ten years, holding true to the integrity of the ingredients has paid off in our customer base."

2x4 Diner

72004 River Road, Wainfleet

A classically trained chef walks into a greasy spoon. While it sounds like the lead-up to a great punch line, it's chef Josh Minor's recipe for personal and culinary fulfilment, and it comes compliments of a decades-old diner located in one of Niagara's most rural municipalities.

The 2x4 Diner has been a local landmark on the corner of River Road and Vineland Townline Road since 1957, surviving under a handful of different owners who sought to preserve the unpretentious allure of the country eatery, though with varying degrees of success. Through all the changes, the 2x4 retained its name and with it, its status as a destination for truckers to grab a home-cooked meal when miles from their own dinner table, for locals to welcome their weekends with breakfast, for farmers to compare notes on the year's crops over a cup of coffee and for teammates to refuel after early morning hockey practice. Now Minor is adding his own flair to the local legend, returning it to a glory once common among diners but absent under previous ownership.

Minor, who grew up in Wainfleet, remembers eating at the 2x4 as a child. But nostalgia was not what made him jump at the chance to buy the cornerstone of country dining when it came up for sale again in 2011. After eight years working in the demanding upscale kitchen of a local winery, he decided it was time to trade tasting menus for the chance to watch his daughter grow up.

Minor brought with him professional culinary skills, honed under pioneering Niagara wine country chef Michael Olson and others, to the 2x4's more laid-back approach to dining. That includes using local ingredients in the blue-plate specials when possible. All the better that farmers are both his neighbours and his customers. With Minor behind the burner now, it's not uncommon for growers to come to the 2x4's back

Josh Minor, chef-owner of the 2x4 Diner in Wainfleet. *Photo by Nathaniel David Johnson.*

door offering bushels of their harvests. Minor welcomes the unsolicited sales pitches because that approach to food should be as common in casual dining as the white linen establishments where he got his start, he says.

"That's what diners used to be about—a community-oriented spot," Minor explains. "I also wanted to do what diners did thirty to forty years ago when everything was made from scratch."

Minor relies on a local butcher for his cuts of meat, rather than a restaurant supply company. He smokes his own pork and makes his own corned beef. It wins him customers from all corners of Niagara and raises the proverbial bar for other "old school" diners. "If you look within a ten-mile radius from here, there are probably eight diners, but how many are doing things from scratch?" Minor says. "People come in and say, 'I love that you know how to cook.'"

SupperMarket

111 Garrison Village Drive, Niagara-on-the-Lake

Wednesday nights in Niagara-on-the-Lake haven't been the same since Lauren O'Malley Norris got her hands on them in the summer of 2012. The graphic designer turned farmers' market manager made midweek into an event when she created the SupperMarket, an evening of building community over small plates of made-to-order food.

It was intended as the sequel to the town's Saturday morning farmers' market. O'Malley Norris wanted the SupperMarket to provide gourmet fare for families to nosh as they topped up their weekend market purchases. There would be food trucks, farmers, restaurants, wineries and an open invitation, spread through social media and quick-witted newsletters, for all to attend.

She did it in the most unlikely of places, too: a parking lot and patch of grass in front of a strip mall. With a vineyard across the road—a secondary highway at that—and the skeleton of a new housing development next door, little about the location said destination, and yet, it turned into one for much of north Niagara.

The SupperMarket started as an eight-week trial, just to gauge response. Five hundred people showed up that first night in Niagara-on-the-Lake, an evening ripe for disaster with only one generator to share among twelve vendors clamouring for power. Something about the charge from casually gathering over thoughtful, unique food brought out only good spirits that night, however.

Even more people showed up the next week. By the end of the eight-week run, O'Malley Norris was clocking two thousand people in search of fish tacos, roasted corn on the cob, a glass of wine to cap their day and a pint of tomatoes to take home and see them through until Saturday's farmers' market.

With picnic tables and barrels meant to be shared by those eating, O'Malley Norris created a setting where strangers could make one another's acquaintance and marvel together at the cohesive community before them under setting suns and hazy skies.

Thanks to O'Malley Norris and her SupperMarket, Wednesdays became the new Friday. Social media feeds filled up with photos of casual meals enjoyed al fresco and rave reviews to tempt those who hadn't yet paid a visit. O'Malley Norris was thrilled with its success, but she was also mindful of the side effects that the incredible popularity brought on by crowd-sourced marketing could have on her project.

"I never wanted it to be trendy and hip. I wanted it to be a place where everyone could go and belong," she says. "I didn't want it to be exclusive. I wanted it to be inclusive to young people, families, older people. That diversity helped the inclusivity of it. You didn't have to dress a certain way or look a certain way."[112]

Though she no longer oversees the SupperMarket, the Wednesday evening do still attracts thousands of people. Her model has been copied in other Niagara cities, including St. Catharines, where the city-run farmers' market moved to a supper time slot on Tuesdays with the hope of bolstering business on its slowest day.

O'Malley Norris now uses her knack for bringing people together to host market-style events at other locations suitable for the community-building act of eating. "It's the pure thrill I got from bringing people together to be happy together," O'Malley Norris says. "There's a joy of looking over a sea of smiling faces and seeing they're being fulfilled."

Minor Fisheries

176 West Street, Port Colborne

Given the Niagara peninsula is flanked by water, it would be easy to think local fish and chips would be a mainstay on local menus. Yet despite having Lake Ontario to the north, Lake Erie to the south and the feisty Niagara

River to the east, most of the deep-fried bliss found here comes compliments of an ocean.

Only one place makes local fish its daily special. Minor Fisheries, headquartered in a Maritime-esque building with red siding on the edge of the Welland Canal near its Lake Erie junction, serves as a beacon for those seeking battered lake perch and pickerel.

Minor Fisheries started in 1948 when Wray Minor chose fishing over his father's butcher business. By then, commercial fishing had been established on Lake Erie for nearly 130 years, and fifty tugs regularly scoured the water to haul in prize catches. Wray's three brothers, Dan, Pete and Bob, soon followed, and together, the family operated two tugs.

Pete and Bob eventually hung up their nets, but Dan and Wray persevered, albeit separately, selling fish to American markets and out of their homes to locals and restaurants. The brothers came together again in 1974 and opened a plant and storefront on West Street on the banks of the Welland Canal, where the family's boats could pull up with the daily catches to be sold fresh or frozen. Business was going swimmingly with a loyal customer base that devoured the lake's two quintessential catches, perch and pickerel, like candy.

By the 1980s, commercial fishing was no longer as easy as dropping a net whenever and wherever a tug chose. Government-enforced quotas were introduced to help manage fish stocks. The fishery was hit hard in the 1990s, when Ontario's Ministry of Natural Resources slashed those annual catch limits for perch by as much as 80 percent to bolster flagging stocks. Pickerel was booming, but the predatory fish enjoyed eating perch as much as Minor's customers. Their appetite took a toll on perch numbers, and to stay afloat, the Minors began purchasing quota from other fishermen, who decided times were too tough to continue relying on the lake for their livelihood. It took buying out three other fisheries for the Minors to return to being a major player with the same amount of fish that only one quota had provided just a few years earlier. In 2012, they bought out a fourth.

The problem was, the drastic decrease in perch stocks meant a price increase at the counter. It was enough to drive some customers to choose those cheaper ocean catches instead.

Times were as tumultuous as Lake Erie during a storm, but the family weathered it by expanding their business again. The Minors added the restaurant at their West Street store to avoid laying off workers. The family was already doing fish fries for several local service clubs, so cooking up individual orders of perch and pickerel for hungry locals only made sense.

"It's just something in you. You just want to keep going," says second-generation fisherman Rod Minor, a gregarious wall of a man who looks every bit a mariner—a real-life version of Brutus from Popeye with lake water in his veins.

Today, fish stocks are healthier, and the Minors, now with the third generation entering the business, annually net 27,200 kilograms of pickerel, 91,000 kilograms of perch and 435,000 kilograms of smelt between Point Abino in Niagara and Port Stanley farther west along Erie's shores.

Many of the customers who strayed in the '90s have returned, and the Minors pad their business with sales to restaurants in Port Dover in nearby Norfolk County. Fish fans can be found every Easter, just after the Minors start their season on the water, lined up out the door of the restaurant and shop, waiting for the year's first fresh catch. When the weather warms up, the restaurant's small patio opens for diners to bask in the sun, breathe the lake air and enjoy Erie's sweet bounty the best way Rod knows how.

"Deep-fried is always the best," says Rod, who now runs the fishery. "It's not the healthiest, but it's the best."

Cibo Osteria

16 Ontario Street, Grimsby

Little about a bedroom community says dining destination. Tony Macri noticed that immediately in 2007, when he moved to Grimsby, a place where Hamilton- and Toronto-bound commuters laid their heads at night before joining the next day's grind.

The most obvious void to Macri, who brought his talents as a pizza maker to town, was Italian food. So the former Torontonian took it upon himself to fix that with Cibo Osteria, a "throwback restaurant" to the Italian eateries of old with their simple, traditional offerings of pizza, pasta and veal. There would be no Italian *nuovo* cooking, where the eggplant Parmesan is an expensive piece of art that leaves diners unsure of just how to eat it. Instead, Macri's from-scratch offerings would be the kind of comfort food that would make restraint difficult when they arrived at the table.

"If you're going to eat here, it's like eating at my mom's house," Macri says. "We're not going to give you a fancy garnish for your plate. We're going to give you good food that's fresh."[113]

Tony Macri of Cibo Osteria in Grimsby shapes pizza dough for crust. *Photo by Nathaniel David Johnson.*

The restaurant operates much like an Italian home kitchen. Family members take up their posts in the tight galley kitchen to help out. Each morning, Macri arrives early to work to crush the first task on his to-do list: make fresh tomato sauce. Once a week, an aunt takes over a corner of stainless steel counter to make ravioli stuffed with ricotta for the Thursday feature.

Macri also does his own butchery, paying a visit to his favourite meat shop for veal and then returning to the Cibo kitchen to do fresh cuts. He buys bushels of local hot peppers in season and flash freezes them so they're readily available for recipes year-round. Oenophiles can wash it all down with house red or white—on tap—from Niagara's Vineland Estates Winery.

Now, more than just a bedroom community, Grimsby is a dining draw, thanks to Macri's Cibo Osteria. People come from throughout the region to fill up on his unpretentious Italian home cooking.

In the summer, Macri can be found getting back to his roots, cooking and serving pizza from the restaurant's wood-fired oven on the seasonal patio. It takes centre stage during the warm season, turning out traditional thin-crust pies in ninety seconds. Two additional chefs tackle the cooking to round out the rest of the menu. Nothing is pre-fab, nor will it ever be, he says.

"That's the number one priority for us, and it's never going to change," Macri asserts. "That may mean more work for us, but that's never going to change."

The Smokin' Buddha

265 King Street, Port Colborne

It was a world of influence that resulted in a radio ad sales rep trading the airwaves for an induction stove. Kevin Echlin wasn't feeling much love for his media job when he decided to give it up and take a chance on the sometimes inhospitable hospitality industry, eventually opening up one of Niagara's most popular multicultural eateries.

But first, there were stints as a busboy, slinging beer and chicken wings at a local tavern in Port Colborne, even working on a mushroom farm in Hiroshima, Japan, where he lived and learned about food in the island nation for two years. There were stops in Thailand, too. Memories were created that would one day become muses for menus at Echlin's Smokin' Buddha, where Thai, Japanese, Korean, Mexican and Indian fare are served. The restaurant brought global flavour to a small town where international dining was otherwise limited to Chinese or Italian.

"I find Asian cooking to be very easy but so broad. Growing up with a meat-and-potatoes background in an English-Irish home, the meat was always very well done. Gravy probably wouldn't have been invented if it weren't for the English," Echlin says with a laugh. "Asian food pushed my tastes. When you're staring at a soup bowl with a fish head in it, you wonder, 'Am I going to come out of this thing?'"[114]

He did and it was with inspiration for a new career path to boot. But the road to restaurateur was a winding one with Echlin first trying his hand in 2005 at selling Thai curry kits out of a Coleman cooler at the Port Colborne farmers' market. It was a test to see how hungry people were for what he was cooking. He wasn't convinced he had much in the way of big sellers, but his wife, Kyla, knew better, encouraging her entrepreneurial husband, who recruited friend Mike Blake to help.

Within ten minutes of opening their stand at the market, a request came in for them to do catering. Had Blake not been there whispering in Echlin's ear to say yes, who knows what would have happened. With only a rice cooker and a set of Wiltshire knives, a new branch of the Buddha business was born. Meanwhile, demand for Echlin's *prêt-a-manger* food at the market grew. Samosas, enchiladas and sushi rolls made with the fresh vegetables Echlin bought at neighbouring stalls were soon added to the repertoire, and in 2006, he was peddling them at other farmers' markets in nearby Fonthill and Welland, too.

Echlin borrowed fridge space from a local grocery store and relied on the kitchen at the local branch of the Royal Canadian Legion to do prep. Eventually, he outgrew the veterans' hall and, while searching for a new space, found a vacancy housing old kitchen equipment in Port Colborne's former train station. With help from cuisinier Jack Redmond, Echlin, in his uniform of shorts, a T-shirt and Birkenstocks, would prepare for market under the glow of construction lights and to the cacophonous hum of passing ships in the nearby Welland Canal. Every cent Echlin made went into buying restaurant equipment, but it was a loan from his mom—Echlin's car put up as collateral—that helped him trade the camp stove he had been using for a professional and permanent kitchen. The Smokin' Buddha restaurant opened in that old train station next to the Welland Canal in 2007. It had twenty-four seats that filled by 6:00 p.m. on the first night. The restaurant was a hit because of its diverse menu that catered to many tastes and diets, including those of vegetarian and gluten-free diners.

More than seven years later, vacant tables at the Buddha are a prize find. Every service also brings in new customers from throughout Niagara and beyond, thanks to being profiled in 2013 on the Food Network's *You Gotta Eat Here*. The fame hasn't caused Echlin to abandon his roots. He still sells his food at local farmers' markets, and you can still catch him in his Birkenstocks.

"There are bigger markets where I could be making more money, but I'm not greedy," he says. "I like the life I have here. I just want to make great food that people can enjoy."

Notes

Chapter 1

1. Len Troup, interview with the author, September 5, 2013.
2. Tiffany Mayer, "Tilling for Tomorrow," *St. Catharines Standard*, March 4, 2008.
3. John Gardner, Ken Slingerland and Pam Fisher, Ontario Ministry of Agriculture and Food, "What You Should Know About Fruit Production in Ontario," June 2004, omafra.gov.on.ca/english/crops/facts/04-045.htm.
4. Ibid.
5. Ontario Tender Fruit Producers Marketing Board, "Peach and Nectarine Facts," ontariotenderfruit.ca/peach-facts.php.
6. 2011 Agriculture Census, "Niagara at a Glance," omaf.gov.on.ca.
7. Gracia Janes, "Preservation of Agricultural Lands Society (P.A.L.S.: The Fight for the Fruitlands," in *Environmental Stewardship: Studies in Active Earthkeeping*, edited by Sally Lerner (Waterloo, ON: University of Waterloo Dept. of Geography, 1993).
8. Mayer, "Tilling for Tomorrow."
9. Jerry Winnicki, interview with the author, November 15, 2013.
10. United Nations Department of Economic and Social Affairs, Population Division, *World Population to 2300* (New York: United Nations, 2004) un.org/esa/population/publications/longrange2/WorldPop2300final.pdf.
11. Ontario Ministry of Agriculture and Food, Provincial Field Crop Statistics, omafra.gov.on.ca/english/stats/crops/index.html.
12. Wainfleet Historical Society, *Chronicles of Wainfleet Township: 200 Years of History* (Wainfleet, ON: self-published, 1992).

13. Joseph Rider, *The Way It Was: My Life Story Including a 40-Year Cannery Career* (N.p.: self-published, 2012).
14. Samantha Craggs, "Another Blow to Farmers; CanGro Closure Would Have 'Major Repercussions' for Tender-fruit Growers," *St. Catharines Standard*, January 10, 2008.
15. Mayer, "Tilling for Tomorrow."
16. Jenifer and John Smith, interview with the author, September 20, 2013.
17. Paul Laprise, interview with the author, December 4, 2013.
18. Frank Cronshaw, interview with the author, December 4, 2013.
19. Torrie Warner, interview with the author, October 7, 2013.
20. Art Smith, interview with the author, February 28, 2014.
21. Foreign Agricultural Resource Management Services, "Seasonal Worker Program Carries on Successful Tradition," February 25, 2014.
22. Ontario Fruit and Vegetable Growers' Association, "Board Briefs, March 2014," ofvga.org/readnews.php?ID=2014-04-02%2016:44:29.
23. Jeff Tigchelaar, interview with the author, January 11, 2014.
24. Murray Bering, interview with the author, December 8, 2013.
25. Richard Bering, interview with the author, December 8, 2013.
26. 2011 Agriculture Census, "Niagara at a Glance," omaf.gov.on.ca.
27. Albert van der May, Thies Bogner and John Van Kooten, *Floral Passion* (St. Catharines, ON: Vanwell Publishing Ltd., 2005).
28. Bob Martin, interview with the author, November 2, 2013.
29. 2011 Agriculture Census, "Niagara at a Glance," omaf.gov.on.ca.
30. Marco Chown Oved, "Egg Fight: Quotas Holding Back Organic Farmers," *Toronto Star*, October 7, 2013.
31. Paul Kent, interview with the author, March 10, 2014.
32. Albert Witteveen, interview with the author, October 23, 2013.
33. Linda Crago, interview with the author, December 6, 2013.
34. Jordan Brock Fowler, interview with the author, September 9, 2013.
35. Rick Ladouceur, interview with the author, September 18, 2013.
36. Shirley Ladouceur, interview with the author, September 18, 2013.

Chapter 2

37. Arden Vaughn, interview with the author, September 9, 2013.
38. Alun Hughes, "The Early History of Grapes and Wine in Niagara," in *The World of Niagara Wine*, edited by Michael Ripmeester, Phillip Gordon Mackintosh and Christopher Fullerton (Waterloo, ON: Wilfrid Laurier Press, 2013).

39. Anthony B. Shaw, "The Niagara Peninsula Appellation: A Climate Analysis," in *The World of Niagara Wine*, 159–61.

40. William F. Rannie, *Wines of Ontario: An Industry Comes of Age* (Lincoln, ON: William F. Rannie, Publisher, 1978), 37.

41. Tiffany Mayer, "Farming by Heart," *Niagara Magazine* (July/August 2011): 20.

42. Rannie, *Wines of Ontario*, 32.

43. Ibid., 33.

44. Ibid., 35.

45. Linda Bramble, "The History of VQA," in *The World of Niagara Wine*.

46. Donald Ziraldo, interview with the author, February 7, 2014.

47. Bramble, "The History of VQA."

48. Paul Bosc Sr., interview with the author, February 13, 2014.

49. Paul Bosc Jr., interview with the author, February 13, 2014.

50. Bramble, "The History of VQA."

51. VQA Ontario, vqaontario.com/Appellations/NiagaraPeninsula.

52. Bramble, "The History of VQA."

53. Canadian Vintners Association, "Ontario Wine and Grape Industry Fact Sheet," canadianvintners.com.

54. John Schreiner, *Icewine: The Complete Story* (Toronto: Warwick Publishing Inc., 2001), 12.

55. Ibid., 164.

56. Charlie Pillitteri, interview with the author, February 27, 2014.

57. Jenny Lee, "Asian Counterfeiters See Canada's Icewine as Liquid Gold," *Vancouver Sun*, June 25, 2013.

58. Tiffany Mayer, "NiAGara Farm Heroes and Agvocates: Jens Gemmrich of Frogpond Farm Winery," *Eating Niagara*, November 30, 2011.

59. Tiffany Mayer, "Organic and Biodynamic Wines," *Edible Toronto* (Winter 2012–13): 12.

60. Mayer, "NiAGara Farm Heroes."

61. Allan Schmidt, interview with the author, February 19, 2014.

62. Winery and Grower Alliance of Ontario website, wgao.com/industry-facts.

63. Monique Beech, "Big Wineries Split from Council," *St. Catharines Standard*, November 19, 2009.

64. Ibid.

65. Tiffany Mayer, "Raising a Glass to Niagara Beer," *St. Catharines Standard*, January 22, 2013.

66. Ibid.

67. Tiffany Mayer, "Raising a Glass to Silversmith Brewery," *Eating Niagara*, August 8, 2012.
68. Grimsby Museum Collection, "Grown in the Garden of Canada: The History of the Fruit Industry in Grimsby, Ontario—John Hall of Kittling Ridge Explains the History of Rieder Distillery," transcript of interview, January 26, 2009.
69. Dan Kislenko, "Wines & Spirits: Ontario Whisky Maker Has Three New Products," *Waterloo Region Record*, September 22, 2012.
70. *CBS This Morning*, "Micro-Boom: U.S. Craft Distilleries Elevating American Spirits," May 3, 2013.
71. Geoff Dillon, interview with the author, February 4, 2014.

Chapter 3

72. Emil Rinderlin, interview with the author, November 16, 2013.
73. Val O' Donnell, Gracia Janes and John Bacher (Preservation of Agricultural Lands Society), "Presentation to the Honourable Carol Mitchell, Minister of Agriculture, Food and Rural Affairs. March 22, 2011," menu.
74. Michael Olson, interview with the author, November 25, 2013.
75. Anna Olson, interview with the author, November 25, 2013.
76. Tony de Luca, interview with the author, October 17, 2013.
77. Mark Picone, interview with the author, November 10, 2013.
78. Ryan Crawford, interview with the author, November 7, 2013.
79. Nathan Young, interview with the author, January 4, 2014.
80. Paul Harber, interview with the author, January 4, 2014.
81. Nicolette Novak, interview with the author, November 18, 2013.
82. John Laidman, interview with the author, November 23, 2013.
83. Justin Downes, interview with the author, December 15, 2013.
84. Tiffany Mayer, "El Gastrónomo Vagabundo: Putting Pedal to Metal to Feed a Peckish Population Pining for Gourmet Street Food," *Edible Toronto* (Summer 2011).

Chapter 4

85. Don Fraser, "Local Unemployment Rises to 9.5 Percent," *St. Catharines Standard*, March 14, 2009.

86. Don Fraser, "Health Care, Self-employment Brighten Otherwise Grim Job News," *St. Catharines Standard,* May 8, 2009.

87. Allan Benner, "Niagara's Unemployment Worst in Province," *St. Catharines Standard,* January 12, 2014.

88. Paul Forsyth, "Hungry for Healthy Food," *Niagara This Week,* February 21, 2014.

89. Scott Ritchie, interview with the author, August 22, 2013.

90. Jane Hanlon, interview with the author, September 3, 2013.

91. Susan Venditti, interview with the author, November 11, 2013.

92. Karrie Porter, interview with the author, November 4, 2013.

93. Lexington Co-operative Market, http://http://lexington.coop/info.html.

94. Vivian Yee, "Food Co-ops in Gentrifying Areas Find They Aren't to Everyone's Taste," *New York Times,* February 11, 2014.

Chapter 5

95. Mario Pingue Jr., interview with the author, January 11, 2014.

96. Martin Gemmrich, interview with the author, January 20, 2014.

97. Rebecca Nigh, interview with the author, February 9, 2014.

98. Jan Campbell-Luxton, interview with the author, January 13, 2014.

99. Melissa Achal, interview with the author, February 26, 2014.

100. Anne Marie Owens, "Lord Mayor of Niagara-on-the-Lake Built Greaves Jams," *National Post,* March 31, 1999.

101. Angela Redekopp, interview with the author, February 6, 2014.

102. Tiffany Mayer, "Niagara 'Foodpreneurs' Cater to Different Tastes," *St. Catharines Standard,* July 3, 2011.

103. Adriano Marinelli, interview with the author, January 18, 2014.

104. Steve Murdza, interview with the author, January 12, 2014.

105. Statistics Canada, "Production and Value of Honey and Maple Products," 23-221-X, June 19, 2013.

106. Wayne Philbrick, interview with the author, January 15, 2014.

Chapter 6

107. Ray Sheehan, interview with the author, February 24, 2014.

108. Simon Kelly, interview with the author, December 19, 2013.

109. Angela Peebles, interview with the author, December 19, 2013.

110. Bruno Aldo Carusetta, interview with author, January 26, 2014.
111. Ruth Anne Schriefer, interview with the author, December 20, 2013.
112. Lauren O'Malley Norris, interview with the author, December 1, 2013.
113. Tony Macri, interview with the author, January 4, 2013.
114. Kevin Echlin, interview with the author, December 21, 2013.

Index

About the Author

Tiffany Mayer is an award-winning journalist who discovered her passion for agriculture journalism in a classroom at the University of Regina and her love of local food standing in a cucumber field in Ontario's Norfolk County.

She has written about farming and food for a range of publications, including the *St. Catharines Standard*, *Edible Toronto*, the *Western Producer* and the *Toronto Star*.

When she's not writing, hitting the nearest farm stand or enjoying a meal, Mayer can be found writing on her blog, Eating Niagara, or leading The Garden of Eating–Niagara, the nonprofit she founded that harvests fruit for social agencies in Niagara.

Mayer lives in St. Catharines with her husband, Steven; their daughter, Olivia; and their three felines.

Photo by Ryan Hewko.